Interfaith Families

Interfaith Families
Personal Stories of Jewish-Christian Intermarriage

Jane Kaplan

Foreword by Phil Donahue, talk show host

Seabury Books
An imprint of Church Publishing, New York

A catalog record for this book is available
from the Library of Congress

ISBN 1-59627-011-X

Church Publishing Incorporated
445 Fifth Avenue
New York, NY 10016
www.churchpublishing.org

5 4 3 2 1

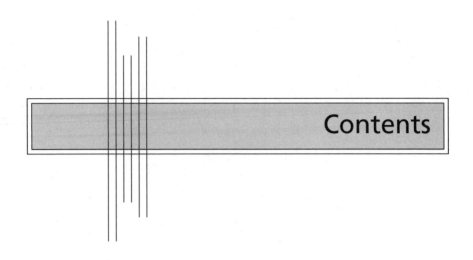

Contents

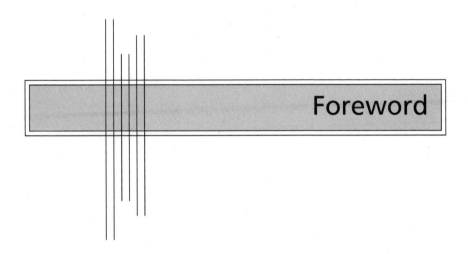

Foreword

This book is more than a collection of stories of Jewish-Christian intermarriages. It is an astonishingly honest look inside the hearts and minds of married people of different faiths. Ms. Kaplan brings the best gifts to this very personal inquiry: an unusually insightful and well-focused interviewing skill and compassion for the very personal nature of the issues. This book is an act of love and respect for the people who have endured what for some was a terrifying discovery: being in love with someone of another religion, another culture, another set of rituals and values. It is a genuine page-turner with Jane Kaplan as the guide on journeys that begin with, "What will my parents say?" and proceed into the most sublime questions of life itself: "Who am I? Who is my spouse? And who shall our children be?"

—Phil Donahue

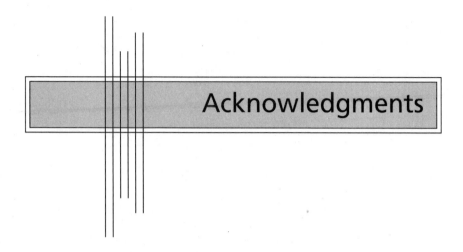

Acknowledgments

Thanks first and foremost to my husband Harry and our children Jacob and Elise for their consistent enthusiasm and support during this entire project. Many thanks also to my agent Ron Laitsch, and to Suzanne Staszak-Silva at Praeger for her clear and insightful guidance in shaping this book. I greatly appreciate Phil Donahue's extreme generosity and encouragement. And I want to thank John Ware for his early help with the original manuscript.

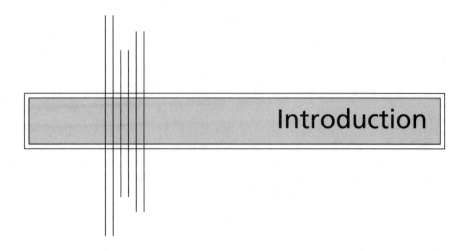

Introduction

* * *

When we decided to get married, I remember my mother trying to talk some sense into me. She would say, "Just keep in mind that religion becomes a very, very sensitive issue, and marriage is difficult to begin with. You have so many issues that differences in religion make everything harder." I just completely ignored her. Then we started planning the ceremony and had a real tough time trying to find someone to marry us. And that's when I really started getting very discouraged, very disillusioned.

* * *

Stephen and I didn't know what we were going to do about children. He wanted them brought up with some religious background, and it made the most sense for them to be Catholic because that's what he is. On the one hand, I had never been very active in Judaism. I didn't go to Hebrew school. I never had a bat mitzvah. And yet I identified so strongly as a Jew that the idea of raising my son as a Christian was making me impossibly uncomfortable. I just couldn't do it.

* * *

We belong to both a church and a synagogue. We each attend the other's house of worship. Whether we are going to the church or the synagogue, we go together, because we're a family. I don't want to send a message to Ellen's church community that I would send her alone. And she feels the same way when I want to go to synagogue.

* * *

This book is intended as an unbiased and nonjudgmental forum for the issue of Jewish-Christian intermarriage. It is made up of fifty-one stories that I compiled by interviewing men and women from around the country and editing their material. There is no single religious point of view that prevails in the book. There are no "right" or "wrong" answers to the questions that are raised. Instead, both Christians and Jews are given a chance to talk freely about how they have been handling the many aspects of intermarriage and how they feel about the choices they have made.

I am not part of an intermarriage myself. I became interested in the topic over the years because a number of my close friends and relatives are in intermarriages and have confided in me about the various issues they were confronting. Many of them have read one book or another on this subject, as I have. The books tend to either be surveys of the issue or represent only the Jewish or Christian point of view. They never seem to include very much in the way of personal stories. People I spoke with were very interested in a book that would have a more personal format and would enable them to learn firsthand about the variety of situations intermarried couples have encountered. They told me they had a great desire to compare other people's stories with their own in order to gain insight into their own lives.

After I decided to do a book about Jewish-Christian intermarriage, I spent many months researching the topic thoroughly. I read everything I could find on the subject in order to determine the issues that should be included and the points I wanted to bring out. Based on my research, I developed a lengthy set of interview questions and topics to explore. This interview guideline included all of the important issues and aspects of Jewish-Christian intermarriage. My goal was to find people who could articulate each of the varied points of this issue in personal and compelling ways.

It took a long time to find the individuals to include in this book. I started out by asking everyone I knew to recommend possible couples and then went on to ask those couples whom they knew, and again whom the next set of couples knew. I preinterviewed by phone everybody who seemed as if they might have something valuable and unique to say. I then chose the individuals I wanted to interview more fully. I did the actual interviews in person if possible, or I recorded the material over the phone if someone lived too far away. In this way, I was able to reach people all around the country and obtain their stories.

As I researched this issue, I learned that each year the number of Jewish-Christian marriages in this country has continued to rise. And indeed I was able to find many individuals who wanted to participate in this book; I initially talked to more than three times as many people as I was ultimately able to use. I interviewed men and women at all stages in their marriages about a wide variety of both practical and emotional issues. My voice was not added to their stories, and there were no experts who stepped in to comment on the material or to offer their interpretations. The ideas and feelings expressed were unfiltered, and the stories seem to me thoughtful and honest and passionate. They were told with the kind of details only someone experiencing a situation firsthand could know.

People willingly shared very personal parts of their lives with me. But in most cases they didn't want to do it publicly; often, there were things they told me that they preferred not to reveal to friends or family members, or even to their own spouses. I have protected their privacy by changing their names and, in some cases, other details that might identify them. At times, if their perspectives differed sufficiently, I have included the stories of both the husband and the wife. But because of the highly personal nature of the feelings expressed, I interviewed each member of the couple privately.

Although there are many common denominators, I think each story has its own unique perspective. In one, both the husband and wife wanted a chance to pass their own heritage on, so they decided to raise their daughter as a Christian and their sons as Jews. In another, a Jewish woman agreed to raise her children as Catholics, but when her son was born she couldn't go through with it, so the couple compromised by becoming Unitarian. There is a Catholic man whose Jewish wife did not want their children baptized, but after twenty years of Catholic education he felt he had to do something, so he secretly baptized his children himself one day when his wife was out. And there is a Christian woman who converted to Judaism and seems to be happily leading the perfect Jewish life but is really feeling she "wimped out" by converting, in trying to make herself acceptable to people who didn't like her the way she was.

There are a number of stories in the book from people who have converted. Although the husband and wife were both part of the same religion after the conversion took place, I have included them as intermarried couples for two reasons. First, in some cases the conversion did not actually occur until after the marriage was already underway, or even until after the children had been born. Second, the two individuals came into the marriage with very different family and cultural backgrounds, which continued to affect them even after the husband or wife had converted.

As I put together this book, some clear patterns emerged about Jewish-Christian intermarriage. These findings are the result of my own observations after researching and interviewing so many people about this issue. They are based not only on the individuals who have been included in the book, but also on all of the others I spoke to along the way. The patterns I found are strongly reflected in the book in terms of the number of couples who are in particular situations.

- A large number of intermarriages have taken place between Jews and Catholics, rather than between Jews and Protestants.
- There have been many Christians who converted to Judaism but very few Jews who converted to Christianity.
- Far more of the intermarried couples I spoke to have chosen a Jewish orientation for their family rather than a Christian one. Even if the Jewish person was fairly nonreligious, he or she often still wanted to have Jewish children and a Jewish home.
- There have been very few situations in which a woman who strongly identified as Jewish was willing to let her children be raised as Christians. She may have said that they could learn about both religions or that they didn't have to learn about either religion, but it was rare for her to agree that her children could be raised completely as Christians.
- Many times, a Christian woman married a Jewish man who was not very active in Judaism. The woman agreed that their children and home could be Jewish but insisted that the family become more active in Judaism in order for religion to be a genuinely meaningful part of their lives. The Christian woman was often actually the catalyst for the family to lead a more active Jewish life.

The biggest choice an intermarried couple has to make is whether one religion will be dominant in their family, and if so, which one. Everything the couple does—how they handle their wedding ceremony, the holidays they choose to celebrate, how they raise their children, and the types of relationships they have with their own parents and other family members—is influenced by this decision.

Because this particular choice is so central to the lives of intermarried couples, I have used it as the basis for structuring this book. The book is organized according to the choices different couples have made. There are couples who chose a more Jewish orientation for their homes and families, and couples who chose a more Christian orientation. There are some couples who decided they wanted to incorporate both religions into their lives, and some who decided they wanted a different alternative altogether. There are spouses who chose to get only minimally involved in a religion that was not their own, and others who decided to convert. By arranging the book in this way, it is my hope that readers will be better able to answer the question, "What will my life be like if I make that choice?"

I greatly appreciate the candor of the men and women I interviewed for this book. Taken together, I believe their stories explore the issue of Jewish-Christian intermarriage in an intimate and thorough way. Somewhere in these pages, readers are likely to hear their own voices and gain insight and support for making their own decisions surrounding this issue. I think the book may be useful to couples who are considering intermarriage, as well as to those couples who are already married and dealing with the situations explored in these pages. I also believe this book can bring more understanding about Jewish-Christian intermarriage to the family members of these couples. Finally, my hope is that all readers will come away with an awareness not only of the complexities of this issue, but of the many possibilities of dealing with it that exist as well.

1 Choosing a Jewish Family Life

The couples in these stories have all chosen Judaism to be the primary religion in their homes and families. There are stories about men and women who are adamant about wanting to raise their children as Jews even though they aren't particularly religious themselves. In some stories the Jewish husband or wife clearly would like more help from their spouse in handling the religious responsibilities for their children, and in others they are very appreciative for the support they do get. There are stories in which Christian spouses talk about missing Christmas and the other holidays they enjoyed in their own homes when they were growing up. And there are stories in which the Christian man or woman is able to become comfortable in a Jewish family and community, while in other stories they are still struggling to fit in. Deciding to have a Jewish family life is the choice that many interfaith couples make, but there is a great deal of variety as to how each individual handles that decision at different points in his or her life.

Kim grew up in a small city in Wisconsin. She is in her mid-forties and works in the field of education. Kim experienced a number of conflicts and a feeling of not being accepted as she explored ways to fit into a Jewish family and community. It has been difficult for her to find a comfortable level of participation in a religion that is not her own.

🕸 KIM (TO BE FOLLOWED BY HER HUSBAND, JEFF)

* * *

When I was a child my parents would have described us as Protestant although we changed around quite a bit. My parents are very liberal. I think they had trouble with organized religion. They both cast off Christianity fairly easily as adults, but when we were kids they still wanted us to have some religious participation.

* * *

The churches I remember going to with my parents were Presbyterian. I absolutely hated going to Sunday school, and I never felt like I was very much connected to Christianity at all. Religion was sort of a nonissue for me.

Growing up, I really didn't know any Jewish people at all. Then I went to do an internship during college, in Washington, D.C. There were people from all over the country. My roommate was Jewish, from New Jersey, and she was really a character. Also, there were a lot of Jewish people in the building. I learned something about Judaism and being Jewish by osmosis.

I met Jeff when I came to Chicago for graduate school. He was working at the Peace Corps, and I was working in a woman's organization. I didn't meet many men, and I was kind of concerned about that. I was in my mid-twenties. I wanted to get married some day and have kids. Jeff and I started dating, and we became good friends and just kind of took things slowly.

Religion was not an issue for us. Jeff was not particularly hooked into any Jewish community or culture. He didn't go to temple. He wasn't a very Jewish person. And by the time I met him I was really nonreligious, so I honestly didn't think it could be a problem at all. It was, however, an issue with his family, which I didn't find out about until later. I would say I was very naïve about what it really meant to marry someone who was Jewish. I don't think I thought it could make that much difference.

I'll give you an example of what happened. Jeff's parents live in New York. When I first went to meet them, they were living in a community that was 99.9 percent Jewish. First of all, I didn't know this. I didn't realize that so many people in the community were Jewish, and I really didn't know that much about Jewish culture. All I can say is that it felt like I was walking into a Woody Allen movie. It was all these intense people with strong New York accents. I know it sounds very stereotypical, but that's how it was. It was funny in a way. It was exotic to me.

This was fairly early on in our relationship. We might have been living together by then. And Jeff was bringing me home to meet his parents. He had not really dated a lot of women, so I think it was a big deal for his parents that he was bringing someone home. Of course, I never thought at all about what they must have been feeling because I wasn't Jewish.

But when I got there, everyone was very nice. We had a big meal, and his whole family was there. I'm sure they were all there because they wanted to see whom Jeff was dating finally. We were sitting at the table. Everyone was eating except his mother, who of course was running around in the kitchen. She never sits at the table. So there is this crowded table with this big family. All of a sudden, there's a moment of complete silence. Then his older brother says, "Well, at least she's not black." And then they all laughed uproariously.

Since then, I've come to know this family. I don't think the brother who made that remark is really a racist, and I don't think he was trying to hurt me. He is just a funny, irreverent person. Anyhow, Jeff is laughing. Everyone's laughing. Of course, I've never forgotten this because it was really quite a moment. And I'm thinking, "Should I laugh? Am I being insulted here? What is this?"

The flip side of it is that my parents simply thought it was interesting that I was dating someone Jewish. They certainly didn't mind. It was shocking to me that it was such an issue for his family. After that dinner was when I started to realize that this really was a big deal and that Jeff's parents were going to care.

Jeff and I bought a house together, and then decided to get married. The one thing that Jeff's parents must have gotten him to promise at some point is that we would raise our kids to be Jewish. I'm not quite sure how that came about. I really think it was more important to Jeff's parents than to him, but he said we had to agree to do it. I said, "Okay, that's fine," because I didn't participate in anything religious of my own.

We decided that we should have a rabbi marry us, and we started hunting around, which is what people do. We found one at a Reform temple with mostly older people. I think this was the temple's way of building up their congregation. We had to go to services there every week and participate in an interfaith couple's luncheon once a month.

I was very nervous. We didn't want to have a big wedding. I didn't want to have a lot of misunderstandings or tension, which I knew we might have if particular members of the families were there. So we got married in the rabbi's study. I cried through the whole wedding, which my mother-in-law thought meant I didn't want to get married. Then the next day we had a reception at our house with all of our friends, and it was wonderful. We were supposed to continue going to temple, but we only went once or twice and then stopped.

I think it would have helped me to talk to people who were in relationships like ours. I think the hardest thing for me has been figuring out where I fit in a Jewish family. And I do think that I have experienced some feelings that people didn't accept me because I wasn't Jewish, which I didn't expect at all. I just didn't think about it. I think it would be helpful for people to understand that there are some Jewish people who don't want their family members to marry outside the faith and that it is something you have to deal with. It doesn't mean you shouldn't do it, and it doesn't mean it won't work, because it obviously works for a lot of people. But I think there were many times when I felt really insecure about what I was doing. Luckily for me, Jeff's family doesn't live near us. If they did, it may have been a lot more intense.

Jeff would have liked for me to convert. He probably thought that would make things easier. But it was very clear to both of us that I wasn't going to because that seemed dishonest to me. I never felt like, "Wow, Judaism is my religion." I told him, "This is all you're going to get. I'm not going to convert, so don't even hope for that." I just feel like I can do only so much, and I can't do more than that because then I cross into something that feels false. I think Jeff knew that he should be satisfied with the fact that I agreed to raise our kids in the Jewish faith, when of course I had no idea what that meant. I really had no idea.

We have two daughters. Raising your kids to be Jewish . . . I think it's very difficult. Again, I think what helps is to talk to other people who have been through it, which I really didn't do. I didn't even know the questions to ask. Maybe I should have, but I was very naïve. Knowing what I was going into would have helped. It's not as easy to raise your kids in the Jewish faith as raising them to be Protestant. Not only do they have to go to Hebrew school two or three times a week, but you also have to take them there or get in a car pool. They learn another language and have homework that you can't understand. There are so many things. It's a huge commitment, and I had no idea. I really didn't know. I didn't know that you start when you are so young, or about all the work you have to do to get ready for a bar or bat mitzvah. But once I said I would do it, I just couldn't go back. I'm sure some people do. Some people say, "I didn't know I had to do all this, and I'm not doing it."

Most importantly, it is very awkward to be in a place where you agree to raise your kids a certain way with a spouse who doesn't buy into it all as much as maybe he should. Jeff is culturally Jewish, but he is not very much of a practicing Jew. I don't think religiously he is all that hooked into it. When we were first married, we didn't really think about anything having to do with Judaism. Jeff never even went to services for any of the holidays until our kids were older. Over the years, we have occasionally gone to Passover seders at my friend Rena's house. We have a lot of Jewish friends, so we will do things at their homes sometimes. But we don't really do many Jewish things in our own home.

I feel like I always have one foot in each camp. "If we're raising our kids in the Jewish faith, let's do it right. Let's not do a half-assed job. For the holidays, let's have a meal. Let's do our own seder." Jeff simply won't. He might say, "Oh, that sounds like a good idea." But he does not participate. He does not cook, or even think about what should be included for a holiday meal. He would like me to do it all, to make it happen, and if I don't do it then it's, "Maybe we just won't do it."

It feels wrong to me. We have said to our kids, "You're Jewish." Every other Jewish kid is having a seder, and why aren't we? So then I start to feel guilty that we are not giving them what we should. I say to myself, "Well, this isn't my problem. It's up to Jeff." But I want us to follow through on what we are trying to teach our kids, and that involves both of us.

When Jackie, our oldest, was preschool age, we started hunting around for a temple. We joined a Reconstructionist synagogue. There are a lot of people there who I really like. And I always feel that, when I'm there, people think it's fine that I'm there. But still, many times I feel like an outsider. I don't feel unwelcome, but I don't really feel a part of it. That's hard for me because of my personality, which is that whenever I'm involved in something, I like to be really involved. I don't like to just observe, which is what I do at our synagogue. I have struggled a lot with that. "Should I get more involved? But I'm not Jewish. What is my role? What should I be doing?"

I don't want to be Jewish, but I want to be accepted, to fit in. I think part of what holds me back are all the issues I have with Jeff, about what he should be doing and what he is not doing. But also, I really think that if I had married someone of any of the Christian religions, it would have been much easier for me to fit in. I think Judaism is exclusionary in some ways. That's been my experience. I think a lot of times people could go a little more out of their way to explain about something that is unfamiliar, or to ask you to participate.

I've kind of made my peace with the way things are, but I'm not crazy about it. I say to the kids, "If I hadn't married your dad, I'd probably go to the Unitarian church." I know I'd fit right in there, and I'd probably be on committees and I would be involved. But I just feel like I can't quite do that at our synagogue. Half the time I get stuck on the Hebrew words. I don't know about so many Jewish things. I do take the kids to services once in awhile, especially now that Jackie's bat mitzvah is coming up.

About a year ago, I had a very emotional episode about Judaism. It happened at one of the really long High Holiday services. While you're sitting there, you have a lot of time to think. I felt so excluded because there was so much I couldn't understand, and I'm thinking I should have learned Hebrew. I was really kind of upset, and I told Jeff that I thought raising the kids in the Jewish faith might be a mistake. What was I doing? Are the girls going to look back at me someday and say, "What were you thinking? Who are you?" It just struck me that I had made this huge decision to do this, and I felt so alienated. I felt like here is something my kids are going to be and I'm not, and I never will be. Is that what I really want to do? I had such a strong feeling of regret.

At that particular service, several things were going on. The rabbi was talking about how we are a family, and we all come here together, and I felt that he was talking about Jewish people only. And yet at the synagogue we belong to, there are many people with all kinds of backgrounds. That's one thing we liked about it. It would be nice if that could simply be acknowledged or recognized during the service. Because at that moment I felt that the rabbi was saying that the holidays are when Jewish people come back together, and let's try to keep that going. I thought, "Who am I sitting here? I'm not Jewish and this is not my family." Everyone was speaking Hebrew. Everybody seemed so connected. I felt so separate. I tried to tell Jeff what I was feeling, and his reaction was, "Well, I don't think the rabbi was saying that."

I want Jeff to understand, but he really doesn't. I might say something about how I feel excluded because I am raising my kids in a culture that I am not a part of. He will jump in immediately, not to say, "Oh, that must make you feel bad," but more like, "How could you say that? It's not true."

It's not that I mind raising the girls to be Jewish. I really think it's been great, and I do think of them as Jewish. They both identify as Jews, and I am grateful for that. I think that Judaism is a wonderful culture. The part that bothers me is that I am the one who has had to make this happen. Without me, it wouldn't be happening even to this degree. And I could have refused. But that's not how it is.

I think Jeff should be eternally grateful to me, and he is not. He is not grateful, and I don't know why. I think he should think I'm the best thing that happened to him because I agreed to do this, and because I've tried so hard. I've never been able to figure it out, and it's absolutely infuriating.

There was one time last year when I told Jeff, "You know what, I give up. I'm not going to do anything Jewish." I threw out my Jewish cookbooks because I was the only one using them. I said, "I'm not doing this anymore. This is your thing. I said we could raise our kids Jewish. I've never done anything that would block them from being Jewish. I'm totally accepting of them being Jewish, but I'm not going to be as involved in it because I think it's dishonest the way we are doing it, which is not much at all."

Jeff was really upset about the cookbooks. That was hard for him. "What are you doing?" I can't get him to understand. He doesn't understand. He never will, and I've kind of given up on it.

I tried to talk to my friend Rena and her husband about it. I told them about throwing away the cookbooks and about feeling alienated at the synagogue. They are both very Jewish, and when I told them my feelings they were shocked. I could tell how uncomfortable they were at the time, and later Rena told me she felt I was being anti-Semitic.

I said, "It's not anti-Semitic, it's me. It's my feelings." I was so upset. She said, "We never thought you would say anything anti-Semitic." I said, "You're right, I wouldn't." I was absolutely furious. I said, "Do you think I would have gone through all this, married a Jewish person, and raised my kids to be Jewish if I were anti-Semitic? How can you turn around and call me that? Are you kidding?" I realized eventually that she was not hearing just my feelings, but was reacting to what she felt were criticisms and judgments against Judaism. It's hard to communicate what you feel without being accused of being anti-Semitic. Even Jeff sometimes thinks I'm being anti-Semitic.

What a lot of people don't get is that it's not that easy to become a Jew. Jewish people do not go out and look for new Jewish people to bring in. A lot of Christian religions do. They welcome you in. They want you. They're evangelical. Their mission is to help you see their way. But Jewish people do not do that. That's just not part of the faith. And I think a person coming in, even a little bit, has to recognize that.

Jeff is also in his forties and is originally from the East Coast. He and Kim met when they were both working in the Midwest after college. Jeff has a great deal of ambiguity about how active a Jew he really wants to be. This has been a complicating factor as he and Kim continue to struggle with this issue.

JEFF (PRECEDED BY HIS WIFE, KIM)

* * *

I really wish I were more Jewish than I am. This is sort of an embarrassment to me, but I never did much on my own in terms of religion. I probably did less in college than I did when I was younger. It was just not my focus. It was not a priority.

* * *

I grew up in a very liberal, Reform family. Both my parents were Jewish, but it was not a religious household. We celebrated the holidays in pretty simple ways. For example, our Passover seder was very, very condensed.

I think for me Judaism was more of a way of life than an issue of going to temple. We would only go to temple on the major holidays. I went to Hebrew school and got bar mitzvahed at thirteen. That was it. I didn't particularly like Hebrew school, but I don't think that's unusual. Most people didn't like it.

I got my undergraduate degree in 1977. I didn't meet Kim until the mid-'80s. Kim is Christian, but she wasn't really religious. When we began to get serious (and I know this is hypocritical), I asked her about having the kids raised Jewish. I told her that's what I wanted. Why did I care? I think it was a comfort level. I felt more comfortable with Judaism than any other religion. And I knew it would be easier with my family. So that was it.

She never hesitated at all. There was never any pause. She just agreed. In retrospect, I don't think she really fully understood what would be involved. Kim didn't grow up in an environment where there were any Jews.

This whole topic of religion was just sort of blurry and distant before we had kids. Once you have kids, of course, everything changes. There is confusion because you feel like now you have to do something more, but you aren't used to doing more, and it gets to be a problem.

I'm in a situation where I am not particularly religious but I still feel Jewish. That's a very hard thing for Kim to understand. She says, "If you feel Jewish, why don't you practice it? Why don't you participate more in the holidays and help establish traditions in our home?" I try to explain to her that Judaism is more than just a religion to me. It is the way I grew up . . . the way of life, the people I knew, and the things we talked about. I'm a lot less comfortable or knowledgeable about the religious parts.

The thing is, when I was growing up, I didn't have to do anything to be Jewish. We were Jewish no matter what we did or didn't do. And if I had married someone who is Jewish, it would be easy because the kids would automatically be Jewish. I wouldn't have to do much. But as it is, if I want my kids to be Jewish, I have to do a lot more. And so far, I haven't done that good of a job.

In retrospect, and it feels very foolish on my part, I made some big assumptions when Kim and I got married. I had always told her that Judaism is a great way of life and how much I like the values. I thought she would naturally get involved in Judaism because she would see the merits. And she does get involved to an extent, with things like cooking Jewish foods, but it's not as much as I thought. Really, the burden of raising the kids to be Jewish has fallen on me, and I haven't been that good about pushing myself.

I know it is selfish on my part, but it would be nice if Kim could play a more active role in helping with doing more at home. And I wish she were a little more engaged with Judaism than she is. But she's not a Jew, she never wanted to convert, and I can't expect her to do more than she has.

There have been times when the kids say, "Why don't we do more Jewish things at home?" That really hurts. It's my responsibility, but it's hard for me. I feel guilty that I haven't really made the commitment to teach them about Judaism. Part of my issue is that I don't feel I have the knowledge or background to drive that commitment. I feel like I don't know enough myself, and that I should take the time to learn more myself so I have more to give to them. I have to admit that I have torn feelings about really investing the time and energy to do all that.

My oldest daughter's bat mitzvah is coming up. It's embarrassing to me that I don't remember much, and that if I am going to be able to help her I will have to get a tutor to work with me on my Hebrew. There are certain phrases I remember but I really lost the skills in Hebrew, and I feel like I need to be better. The pressure is on my daughter, but I feel like it's on me too.

I probably didn't think about this issue as much as I should have at the beginning. Part of that is because I was young, and thought things were just going to fall into place. I think it would have been helpful to have given this a lot more thought early on. I could have found a rabbi I was comfortable with to help me address some of these issues, or had more discussions with people in similar situations. But I didn't do any of those things. Kim and I kind of learned as we were going through it. It would have been easier on both of us if I had realized the role I'd have to play in this whole process. I just hadn't known that in a situation like this, I would have to do a lot more than I would on my own if I really want to raise my children to be Jewish. And that is what I want for them. I want my children to see the value of being Jewish, and to be committed enough that they will maintain their religion when they are older, even if they become involved with someone of a different faith.

Karen is in her late forties or early fifties. She works as an artist in a variety of different mediums. Karen appeared to me to be a strong and passionate woman who has worked hard to handle this issue with integrity. She decided she could make major changes in her life for her husband but only if he was sure himself of what he really wanted.

✖ KAREN

* * *

I was born in Prague, Czechoslovakia. I really grew up in Montreal, though, because we moved there when I was five. My mother was Catholic, and my father really wasn't anything. The way the school system was set up in the '50s and '60s was that if you were Catholic you went to the Catholic school, which was part of the public school system. And if you were anything else, whether it was Protestant or Jewish or whatever, you went to the Protestant school. So being at least partly Catholic, I went to the Catholic school.

* * *

As a child, I was actually quite devout in the sense of being very spiritual. I believed in the goodness of God. I was always getting into trouble in school. We had religion classes every day, and I would ask questions like, "How come Jews and Muslims and little babies in Africa who have not been baptized . . . how come they can't go to heaven even if they are good people? If God is all you say he is, how come they don't get a shot at heaven too?" I never got straight answers to these questions, and I didn't like that. So that was one of the big injustices I found with the religion.

My parents never went to church. My mother would only go on Christmas Eve, basically to hear the music and to see the pageant. But I went to church every Sunday. I was terrified of mortal sins, you see, because if you don't go to church you commit all these mortal sins and if you commit too many of them you go to hell. After a certain amount of sins, it adds up. I was terrified of hell.

I met Stuart just after I had finished graduate school here in the States. He was running an arts program for kids. There was an immediate attraction. Stuart is Jewish from New York. He went to an Orthodox synagogue growing up. His family was somewhat observant, but not really Orthodox. They didn't keep kosher. Stuart grew up with the orientation that there was no question he would marry a Jewish woman. His parents didn't even want him to hold hands with anyone unless she was Jewish. They weren't so dog-matic as to say that all women who are non-Jews are trash or filth. They weren't like that. It's just that Judaism was really, really important in their family.

In my family going out with someone Jewish wasn't too big a deal. I think if I were involved with someone who was black or Asian it would have been more of an issue. But I have to say that there really was a certain level of anti-Semitism in our family. It was mainly in the form of stereotypes. "Jews have all the money. They are the bankers. Jews run the world. Jews are stingy." These things weren't expressed blatantly, but they were subtle, under-lying messages that would come out in little jokes here and there. These kinds of stereotypes were made about Jews and about other races. I think it had to do with my parents being immigrants, and needing someone to kick around.

By the time I met Stuart, I had moved away from being a practicing Catholic. The important thing for me was honesty and knowing what it is you want out of life in terms of religion. I wasn't associated with any church at that point. Stuart was obviously Jewish, but he didn't belong to a temple when I met him. He was one of these confused people, who I still have a hard time understanding. Around the High Holidays he would get nervous, and he'd start pacing the floor. "Oh, my God, I have to go to services, but where am I going to go? What kind of place do I want to go to? What do I really want to do?"

He'd go back and forth. I mean, he would get totally nuts, which was a little crazy to me because in growing up Catholic the rules were so different. I would say, "Well, then, just go. What's with all this questioning? Either you are Jewish or you aren't. Either you want to practice your religion or you don't. Why are you so confused about this?" I kind of understand a little bit more now, because I know that Judaism is more than a religion and you can feel very Jewish and still not want to be religious. But I have a somewhat hard time understanding it.

Stuart and I were together for a long time. When we started getting more serious, it took us a long time to make up our minds as to what we were going to do with our lives in terms of marriage. And when we eventu-ally did decide to get married, Stuart said he thought it was very important that he have Jewish children. I didn't have a problem with that. They weren't going to be Orthodox Jewish. I would have had a problem if he had wanted that, but then he probably wouldn't have been with me in the first place.

The only thing I said was, "I need you to get your act together, because if you're going to ask me to give up Christmas, you have to be very clear about what you want." To me, fairness was the big issue in all this, and being honest. I think that if you're going to ask someone to let go of something that's important to them, you'd better be honest with yourself about why you're doing it. Christmas has always been the holiday that I really loved, and I knew it wasn't going to be easy to give it up. I was prepared to do it and I was prepared to have a Jewish home if Stuart so wanted to have Jewish children, but he had to be pretty clear. There couldn't be any of this "I don't know what I'm going to do" business. Also, I didn't want to send my children a confused message. So I really needed him to get himself together about all this. He said, "Yeah, yeah, sure. I'll do it." I said, "Fine," and that was it.

We decided to get married in November. The High Holidays were a month or two before the wedding. We wanted to go somewhere for services where we would be comfortable, but we really didn't know where to go. This was a pretty nervous time for us. We would be getting married soon. It felt like a very big step to us. We had been together for six years, and living together for three years. This wasn't something we were doing lightly.

We ended up going to High Holiday services at a temple that a close friend of ours belonged to. It was a huge place, and there were tons and tons of people. We were in the overflow area in a smaller sanctuary, and the assistant rabbi was the one giving us the sermon. He started to talk. His sermon was all about how the Jewish family is falling apart for two important reasons. "The first reason," he said, "is that there is a large gay community of Jews who no longer have intact Jewish families." The congregation didn't like this. There were murmurs in the audience, and the shuffling of chairs. "And the second reason that the Jewish family is falling apart is because of the 'shiksas' out there who are taking away our prime Jewish young men."

He actually used the word *shiksa*. At that point, some people got up and walked out. I was so upset. It was not what we needed to be listening to. Stuart was appalled, as was the friend who belonged to that temple. It turned out that there was so much outrage after this sermon that the assistant rabbi was fired. It is almost funny in retrospect, but at the time it was horrible.

We rented a room at a hotel for the wedding, and a judge married us. We wrote our own ceremony, and it was really lovely because we incorporated Jewish traditions and also some Czech traditions. We each broke a glass.

I have to tell you about something that happened. This was one of my mother's funnier moments. My mother made me this quite wonderful wedding dress. So there we are in the hotel room the day of the wedding, and she's doing the final fitting. It had to be so perfect. My uncle is sitting there talking to us, and my mother says to him, "Thomas, what do you think? Karen is marrying a Jew. I can't believe she is marrying a Jew. My luck, she picks the one poor Jew to marry. Can you believe it?" I'm sitting there thinking, "Oh, my God. What are we going to be in for?" She was dead serious. Then she says, "But you know what? Maybe it's not so bad, because Jews really take good care of their wives. They buy them good things. I don't think I have anything to worry about."

"Yeah, right, mom. Stuart is really going to go out and buy me diamonds and fur coats." To this day, she believes that about Jewish husbands. Not the diamonds and fur coats part. That's not who I am and we couldn't afford that anyway. But she is convinced we have the best marriage in the world. She should only know. We have a decent relationship. But according to her, we have the ideal relationship, we have the greatest home, and the reason is because Jewish men are good to their families. That's why Jewish men don't get divorced. They stick by their families. They take care of their children. "Look at your husband and how he takes care of your children. Jewish men do that." She's got it all figured out. And stereotype or not, I'm not going to change her mind at this point. She's 88 years old. She can go to her grave thinking we have the best relationship and the best family. It makes her happy.

We have two children, Jacob, who is 16, and Lizzy, who is 12. They are very much Jewish. Jacob went through a bar mitzvah, and it was wonderful. When I got pregnant with Jacob, and we found out it was going to be a boy, Stuart got really nervous because he knew he wanted to have a bris. Well, not only had I not converted, but we didn't even belong to a temple at that point. We didn't know who to even talk to about it. We made some calls ourselves, but we couldn't find any mohels who would perform the circumcision if the mother wasn't Jewish. So what to do?

We finally went to talk to a rabbi who was on the board for a battered woman's shelter in our neighborhood. We thought, "He's on the board for this shelter. He's got to be a somewhat liberal person." We called him up and explained the situation. He told us to come in and talk. We spent two hours with him, and he was a huge help. A lot of the conversation centered on my commitment to raising our kids to be Jewish. I turned to Stuart and said, "I am saying to you in front of a clergyman that I am going to make the commitment for this child to be Jewish, to go through a bris, to go through a bar mitzvah, to go through all the Jewish rituals that need to be done. You have to make a commitment to me that you are going to maintain the Jewish religion. This is not going to be just me. It is not something that I am going to do by myself. You have to make a commitment to yourself about this." So he did.

That rabbi was so wonderful. He said, "I'll find you a mohel. Don't worry about it." It was a tremendous relief. I guess he had an arrangement with this one mohel, and it was like, "Don't ask, don't tell." The mohel must not have asked much about us, and the rabbi didn't volunteer much information. So Jacob was born, and we had a bris at the house, and the mohel came and did it.

I'm very proud of my children and how they've absorbed the issues about religion and culture in our family. Jacob, especially, has always had a great sense of humor about things that would come up. I remember one night when he was about seven. It was Christmas time, and we were driving home. We drove down this street where there was a big manger set up outside of someone's house. The manger was pretty gaudy, but Lizzy loved it. Lizzy was two or three at the time, just a toddler. She loves little things, especially little babies, and as we drove by the manger with all those lights she said, "Look at the cute little baby Jesus. I love that little baby." Stuart is whispering to me, "Oh, my God. Lizzy is going to want to be Christian." And Jacob said immediately, "Time to get this girl to Hebrew school."

We've definitely had a lot of funny incidents. But some things have been difficult. I always get melancholy at Christmas time. When I was growing up, Christmas was a real family holiday. You had to be home for Christmas no matter what. The one Christmas I missed was when I was living in Europe for a year. I was so homesick. I love the smell of the Christmas tree, and the lights, and my mother baking cookies, and all the excitement. It was always a very big deal. Not having a Christmas tree . . . that's been very hard. The one thing Stuart absolutely could not stomach was a Christmas tree in his house. I understand why he doesn't want one. For him it's such a strong symbol of Christianity. I totally understand it intellectually, but emotionally I have a hard time with it. Part of it is that he doesn't want to confuse the kids. But my argument is, "Well, if we teach them right, they won't be confused."

What we do is we go and visit my parents at Christmas. We have Christmas at their house and we give Christmas gifts, but it's not a religious thing. The way my family celebrates it, it never has been. We never had a manger under the tree or anything like that. Stuart is willing to go to anybody else's house for Christmas. It's just that he does not want Christmas in our house. That would be just awful for him. As a matter of fact, we did have Christmas once when our kids were little. Jacob had severe asthma when he was a baby, and when he was about two years old he was having a terrible time with it. He ended up in the hospital. He got out right before Christmas and we really couldn't make the trip to visit my parents with him, so my parents came to our house. Stuart actually relented and we had a Christmas tree up for two days. I loved having the tree. Stuart was very conflicted and upset the whole time we had it. As soon as my parents left it had to go out. I mean, they walked out the door, and two minutes later the tree was gone.

There are differences between Stuart and me that I know have to do with how we were each raised. An hour of religion every day for 13 years, 5 days a week, really sticks with you. It's a horrible tension that you live under, even if you're not consciously thinking about it all that much. For example, Stuart doesn't have the kind of guilt that I do. One time we were talking about life, and I happened to mention that I am terrified of going to hell. He looked at me like I was totally off my rocker. He asked me why I was really worried about that. "Well," I said, "It's because of all my mortal sins." "What sins," he asked, "Have you ever killed anybody? Did you ever rob a bank?" "Well, no." "Did you ever deceive someone so much that it injured them in any way?" "No." "So what have you done that was so bad that warrants you to think that you would go to hell with the Hitlers and the Idi Amins of the world?" And I said, "I don't know. But I haven't gone to church. That's what it is. What have I done that is so horrible? I left the Church."

Jacob is in his thirties and works in radio and theatre. It has taken Jacob and his wife Diane a long time to become comfortable together as a couple. One reason for that is because they each had to work out their separate ideas about religion and the place it was going to have in their lives. It became clear fairly quickly that even though Diane was the one making more of the obvious changes, there were a number of changes Jacob needed to make as well.

✖ JACOB (TO BE FOLLOWED BY HIS WIFE, DIANE)

* * *

I grew up leading a dual life. At home we really didn't do a lot in terms of practicing Judaism. We did things for the High Holidays like typical secular American Jews. We didn't celebrate the Sabbath that much. But when my sisters and I were ready to start school, my parents decided that they wanted to give us more of a Jewish education than they had. They sent us to an Orthodox day school. And the things I learned at the day school were very different from what I got at home.

* * *

My parents really chose the Orthodox school because it was the only day school in our area. And to be honest, I'm glad they did. I went to that school from kindergarten to eighth grade, and I really cherish the education I got there. It was difficult at times because I would learn things during the day about what Jews are supposed to do, and then come home at night and not practice anything I learned. Also, we would all bring our lunches to school, and people around me would be eating their kosher food, and I knew my mom had packed me something like pressed ham for lunch. So there were times when I would be thinking, "This is all pretty strange."

I definitely had a strong Jewish feeling. I got involved in a youth group, and I'd go to weekend retreats and conventions. We had some really good teachers at these events. There was one in particular who I thought was just great. We would be standing around in the temple and singing songs at the end of Shabbat. All the lights were off, and we would just be looking at the candle for Havdalah. This teacher would tell us stories. He'd say, "You know, we are all together in here, and we're singing these songs. And outside is a man who is 30 years old who is looking inside. He is saying to himself, 'I used to do that, and I want to do that again.'" He sort of instilled that feeling in me of not wanting to ever let go of Judaism, and he did it in a very loving way. This was when I was in the seventh or eighth grade. It was a very long time ago, but I definitely carry those images with me.

After grammar school I pressed hard to go to a Jewish high school in a nearby city, because that's where some of my friends were going. But my parents were dead set against it because they didn't want me living away from home. So I went to a secular school. I did continue studying Gamora with a rabbi at the day school, but that kind of stopped after my freshman year.

When I started to date, I usually went out with Jewish girls. I don't think I made a conscious decision to do that. I think it's more that those were the girls I met and was attracted to, and just ended up going out with. Whether or not I went out with Jewish girls was not something I considered to be a big concern of my parents. I remember talking to them one time, and describing a conversation I had with some of my friends. I had said that I thought my parents didn't care if I dated Jewish girls or not. When I told this to them they seemed surprised, and my mother said, "Well, why do you say that?" That was the first time I ever really sensed that they might have some feelings about this issue. But it certainly wasn't something they reminded me of every day.

Honestly, I have always had a sense that I wanted to have Jewish children. I felt that even when I was dating non-Jewish people, which I did more of from the time I went to college. One of the things that had been instilled in me was that assimilation equals death. That was a lesson from my grade school days. For a long time I wasn't worrying much about any of this because I wasn't ready to get married or have kids. But I've always known that when I was ready, it would be important to me for my kids to be Jewish.

I met Diane at a small birthday party for a mutual friend of ours. I was thirty-one at the time. Diane grew up in a family that is very much Southern Baptist. Her father is a minister of music, which is similar to being a cantor. Her entire family sang in the choir, and they were at church at least a couple of times a week. A lot of the people in Diane's religious community had a very black and white view about religion. They felt that the Bible is the word of God, and you should just follow its tenets without a lot of questioning. Diane's parents differed in that they always said to their children, "If you have questions, you need to pursue them." So Diane did, and she really became disaffected with some of the ideas she had been raised with. She began looking at other religions, and when I met her she was reading about Buddhism and Hinduism and those sorts of things.

I told Diane fairly early on that I wanted my kids to be Jewish. I think she was a little reluctant at first, but she was willing to consider it. She didn't say no. She wanted to learn more about Judaism. We tried going to a few different synagogues. Gradually Diane became more comfortable with the idea that raising her kids to be Jewish was something she might be interested in pursuing, and something she would be willing to do. The interesting thing is that she said, "Look, if I'm even going to consider doing this, we are not going to have Judaism in our lives in name alone. This has to be something we will be involved in, and something we will embrace."

We started each week to celebrate Shabbat. We began lighting the candles and saying the prayers. And we began going to temple on a pretty regular basis, which is way more than I did at any other time in my life. I knew that if I were involved with somebody who was Jewish and not particularly religious, there wouldn't have to be as much of an incorporation of Judaism into my life. And honestly, I didn't know how I felt about all of this at first. As a kid I had enjoyed the particular Jewish experiences that I chose to be involved in, but I had never especially liked going to temple. That didn't give me the same kind of spiritual feeling as I got from those small youth groups. So I was a little reluctant about doing too much until we discovered and got involved in this temple that we are now in. It's a Reconstructionist temple. It has a large number of interfaith couples, but they are all interfaith couples that have chosen Judaism as the religion they are going to follow. The feeling is that the people who are part of this congregation have chosen to be part of a Jewish community in a very conscious and nonobligatory way. And the atmosphere there truly is spiritual. The first thing Diane and I did when we discovered this temple was to join the chorus. Diane is a fine singer, and I'm an adequate singer, so that was a good place for us to start to get involved.

Before we actually made a commitment to each other, we definitely looked into as many aspects as we could of an interfaith marriage. We tried to figure out how everything would really work. We read books that talked about, "the December dilemma," which was something we were already dealing with. We don't have a Christmas tree, but the smell of greenery around the house at that time of year is something that Diane really likes. So we do put up greenery, along with some dangling stars of David. I would prefer not to have any of it. I don't particularly care one way or another about the Star of David, but I would certainly rather not have anything Christmas tree-ish. But I go along with it because I know there have been an awful lot of compromises on Diane's part. It's true that when we got together I had a more specific view of what I wanted than she did. But still, she's done a lot.

When we actually did decide to get married, we wanted to have our wedding in this Reconstructionist temple that we had been going to. We talked to the rabbi, and he agreed to marry us. He suggested some more books for us to read to prepare for the wedding. We read them and we talked about them. They had questions about money and dealing with families and things like that. Some of the books had little exercises that were kind of silly, but we went through a few of them, and they did expose some cultural differences between us. So we really did do a good amount of preparation.

We had a Jewish wedding. It was in the synagogue, and our rabbi officiated. Would an Orthodox person consider our wedding ceremony Jewish? Well, probably not. I think that our rabbi left out some particular phrase that is usually always included, because Diane wasn't Jewish. A few people picked right up on that. After the ceremony my uncle said to me, "That was a nice wedding. It wasn't a Jewish wedding, but it was a nice wedding." But in our opinion, it was a Jewish wedding.

Jamie was born just about a year after we got married. Diane had not yet converted. Was it an issue for me that she didn't convert before we had a child? Maybe just a little bit. We did have the brit mila, the bris. And there is a certain thing to say at that time for a converting child, which we did, because when Jamie is six months old, we'll do a formal conversion for him in a mikva. Even the Orthodox will recognize a conversion of a child who does that. It was Diane's idea to have that happen, just so that he would never have any problems over whether or not he is really Jewish.

Diane has always talked about converting. She has even said to me, "I am probably going to convert." I have never directly said to her, "I want you to do this," or "I need you to do this." Not even once. But on the other hand, I remember reading somewhere about a couple in which a Christian woman is married to a Jewish man. They really don't have the best communication. Years go by, and one day they talk about the fact that the husband is sorry that she never converted. And she said, "Well, you never asked me to." So even though I don't want to push Diane to convert, I have definitely let her know that it's something I would love to happen if it's right for her. I would never press for it. I let her know what I want, and then I've made an effort to completely let the subject go so she can figure out for herself what she wants to do. There is no real promise of the conversion. I think she probably will do it, but it has to be in her own time.

Now that we have Jamie, we have a lot more contact with Diane's parents. Her parents are as liberal Southern Baptists as you can get, but they grew up in a culture in the South that is pretty narrow-minded. I think that in some ways they feel kind of stuck in this narrow-minded denomination that they don't necessarily share a lot of the feelings with. But still, they're sensitive about what they perceive as criticism of their community. Diane has said to me recently that her parents don't think I have any respect for their religion. And in some ways I don't totally respect it, but at the same time I don't think that they do either.

It's a little tricky. I think that some of what her parents are feeling has to do with the fact that Diane has been talking to her mother lately about the possibility of her converting. Her mother kind of got a little upset and questioned why Diane would be doing this. We think her mother feels a little caught in something that she doesn't totally believe in herself, and it makes her sort of defensive. So I don't know exactly what is going to happen with all that.

It is very possible that my in-laws are going to be moving close to us sometime soon. That means they would be the relatives that will be the nearest to us and to Jamie. I was thinking the other day that one of the things I really valued as a kid was having my grandmother sing me Yiddish songs. There were all kinds of other little Jewish things that she did that had an influence on me as well. I really loved that. Diane's parents have their own music and their own traditions that they'll be sharing with our son. And I don't exactly know how that's all going to play out. He'll still be hearing the Yiddish songs because Diane and I will be singing them to him. He'll be hearing them from his parents in his own home. So that will be a very different experience than the one I had growing up.

We've talked a little about whether we might want to send Jamie to a Jewish day school. I certainly valued that experience. But Diane didn't have that same kind of experience, and she's not particularly for it. She has a problem with the concept of Jewish day schools as being separate and exclusive. The concept of a chosen people is something that she is not so fond of. It's extremely important to me that my child have a strong Jewish identity, and I do think that one of the ways he can get that is by going to a Jewish day school. But on the other hand, we plan on having much more of an active

Jewish family life than my family ever did. I think Jamie can get a very strong Jewish identity from the things that we will be doing at home and from the things that we'll be doing at the temple.

One thing I'm so grateful for is that Diane and I have found this particular spiritual place to be a part of. We were just at temple on Friday night, and we had Jamie there with us, and we were singing Hamotzi. There was a whole group of people, and we were all either touching a challah, or touching someone who is touching a challah. Everybody was singing. And I just thought, "I love this. I just feel very blessed that we're here and that we can share this with our son."

Diane grew up in the South. She is extremely close to her parents, and has a lot of good feelings about the community she was a part of when she was growing up. Diane is very conscious of wanting to continue to show appreciation and respect for her own family and heritage even as she is moving in a completely new direction.

DIANE (PRECEDED BY HER HUSBAND, JACOB)

* * *

I was raised Southern Baptist in a town in Alabama. There's no question that a lot of our community was pretty fundamentalist. Most of the Southern Baptist culture in my opinion is very brainwashing. It doesn't really allow you to explore questions. That's the part I had the most trouble with.

* * *

My father is a minister of music. He didn't get involved in the ministry because he felt a calling, which is what a lot of ministers do. He was just a musician who also happened to be a practicing Baptist. Combining his work with his religion was a natural thing for him to do. My family was basically in church every time the doors were open. On Sundays, we kids would go to Sunday school and then to the morning service. Later there would be some sort of youth activity, and then an evening service. The church was the center of our social community.

I will say that my parents were not as conservative or fundamentalist as most of the people around them. They actually encouraged me to figure things out on my own. At Sunday school, some of the teachers would say different things that would bother me. The really great thing, and the reason I am the way I am today, is that when I would say to my mom, "I didn't understand this," or "This didn't make sense to me," or "What about so and so, because they're not Christian?" she would always say, "God gave you a brain, and He intended you to use it." That gave me the freedom to think for myself.

I went to a local college, and when I was a sophomore I had what Southern Baptists would call a "born again" experience. I was on a choir retreat, and I decided I had to rededicate my life to being a better Christian. At that point in my life, I had been just kind of flailing around, not knowing what I wanted to do. I'd been partying and all that kind of thing. And what I came to realize was that I needed to start using my brain a little bit more. So for the next year or so I was very much dedicated to being a better Christian. In my family that didn't mean becoming more fundamental. It meant trying to be a better person.

I moved to Atlanta, and away from my parents, when I was twenty-two. I began doing some exploring about my spirituality. I started looking into some of the Eastern philosophies. I attended a meditation group. I tried going to a Baptist church for a while, but I hated it, and I knew that wasn't where I belonged. I just kept looking around. This is something I really struggled with. I'd be up half the night wondering if I really was going to hell if I didn't follow the right path. By the time I was twenty-five, I had completely rejected Christianity. It wasn't just the Southern Baptist part that I wanted to get away from, but all of it. I didn't believe that I could lead the spiritual life that worked for me and be Christian. I was quite dogmatic. I wouldn't even have a Christmas tree. In no part did I want to be connected to Christianity at all.

Jacob and I met at a birthday party for a friend of ours. We flirted at the dinner. He didn't say so that night, but Jacob later told me he thought I was Jewish. We started seeing each other, and we talked about religion right off. Really on our first date, Jacob let me know that one of the reasons he and his old girlfriend broke up was that she wanted to raise her kids Unitarian, and he very much wanted to raise his kids Jewish. I respected the fact that he came right out with that. In my head I thought, "Well, that's interesting." It didn't turn me off. But at the same time I didn't think, "Oh, that would be great."

We took things very slow, and we formed a good friendship. And over the next few years, as we did get more serious, I started looking into Judaism. Actually, the initial problem I had with it was that Jacob did not attend a synagogue on a regular basis. To me, if you're Christian, you go to church. That's a big part of it. So I didn't understand why it wouldn't be the same for someone who is Jewish. Eventually I learned more about Judaism and the different ways people practice it. I told Jacob that I knew I could never be Orthodox. I probably couldn't be Conservative either, because some of the aspects were not quite liberal enough for me. And Jacob didn't like Reform because he didn't like the organ and the choir, or the rare use of Hebrew. Finally we discovered this Reconstructionist synagogue. And I really became attracted to the Reconstructionist movement and what it stood for. And that's when I started getting really serious, thinking, "Could I do this or could I not do this? Could I raise my kids as Jews?"

The thing that appealed to me most about Judaism, or at least Reconstructionism, is that it asks you to question everything. And for me, that's really great. I also sensed that there didn't seem to be an attitude of, "Our way is the only way," which is something I very much disliked about my religion when I was growing up. But it's interesting. What happened is that as I began to get in touch with what Judaism was all about, I also started to think, "We're getting really serious. We're moving along with this. Before we go any farther, I need to slow down and explore my Christianity again." So I went back and talked to a minister, and he gave me some books, and I looked into Christianity a bit more. I started to realize that there are a lot of Christians who are open to different ideas, and who believe that their way isn't the only way. And what's ironic is that at the point I realized I could raise my kids Jewish, I actually realized that I could be comfortable raising them Christian as well.

My entire background revolved around Christianity. I found that despite my relationship with Jacob, and all the things I liked about Judaism, I absolutely was feeling pulled towards my own heritage. I needed Jacob to be willing to explore Christianity. It's not that I wanted us to stop going to the synagogue. And I wasn't asking him to consider raising his children with any element of Christianity. I just wanted him to learn more about it, in the same way that I was learning about Judaism. But he really couldn't do it. He said, "You know, I grew up in this Christian world. That's enough. It doesn't work for me to learn anymore."

We pretty much broke up over that. There were other things involved as well, but that was a definite part of it. His inability to accept my religious background was a big issue. I didn't feel he respected who I was, because I had been raised Southern Baptist. And it's funny, but in some ways even my Southernness bothered him. He made fun of it. And I really wasn't okay with all that. I had to say at some point, "Look, if you are serious about me, and you're talking about how you want to raise your children, you have got to accept me for exactly who I am. My parents are Southern Baptists. Now, they're liberal, but they're Southern Baptists. And if you can't come to terms with that, we can't go any further."

So we didn't see each other for a while. And a few months later I called him to say hello. I had missed his birthday. We started talking, and he was very, very upset. I realized how much he did love me. He was never able to show it before. But once we were broken up, I saw it. We got into therapy together. Nothing drastic happened. It wasn't such an epiphany. We just went along, and we learned to communicate better. Jacob told me that as long as we raised our kids Jewish, he understood that my spiritual path would be my own. I said, "I just need you to understand, I'm not ready to say that I would ever convert." I really needed him to know that. And I really needed him to say, "You don't have to ever convert. That's alright." And that's just what he did say. And he's stuck to that. He has never asked me to convert.

Did he ever actually do anything on his own to learn about Christianity? No. But by that time I honestly didn't need him to do it as much because I could see that he had become more receptive to my background and my family. His attitude had softened and I knew he respected who I was. The fact that he said, "Your spiritual path is whatever it is, and I'm okay with that," was his way of expressing that.

Once I decided I was ready to commit to marrying Jacob and raising our kids Jewish, I told him we wouldn't do it half way. I said, "If we're going to do it, we're really going to do it. I want us to participate in Judaism, and to be very involved." The thing that's beautiful to me about religion is that it gives you a way to continue to ask yourself the important life questions. And why would we want to miss that? It's always been important for me to think of things beyond this earth, and to try to understand life and the big picture, more so than it is for Jacob. There's no doubt that of the two of us, I am the spiritual leader.

About a year ago, shortly after we had gotten married, and I knew I had the freedom to be whoever I was, I started talking to the rabbi about converting. I wasn't pressured by anyone, not by the rabbi, and not by Jacob or his family. His family has always been so loving and accepting of exactly who I am. Of course, it might have been a different story had we said we're raising the kids to be Christians. I'm not a hundred percent sure I'm going to do it. But one of the reasons I decided to go ahead and look into converting is that I was pregnant with our son, Jamie. I don't want my child to ever not understand if he's Jewish or not. Also, I have already made the decision to live a Jewish life with Jacob and our kids. I think I was maybe waiting for a lightening bolt to hit me, or some sort of emotional experience, so I would know it was time to convert. But I realized that choosing to convert is really a very logical decision. "If I'm living this life, if I'm raising my children in this way, why wouldn't I convert?" I'm in a conversion class right now, and that's a lot of what we talk about. "Why wouldn't you do it? Why would you?" Those questions are very important to me. We spend a lot of time wrestling with them.

Another thing that makes me want to convert is thinking about Jamie having his bar mitzvah. I don't want to sit there, and have Jamie feel bad because his mother isn't being honored. I want to be called up to the Torah. And probably Jamie and I will do a lot of the studying together. Hopefully I'll have my own bat mitzvah by then as well.

I'm still very close to my parents, and Jacob has become close to them as well. When Jamie was born, my parents came to the bris. The bris was really hard for all of us. It wasn't hard because it was a Jewish ceremony. It was hard because you don't want to see your eight-day-old child physically hurt and in pain. It was horrible. My parents are very emotional people. They had never been to a bris before. I was wailing. So they're seeing me in pain. They're hearing my baby crying. They were just beside themselves. It was very traumatic. My father-in-law just thought we were a bunch of nuts.

When I first told my parents that Jacob and I would be raising our children as Jews, and that I was considering converting, it was not particularly difficult. They love Jacob, and they were very open to it all. But from the time I actually got pregnant, and especially since we've had the baby, it's been harder. My parents told us that they are afraid they will not be enough of a part of Jamie's life. They are afraid that they will feel somehow estranged, and not as connected. My parents' religion is so much a part of who they are. I think they're worried about having to keep a lot of the things that are so important to them separate from Jamie.

I do think that it will be a little tricky to find ways of including my parents in Jamie's life in ways that still respect who they are and what they believe. My parents are really good people. I don't want them to feel that they need to change anything about themselves in order to have a close relationship with their grandchild. Just this last weekend, we visited them in Alabama. My father is actually serving as an interim minister at a church right now. So we went to my father's church, and he preached. He focused on passages from the Old Testament. He made absolutely no mention of Christ. There was no mention of the Savior, or anything like that. I know he did that to make us feel more comfortable, which I thought was so lovely.

I don't know how much Jacob appreciated what my father did. My parents really need his acceptance, and to know he respects them too. It's not easy for Jacob to sit in a church and be comfortable himself, much less to have his son sitting there with him. I understand that it must be difficult. At the same time, I feel that my dad's gesture was very generous. It was something he didn't need to do. I said that to my dad. "You don't need to feel like you can't mention Christ in your own church just because we're there."

Even though my parents are not the same religion as our children will be, Jacob and I decided that if we were to die, or something were to happen to both of us, the children would go to my parents. Of the four grandparents, my parents are the ones who would probably be able to handle it the best. They understand we want our children to be raised Jewish, and they're okay with that. They don't know how they'd do it, but they'd figure it out. This is something that both Jacob and I agreed on, absolutely. And I think the fact that my parents know they're in our wills makes them realize, "Oh, they really do respect us."

Janet is in her forties. She started out as an attorney but is now working in real estate. Janet found it difficult when she realized that the man she wanted to spend her life with did not share her religion. She has no doubt that going ahead with the marriage was the right thing for her to do. However, she is also very aware of some of the ways in which her life would be different if she had married someone of her own faith.

✖ JANET

* * *

I'm Jewish. When I was growing up, I had a fairly conservative religious education. I was bat mitzvahed, and then I kept going all the way through Hebrew high school. I wouldn't say we were all that religious. We didn't keep kosher. Our Judaism was based mostly on the traditions and the holidays, and was very much tied in with family. I always knew it would be difficult if I married someone who wasn't Jewish. But my parents are also somewhat liberal and understanding, so I figured that whomever I chose would be okay.

* * *

I met Lou at college in St. Louis. My parents were very happy that I was going to a college that was about sixty percent Jewish. They must have thought, "Oh, no problem." But of course I found the only group of non-Jewish people to hang out with. It's funny, but throughout my life I've tended to do that. Anyhow, Lou and I met freshman year, and we were both part of this large, very close-knit group of friends. They all came to my house for Thanksgiving. So my parents knew Lou already, and by the time our relationship became something other than a friendship, it wasn't initially a pressure because they knew him and they liked him. But as I began to realize that this was somebody I could possibly spend the rest of my life with, it was very difficult for me.

I guess I had been coached on all the problems there could be if I married someone who wasn't Jewish. I was torn between being very happy because I thought Lou was somebody I really wanted to be with, and being concerned about what that actually meant for the future and kids and all that. I used to cry over this issue. I would say to myself, "Why couldn't I fall in love with somebody who is Jewish?" It was a difficult thing because Judaism was so important to me and I definitely felt the need to continue to have it in my life. I wasn't sure how that would work.

Lou and I kept going. And once we kind of realized that we were both looking towards a future together, we talked about this issue a lot. I expressed the feeling that it was important for me to be married in a Jewish ceremony. And it was important to me for my kids to be Jewish. Lou comes from a very religious family. He was an altar boy. He went all through parochial school, but he really rebelled against the religion, and just at the point we met, he had stopped going to church. So the issue of religion was an easier thing for him. I was the one who had the stronger feelings. If he had been someone who was more devout, I don't think I would have married him. It wouldn't have worked for me.

We did discuss the idea of conversion. It wasn't something he was comfortable with because he wasn't at all religious in any way, so there would have been no point in him converting. It isn't something I would have asked him to do, anyhow, because I would never have wanted anyone to ask me that. But what Lou did say was that if it was important to me, he would feel fine being married in a Jewish ceremony, and having our kids raised to be Jewish. That was the key for me. And although there have been stumbling blocks along the way, it has been easier for me than for some other people because my husband has been so flexible.

When we decided to get married, my folks asked a lot of questions. My dad was concerned about the kids. And he was also concerned that I wouldn't feel as close with my husband's family. He was afraid I wouldn't have the same kind of relationship that I would if they were a Jewish family. And he didn't think he and my mother would have a close relationship with them either. I think in our case, though, there were socio-economic issues that separated our families more than religion. I think that my parents maybe tied in a little too much with Lou's family not being Jewish, rather than the fact that they were from a whole different walk of life. And I think that even though there isn't the kind of closeness my parents would have liked, in general, it has worked out okay between the two families.

We had the wedding at a hotel. At the time, there weren't many rabbis who would officiate. My rabbi from growing up wouldn't do it. The Conservative rabbi said, "I'm not allowed to do that." The one we finally found was a little flamboyant, and wouldn't have been my first choice, but he was a rabbi. My mother-in-law cried through the whole ceremony as they stood under the chuppah with us. And I thought, "You have to wonder whether she's crying because her first son is getting married, or because he is getting married by a rabbi." But I will say that my father-in-law really got into the whole thing, with the glass breaking, the dancing, the hora, and all the Jewish things. They both really had a great time. They still talk about it. I think it was a really neat wedding. Plus it was something they had never seen before.

I think it was actually my idea to do one other thing related to our marriage. This was for my in-laws. Lou and I both thought they would feel a little better about the whole thing if we had the marriage blessed by a priest. Obviously, we wouldn't have a service. But we found a priest and the two of us went and talked to him for a bit, and he did a little blessing of the marriage. I felt fine about it. He didn't say anything that made me uncomfortable. It wasn't a big deal, and my in-laws didn't come. But we told them about it. And I think it made them feel better because for them the marriage was now somehow more real.

Lou and I have three children. I'm pretty sure the kids would describe themselves as Jewish, especially now that they've been bar and bat mitzvahed. A couple of times I heard my middle one particularly say, "Well, I'm both." And I said to her, "You know, you're really not. Your dad is Christian, but you're really not."

I would have liked my kids to go to a Conservative temple for Hebrew school and Sunday school. I did send my daughter to religious school at the Conservative temple in our area for two years. But at that point, in order to continue we would have had to join the synagogue. So then I had to make a decision. The problem was that the Conservative temple was very unreceptive to Lou really being a part of the temple. They told me that when our kids had their bar and bat mitzvahs, Lou would not be allowed up on the bema to be part of the service. I felt very uncomfortable with their attitude. I said, "You would think you would want to encourage people to stay within the fold and raise their kids Conservatively. Why are you making it so difficult?" But they were just totally unbending.

So we've had to compromise. And that's just the way it is. It's a little difficult for me because we ended up joining a Reform temple that I'm not especially comfortable with. It's not what I'm used to. It's very different from what I grew up with. We picked the Reform temple because they have a lot of intermarried couples there. It was just easier. But what's frustrating is that when we got to my oldest daughter's bat mitzvah, we still had some problems. There was a certain portion of the service that my husband couldn't be a part of, which was the Torah service itself. We were pretty upset about it. At the time there was a rabbi who had been there for thirty-five years, and everybody was afraid to step on his toes and complain about anything. But I decided I had to say something. I went through the cantor, who was the one helping my daughter. I said, "You know, I don't really understand why Lou couldn't be up there during the Torah service. I could understand if you didn't want him to hold the Torah." That made some sense to me, and truthfully, he really wouldn't have wanted to do that anyway. He was happy to participate in the service, but I think that would have been a little too much for him. Anyway, as it turned out, the cantor talked to the rabbi and they said, "That's fine." So he was able to be a part of the Torah service. I walked and carried the Torah, but he walked with me.

For me one of the biggest issues has to do with the High Holidays. The holidays are very important to me. I guess I kind of knew it would be this way, but because family is so important, I find it difficult each year at holiday time when I am hit with the realization that we won't be going to services together as a family. For one thing, my husband is not going to sit in temple all day, which is what I do. So I end up being with my folks and going to their synagogue, because I don't like to sit by myself all day. I do take the kids to the family service at the Reform temple we belong to, but I've never really become a part of it because as a family we don't do much there, and because it's not a place that I've ever felt comfortable. So I don't do the holidays exactly the way I probably would have liked to. And I'm less involved in the temple overall than I probably would have been if I was married to somebody Jewish.

Neil is a businessman who is in his fifties. He was raised to feel that it would not be possible for him to marry someone outside of his own religion. But everything changed for Neil when he discovered that some of the most basic assumptions he had about his life and his family were completely wrong.

✖ NEIL

* * *

Both of my parents are from Europe. They were there during World War II. All of their friends were refugees. I really didn't know any adults who were peers of my parents that were born in this country. My parents sent me to an Orthodox Hebrew day school. We were not observant at home, but at school we were very observant. I was much more educated in general than my parents were. They never had gone to school much during their childhood because the war had happened.

* * *

Almost everything we did at home that had to do with being Jewish was based on what I brought home from school. Neither of my parents read Hebrew or was familiar with the prayers. We didn't do too much about the holidays, because neither of them was from a religious background. But all of their friends, and all of my friends, and everybody in the street that I knew from the neighborhood, everybody was Jewish.

I didn't go out with girls much. When I graduated from high school I had gone out with one girl who was from my school. I also met some girls from a Jewish youth group through the temple, and those were the girls I knew and those were the girls I spent time with. When I started college, I had a girlfriend from that youth group. She was still in high school, and I would come home on weekends to see her.

I didn't exactly go away to college. I went to a college about twenty miles from my house. And when I went there, I became more observant than I had been at home. All through grammar school and high school, my Jewish needs were met at the day school I went to. Judaism had been interwoven into my life. It was my life. When I went to college I thought, "All right, where's the Jewish part?" So I had to create more of a Jewish life on my own.

One thing I started doing was keeping kosher. When I was growing up, my family would eat in Chinese restaurants. We never would try to eat kosher. But when I went to college, eating kosher became an issue for me. Also, when I was at the day school, we used to have prayers every morning. I didn't do the prayers on the weekends or on school vacations. I didn't even think of doing them. But then when I went to college, I decided maybe I should do prayers myself on my own, which I did for a while. I also started Sabbath observance. I went to synagogue every Saturday. Actually, most weekends I went home. I would see my girlfriend, and I'd also go to synagogue.

When I went to college I wasn't really looking to get attached to anybody. The relationship with the girl at home wasn't serious, and eventually it just sort of ended. I didn't want another girlfriend. I was sort of playing around. Marriage was not in my sights at the time. I wasn't thinking about it. I was free and I was meeting girls. And actually I wasn't even meeting any Jewish girls. Being with non-Jewish girls was better because that made it easier for me not to commit.

There was no question in my mind that when I did get married it would be to someone who was Jewish. I wouldn't think of it any other way. In fact, when I started going out with Donna we discussed it. I put it very bluntly. "You're not Jewish. There is no way I'd ever marry you." That was exactly how I felt. "Since you aren't Jewish there is no way in the world we will ever get married. If you want to have a relationship with someone who you might get married to, go find someone else. Otherwise, we can have fun."

As a liberal person in the United States of America, I had my own rationale for saying I was not going to marry someone who is not Jewish. Why is it so important to marry someone who is Jewish? What difference can it make? A person is a person, right?

My rationale was this. "The Jews have been around for thousands of years. They have seemed to make a positive contribution to the world, and for that reason what is it my business, or my right, to sort of end that? Because the question is, why is it that the Jews have made so many contributions to the world, disproportionate to their numbers? How could that be?" And my answer was that there is something innate in the blood, in the gene pool, that makes Jews able to make these wonderful contributions. "How can I do something that might stop it? If you marry somebody who is not Jewish, you are diluting this very pure gene pool." That's how I explained it to myself.

When I met Donna, I was in graduate school. We went out with each other for a fairly long period of time. But at the same time, Donna was going out with other people, and I was going out with other people. It was definitely understood there was absolutely no commitment. There was no future. It would have been a problem for me if I thought there was going to be a future. We sort of drifted apart, and then we broke up. And one day I ran into her and she tells me that she's engaged to someone else. I said, "That's great." It was wonderful for her, and I was happy. I was relieved. That was a good thing. But then I found myself missing her, and I was upset. Her engagement didn't work out, and we got back together again.

I still wasn't thinking about marriage. I was young. I was only twenty-two. I finished school and started working for my parents. I wanted to move out, and get a place of my own. Donna and I decided to get a place together. I told my parents about it, and they got all upset. They did not want me to be serious with someone who wasn't Jewish. But Donna and I still weren't talking about marriage. The subject did not come up at all.

So here I was having this long-term relationship with someone who wasn't Jewish. Then a couple of things happened. One is that I was talking to my mother, and she said, "It's too bad you can't be with Donna, because she isn't Jewish." It had never entered my mind that there was a serious possibility Donna and I would be together. I just never really thought of it. But since I had told them we were living together, my parents were all involved. And I decided we had to break up because my mother was right, and I could never make a commitment to her and what was the point of being together after all this time, and the heck with it. So we broke up.

Then what happened is I took a trip to Germany, and I visited my grandfather who I had never met before. This was my mother's father. My mother's father had divorced my mother's mother during the war, and after that my mother never spoke to her father again. They never communicated. So I had never met him. My friend and I flew to Berlin, and went to meet my grandfather. He was living in the same house he had been in before the war, but the name of the street had been changed. I remember there was a Jewish star on the house, to show that a Jew lived there. The reason he survived the war was because he left Germany to go to Italy. He remarried in Italy, and he was there for most of the war.

My grandfather spoke English very well. He was an educated guy. We took a long walk around the zoo, which was close to his house. We were just walking and talking. I told him "I've got this problem. I've got this girlfriend and I really care about her, but she's not Jewish, and I feel like I can't marry her."

So my grandfather says to me, "What's the problem?" I said, "Well, I'm Jewish and she's not Jewish, and that's that." He said to me, "There's no problem. Your grandmother wasn't Jewish, and neither was your mother." I said, "What?" "No," he said, "Your mother was baptized," and he told me the name of the church where they had had the Baptism. I said, "Oh." He said, "Your mother is not Jewish, your grandmother is not Jewish, and so what's the big problem?"

There goes my gene theory out the window. My whole rationale for not marrying someone who is not Jewish because you're going to dilute the bloodline is gone. I had absolutely believed it. It was the way I had pretty much explained how I was going to live a major aspect of my life. And I certainly had no reason to particularly disbelieve my grandfather. He didn't care. He had no ax to grind. I started remembering other things I knew about my mother's family, and I knew he was telling me the truth.

So now I don't know what to do. I come back to the States, and I'm upset. Donna and I are broken up at this point. So I go to my old friend from kindergarten, and I say to him, "Alan, I might not be Jewish. My mother was not Jewish. What do I do?" Alan is the son of a rabbi, and he is also a rabbi himself. His whole family is very Jewish. He says to me, "You know what, if you think you're Jewish, you're Jewish." And that's it. It took me a while, but eventually I decided to just accept that.

At this point I was pretty angry, and thinking about my parents stepping in and saying they didn't like this relationship with Donna made me even angrier. The first thing I did when I got back home was go to a Chinese restaurant and eat shrimp. The second thing I did was decide to stop doing all the religious stuff I had been doing.

I never confronted my parents about this. I know that the way they handled it had to do with their background. After World War II everybody was sort of mixed up, and people's backgrounds were all pretty vague. Nobody asked a lot of questions. If you said you were a Jew, they were happy to accept you. When my father married my mother, she didn't bother to convert. They just let everyone assume she was Jewish. Even at the Hebrew day school I went to, they were just happy to have anybody and they were not going to challenge your background. Every Jewish kid was a gift, and they weren't going to look any gift horses in the mouth.

Gradually Donna and I sort of worked our way back together. Time went by, and I think probably by now it had been five years that we had known each other. I was getting more and more irritated with my parents, and feeling, "Oh, God. I have worked for years in the family business and I helped build it up and they have plenty of money and it's enough." All the time I worked, I didn't really get any salary. And not having any salary, I wasn't really independent. It just got to the point that I said I have to start taking care of myself.

I decided to move to Minneapolis and start my own business. And that was going to be the end of Donna and me. I wanted to break with everything. So I moved in February, and she came to visit me a couple of weeks later. I had already been finding myself getting attached to a particular woman who was from the same area as Donna, and was Irish Catholic, and a lot like Donna, but obviously not Donna. And I said to myself, "Hey, stupid, you've got the real thing. What are you doing?"

Donna and I went on a trip together, and I proposed to her, and we decided to get married maybe a few weeks later. We had been through so many years of being together and breaking up, that by the time I really decided I wanted to get married to her, and she felt the same way, we wanted to do it as soon as we could. I didn't know what we would do about the religious parts and having a family. I just wanted to be with her. All the other stuff wasn't important. I went to my father and said, "You know what, dad? I'm going to get married to Donna." He said, "This will be the last time I am ever going to talk to you." I said, "Okay, that's fine. Goodbye."

The fact is that I had always had a particular relationship with my family. I was very attached to them. We had a relationship of all for one, and one for all. I was always the star of my family, and I was always the hope of my family. I was the success of my family. They were stunned when I actually decided to marry someone who was not Jewish. Stunned. They didn't think it was possible, and I didn't think it was possible either.

Donna's parents put together this wedding really quickly, and it was at their house. My parents refused to go. My father was mostly the one against it, but my mother sort of went along with him. My mother's mother and her husband came. My grandmother said to my mother, "You're not going to your own kid's wedding? Are you crazy?" I didn't even try to talk them into coming. It made it easier. It was hard enough for me.

As soon as we got married, Donna started making chicken soup on Friday nights. That was it. She knew that I needed this and I wanted this, and she just supported it. She knew that it was important to me and she just did what she could. That's how we started adding a Jewish element to our lives. Making chicken soup was the first step.

Shortly after we were married my mother was diagnosed with cancer. This was a big strain on the whole family. I made up with my parents, and I would go back and forth a lot to see my mother. She died a few months later. I started going to say Kaddish every morning. So now I was doing prayers again. I was starting to do more Jewish things.

After we had been married a little longer, we started talking about the fact that maybe Donna was going to convert. She told me she was thinking about it. I never asked her to convert. I wouldn't dare to ask her because I felt I had no right to say anything about it. Converting is something she had to do on her own volition. It had to be her own idea, and she had to feel this was the best way for us to raise a family. I was very glad when she decided to do it. In terms of kids, it would have been really, really hard if she didn't convert. I just don't know what I would have done. I think that would have put a severe strain on us. I don't know if the marriage would have lasted. I don't know what would have happened. I think she sensed that.

The fact is we did things that were for each other. She understood what I needed, and I understood what she needed, and we were willing to give each other those things. I think she knew I really had to have a Jewish family. I really had to have Jewish kids. I really had to live this Jewish life. And so she accommodated it. And she really had to have me. We wanted to be together, we had to be together, and that's the way we could do it. It's like the gift of the Magi. Each one takes a precious thing and gives it to the other, and I think that's what we both did.

In a way being married to someone who converted is easier. There are many Jewish people who resist the rituals and who resist participating. But for Donna, it's not enough for her to just be Jewish. She feels she has to participate. She can't say, "Well, I'm Jewish, but I don't care about doing all these things." If she's going to be a Jew, she wants to be an active Jew.

The hardest thing . . . it was all hard. Everything sort of came as a natural progression. I started from certain assumptions and as life went on I found out different things and my feelings changed. What really helped me was going to Germany and visiting my grandfather. That was the turning point.

I think the most important thing is that you have to know who you are. And you have to be willing to face up to who you are. I knew who I was at one point, and then I found out I was a little different. When I started out, I absolutely meant what I said to Donna. I said it straight out. "No way in this world will I ever marry you." But as life goes on, sometimes you change.

As far as my kids go, they've got to make their own choices, and I've got to handle them. Those are two different things. They are going to be individuals, and I'm going to be me. And, hopefully, they're going to make good choices for themselves and be happy.

Gloria is in her fifties. She and her husband are both lawyers. Gloria has found it to be a tremendous help to be part of a religious community that is made up of couples in situations comparable to her own. It is a big reason why she is as comfortable as she is with the choices she has made.

❂ GLORIA

* * *

I was raised in a Catholic family. My father grew up as a Southern Baptist and actually converted to Catholicism when he married my mom. We were very involved in our church and in daily Mass. I went to a parish school for both grade school and high school. My social circles and world were all Catholic because of the schools I went to. Certainly, there was an expectation that I would remain Catholic and have a Catholic husband and family. It wasn't really discussed, but that was kind of the assumption.

* * *

I have a very large family. Other than one of my brothers, I was the only one to go to a secular university. When I was making decisions about what college to go to, I remember thinking that I wanted to get out of the world I was in. It wasn't so much that I didn't like that world, but it was very limited. I wanted to experience other people's backgrounds and to expand a little bit. At the university, I still found that people sort of stuck together in pockets. The Jewish kids mainly hung out with the other Jewish kids, and the non-Jews were with the non-Jews. I did have a Jewish roommate whom I lived with for three years. Other than that, I didn't have a lot of Jewish friends.

The first year I was in college, I was involved a little bit with the Catholic center. I wouldn't say I really fell away after that, but I had lots of questions in my mind about the role I wanted Catholicism to have in my life. A lot of the fundamental core values were with me, but I was bothered by some of the dogma. Even though the Catholic Church had been somewhat liberalized, it was still pretty rigid in terms of its doctrines and beliefs. So that raised a lot of doubts in my mind.

Howard and I met in college. I was a junior, and he was a senior. We were both working in our dorm cafeteria, and we met over the mashed potatoes. A few weeks later, we had each finished working and we were sitting in the cafeteria having coffee. We started joking about something, and he said, "Let's just get married." And I said, "Okay, how about next Saturday?" He said, "Well, I can't get married on a Saturday." And this was how I discovered he was not Christian. I remember that I kind of decided at that moment, albeit in a pretty immature way, that this wasn't something that would necessarily interfere with the development of a relationship.

Howard was raised in a Conservative Jewish family. He was bar mitzvahed. His family was pretty active. Both of his parents are Holocaust survivors. They came here after the war. I learned very early on that Howard had dated a number of non-Jewish women. I think he was pretty certain he was not going to marry a Jewish woman. I'm not quite sure why, but his experiences dating Jewish women were not positive, and I think he made some generalizations from that. The first time he brought an Irish Catholic girl to the house, his father told him that if he ever dated a non-Jewish girl again, he did not want him to pray over his grave. He was that adamant. It was that strongly felt. Howard's solution to that was, "Well, I just won't introduce my dad to the girls I'm dating."

We did start dating, and it was a platonic relationship for a long time. We took things very slowly. Obviously he was going to be graduating. Also, there was a whole charade going on with our families. I didn't even meet his parents for five years. And with my family, our relationship was just something that wasn't discussed. Howard did meet my parents and the rest of my family fairly early on. He would sometimes come to our house. But we usually did things with friends, so there was always a group and it wasn't very clear or obvious that we had a special relationship.

Howard and I had met in 1974. We did not get married until 1984. We were both in separate law schools for four of those years. But after that we were together back in Chicago, and it was still another six years before we got married. Religion was definitely a major factor in why we waited so long.

Putting children aside, I don't think either of us felt that this was an issue for us. We had pretty common basic values. But the more we talked about marriage, the more the focus was on children and how we would raise them.

It was interesting. It was exceedingly important to Howard that the kids be raised Jewish. But he couldn't articulate why he felt it was so important. I'd say, "You want to raise the children Jewish, but what does that mean?" He'd say, "Well, I don't really know what that means." For practicing Catholics, the rules are very clear: "You go to Mass, you follow the doctrine." For him it was much more cultural: "I want my children to identify as Jews." Other than that, at the core of his feelings was the Holocaust. He felt it would be a betrayal of his parents in particular but also of the faith and the culture generally for him not to raise his children Jewish. I was very sympathetic to the issues he faced. Also, I had this odd, superficial, very depersonalized feeling which was, "Oh, there are so many Catholics in the world. Even if I don't raise my children to be Catholic, my religion and my culture will go on without me." That sounds a little callous, but I think it was what I felt.

Deciding about children was one hitch in the marriage decision. And then there was another big issue. It almost sounds childlike, but both of us are very attached to our parents. And each set of parents is extremely involved in their religion. My parents are devoutly religious. It is a major part of their lives. I don't know if *religious* is the right word for Howard's parents, but they are devoutly Jewish. For each of them, their religion is so much the essence of who they are. So there was this great fear on both of our parts of just bringing sadness to them. We didn't want to do that.

I had met Howard's parents about five years into the relationship. I met his mother first and got along great with her. She knew we were dating at that point. I met his dad a little later. Howard and I were living together. We had just bought a three flat. His dad is a wonderful handyman, and he was coming over to help out. My first encounter with his dad was when he walked in the door, and I was on the bathroom floor scrubbing and scrubbing to get the stains out. I can honestly say from that moment he fell in love with me. He is a guy who just respects someone who will work hard and really put in some effort. He and I developed a wonderful relationship.

By this point, it had to be clear to everyone that we were serious about each other, but neither set of parents raised the issue. I think that they each had the mindset of, "If we don't talk about it, it will go away." I really believe that is what they thought. So there was no discussion about it at all.

Finally we decided to get married. When we told Howard's parents, their first question was, "How will you raise the children?" And our answer was pretty automatic: "We are raising them Jewish." We wouldn't have gotten married had I not agreed to that. That was satisfactory to them. They didn't ask if I was going to convert. They didn't want any of the specifics. They just wanted to hear the words, "We will raise them Jewish." Once they heard that, I think they made a real effort to put aside a lot of their other feelings so they could accept our marriage.

When we told my parents, their first question was, "If you're getting married, then by whom? Who is going to marry you?" They wanted us to be married by a priest. To them, marriage is a sacrament, and without a priest it wouldn't be valid.

We ended up deciding to get married not by a priest or a rabbi but by a judge that I had clerked for. My parents didn't articulate any opposition at the time, but I discovered recently through some discussions we had that they had prayed and prayed that we would not get married. It was not that they felt the marriage was inherently wrong but that it would be very problematic. They thought we would have an extremely hard time. Also, they were worried about my afterlife, which for them was critical.

I think back to my rationalization of leaving Catholicism, which was, "Hey, if you lose one Catholic, what's the big deal?" From the Jewish perspective, I know that losing one Jew is considered a huge loss. But that's kind of a community view. If you think about it more personally, it's clear that it's not just hard for the Jews when an individual leaves their faith. From my parents' perspective, having to deal with one of their children leaving is as big a loss for them as it is for Howard's parents. And the knowledge that their grandchildren would not be Catholic was especially difficult for them.

My father and mother came to terms with our marriage in different ways. My father is an extremely devout Catholic. He is probably more educated than my mother, because he converted to Catholicism as an adult. But his view was always, "My children come first." He said, "I can be a Catholic and I can still go to my daughter's wedding. I can still support my child." My mother struggled more with the issue of, "What am I allowed to do? Can I go to my daughter's wedding and still be a good Catholic?" She worked very hard to find a way to abide by the rules of Catholicism and yet to still be supportive of me. It is remarkable because I know they each had their own perspectives that they had to work through in order to accept this marriage, and in the end they did.

Howard and I knew we were going to raise our kids to be Jewish. But when it came to the specifics, our approach was, "Well, we'll figure it out as we go along." Our first child, Mark, was born within a year of our marriage. We did not have a bris. The ceremony itself wasn't that important to Howard, and in fact I think he had some discomfort with the whole idea. So Mark was circumcised in the hospital after much objection from my obstetrician, who was vehemently opposed to circumcision. I finally said, "This is not an issue. I can't even discuss it with you. He will be circumcised."

Howard and I used to joke that my mom for sure had baptized Mark when she was alone with him. It doesn't take a lot to do, and I'm sure she would have done it just to be on the safe side. We joke about it, but I have a feeling she really may have done it with all of our kids. In my view, if it gives her comfort, it's fine.

After my son was born we had a daughter, and then another son. When my kids were still very young I became friends with a woman and her husband, Aaron. Aaron was a rabbi with a really strong interest in interfaith marriages and family issues. He was starting a somewhat informal interfaith family network and asked Howard and me to join. We started with a group of twelve families. We met once a month in people's homes. Because all of us had preschool-aged kids at the time, mostly we did activities that centered around the holidays. Then, as the kids started to get older, we became a little bit more structured. We actually hired somebody to work with the kids as a teacher. Anyhow, Aaron eventually decided to leave the congregation he had been with, and this small group of twelve families decided to formalize and create a congregation.

This was about six years ago, and we now have about 130 families, which is incredible. Aaron is our rabbi. The congregation is Reform. And it's not some sort of new religion. It's exclusively Jewish. Because there are so many interfaith couples, there are great discussions about the religious aspects of raising children, as well as all kinds of other family issues. It's a wonderful community to be a part of. Actually, in recent years there has been an increase in exclusively Jewish families who have joined. They like it because of the depth of discussion on a lot of issues and because of the variety of perspectives that are brought to the discussions. For me, belonging to this congregation has made my choice to raise my children Jewish manageable. It helps so much to be with a group of people who understand the difficulty of that choice, rather than simply taking it for granted that it is something I would naturally do.

There are other things that are easier as well because we belong to this particular congregation. At one of the other Reform synagogues in our area, they also have a fairly significant non-Jewish population. But at that synagogue, the decision was made that the non-Jewish members of the congregation could not vote. It's not that I really care so much about voting, but the symbolic statement is that as a non-Jew you really don't belong. There are lots of situations like mine where you have a Jewish man and a Christian woman, and more often than not the woman is the one primarily responsible for the religious training. She has made that leap to raise her children as Jews. And then somebody says, "No, you can't vote. You're not really a part of this congregation." To me, it would have been almost unbearable to be in that setting.

One thing I've always been pretty sure of is that I'm not going to convert. To me, converting means that you reject one thing and then make an affirmative leap of faith over to something else. It's a very spiritual, faith-based decision. That has never happened for me. A lot of the time it seems that when people convert it is less of a spiritually based choice and more of a cultural, almost practical choice instead. But that's not how I would want to do it.

At this point, any ambivalence I do feel about the religious choices I've made has to do with my sense that there is something I have lost in my Catholic upbringing that I haven't yet found in Judaism. I've lost the sense of spirituality that I want to get from my religion. I'm probably going to overgeneralize this, but my sense is that Jews don't tend to look at their religion primarily as a spiritual solace. It is predominantly a cultural tradition that is extremely important. My upbringing is different. I grew up feeling that there is a spiritual reason for your religious focus and that there's a solace you get from your religion that you cannot get from anything else.

I do think that, given our congregation, I eventually might find more of what I'm looking for spiritually in Judaism. There was one High Holiday service that Howard and I were at a number of years ago. I don't really know any Hebrew, but I was becoming familiar with the songs and the chants. I turned to Howard and said, "This is what it's about." Somehow, it felt like a true spiritual moment. It is something that only happens for me in a group setting. It never happens when I'm completely alone. That was kind of the first taste I had that I could get that feeling of solace from Judaism. That's been the thing that I am searching for, that I haven't completely found.

Our kids have always known my background. They are aware that, over the years, I have usually gone to Easter and Christmas Mass. I didn't go so much out of a sense of obligation in the sense of still wanting to be a practicing Catholic. It was more that it just felt right to be in church at those times. It felt very familiar. It was a comfortable place for me to be. Howard doesn't go with me, but he doesn't object. Also, my whole family is right here in the Chicago area, so any gatherings with our kids and my family often seem to occur around Christian holidays.

I think Christmas and Hanukkah are the hardest times of the year to deal with. I think that Jews feel very much marginalized during that time of year, because Christmas is just such an overwhelming holiday. And when you're part of a world that is heavily Jewish, like I am, you realize that the way a lot of Jewish people deal with that feeling of marginalization is by trivializing Christmas. They trivialize the traditions of my family and the traditions I grew up with. I have a very dear friend who is Jewish, and she will never refer to December 25 as Christmas. She always just calls it December 25. I want to say to her, "It's Christmas. Can't you just acknowledge that this is a big day for me?" But I don't say anything. For me, that holiday period raises a lot of tension between wanting to understand the perspective of my Jewish friends and loving and wanting to keep the good feelings of those experiences from my childhood.

This tension manifests itself in our family in a way that sounds so trivial, but it happens every year. We always give our children gifts for each of the nights of Hanukkah. We don't have a Christmas celebration at our house, but the tradition has evolved for us to go to my parents to celebrate Christmas with them. Even though my parents only live about an hour away, we stay overnight with them on Christmas Eve. Grandma makes these great breakfasts on Christmas Day. And of course Santa Claus always comes to Grandma and Grandpa's house. When the kids were little, they knew Santa didn't come to our house, so they would leave notes and say, "We're not home, go to Grandma and Grandpa's." What happens is that our kids end up getting gifts from us at Hanukkah, and we bring gifts to my parents' house for them at Christmas as well. And every year there is a battle between my husband and me over which gifts are the Hanukkah gifts and which are the Christmas gifts. And it suddenly hit me this year why there is this fight and why there is tension over this same issue. Partly it has to do with my feelings about my traditions, but it also has to do with his feelings of marginalization. "If you give the nicer gift at Christmas, does that mean that Hanukkah isn't as important?"

This has been going on for so long, but I could never articulate it until this year. And this year, when we kind of got into that debate, I found myself bursting into tears and saying, "I have given up my whole background. Let me give them a nice gift for Christmas. Can't you at least give me that?"

Howard understood. But he didn't want me to have those kinds of feelings. He has never pushed me to convert, but he wants me to completely embrace Judaism and be willing to kind of put that other part of my life behind me. At that time of the year, though, I usually can't. It's amazing to me that even though we've been together twenty-five years, and married fifteen years, these issues still exist between us.

There are some things that have come up that we have been able to resolve fairly easily. We've talked very concretely about funerals and death. This is something that Howard recently started asking me about. He said, "When we die, if you die before me, what do you want me to do?" In theory I can't be buried in a Jewish cemetery, and yet we have this irrational desire to be buried next to each other. And to me, what he was really bringing up was, "What happens next?" Catholicism is so based on notions of the afterlife and that human desire to stay together. I thought about it. I have always been uncertain about the afterlife part. I said, "I want Rabbi Aaron to be there, and I want to be cremated, because I just don't want to deal with where I'm to be physically buried. And that's it, that's all I want." And I think that as a practical matter Howard kind of feels the same way: "Let's just be cremated."

If you asked my children what religion they are, they would say they are Jewish. A number of years ago I overheard my younger son, Jonah, make a comment about being half Jewish and half Christian. I said, "Well, you know you're not really half Jewish and half Christian. You're Jewish, and you have a mom who is Christian, and that's okay." And he said, "Oh, I know that. I just tell people who don't know me very well and ask me what I am. It's easier to explain that way that my mom isn't Jewish."

Jonah has said other things that let me know he's given a lot of thought to his religious identity. About a year before his bar mitzvah, he and I were driving through an area that was heavily Orthodox. It was a Saturday morning, and there were a lot of people on the street. My son turned to me and said, "You know, Mom, I kind of consider myself an un-Orthodox Jew." And I thought he had come up with the perfect label. He didn't understand exactly what he was saying, but I think he just meant, "I'm connected to those people in some ways, but I'm different from them, too."

My daughter has started to ask me questions about Jesus Christ and the nature of an afterlife and who is going to heaven. I try to explain, while at the same time distancing myself and trying to be objective. I tell her, "Christians believe that Christ is God." I say that I believe Christ was an exceedingly good man who was a role model in all sorts of ways and lived a life that we would want to emulate in terms of values. And we talk about the values, and she sees how she can link many of those same values to Judaism.

My oldest son hasn't asked me much about religion. But lately he has gotten interested in the opposite sex. One day he asked me, "Mom, would you be upset if I married a Catholic girl?" I almost burst out laughing, but then I stopped and thought, "This is a great question and I don't have an automatic answer to it." I made a choice to raise my kids Jewish. To me, it was much more positive than sort of blindly raising them Catholic. And if my son married a Catholic girl, would that all fall by the wayside? What I said to him at the time was, "The most important thing to me is that you find someone who has the same beliefs and values that you do."

But my son's question keeps coming back into my head. I realize that we really are beginning to face that issue of what kind of people our children will marry, and I am surprised at how I think about it. Sometimes being married to a person of a different faith is really hard. As a parent, you don't wish difficulty on your children. Our parents didn't want us to have hard lives. That's really what they cared about. And now that I'm a parent, I am thinking about that same thing. But the flip side of it is that so much in our life together has been positive. I think Howard and I have a relationship that is all the richer because of our differences. And our kids have an outlook on life that is all the richer from our having made that difficult decision.

Elise is in her early fifties and works in the area of historic preservation. She and Eric met when they were both in graduate school. Elise and Eric appreciate the support their parents have shown for them since they first decided to get married. They know their parents mean well and that their intentions are good. But some awkward moments have still come up.

✖ ELISE (TO BE FOLLOWED BY HER HUSBAND, ERIC)

* * *

I grew up in a very Jewish neighborhood in Chicago. The schools I went to were almost completely Jewish. Our home was culturally Jewish, but there wasn't a lot of attention given to what I would call spirituality.

* * *

We joined a Reform synagogue when it became time for me to start Hebrew school and Sunday school. I remember the focus of those classes always seemed to be on who we were and what we were feeling, rather than on the interpretation of Scripture or what the Talmud said. I never got much of a foundation about Judaism through books or institutions. It was all based on what we did at home. I don't think I knew what a mikva was until I was an adult. I learned about the things that my own family did. I understood the very basics about what you're supposed to eat and not eat and how to observe Passover and the High Holidays.

Eric and I met in graduate school in Montana. The more I got to know him, the more I found that his values and his responses to situations were very close to my own. Eric was raised mainly as Protestant. Religion was never an issue between us. The first time it actually came up (and this probably doesn't show very good planning) was in the rabbi's study when we were talking about our wedding ceremony. It was important to me to have a rabbi marry us. The rabbi said to Eric, "Well, I won't require that you convert in order to officiate. However, I would like a commitment from you that you will raise your children as Jews." And Eric simply said, "Yes." That was really the point where we committed to having a Jewish household. Eric went on to study and learn as much as he could. He has always been better read on these matters than I have. His approach to Judaism is much more intellectual than mine ever was.

Probably because we decided to have a Jewish home, my family was very supportive. I think my favorite story about all this is when I was riding up in the elevator with my grandmother. Eric was already waiting for us in her apartment. My grandmother turned to me and said, "Is Eric going to convert?" and I said, "No." We finished the ride in silence. We got up to the apartment and my grandmother started preparing a meal. She couldn't reach the plates on the top shelf. She just turned to Eric and ordered him to get the plates in a way that she would to any of her grandchildren. And I knew at that very moment that it was going to be all right. I think that probably is a good way of describing everyone's reaction: "Well, this isn't what we necessarily wanted to see, but obviously Elise is happy and Eric is a decent human being, and we have to be supportive." I think all of my family members probably went through that. Perhaps my parents in their own intimate moments may have expressed more concern than they did to us in person, but I believe that they reconciled fairly quickly, particularly after they spent more time with Eric and really got to know him.

There was one thing that happened that was very difficult. I can be pretty cavalier about it now, but at the time it was hard. We were at the wedding supper, after the ceremony. There were a number of speeches and toasts. My father-in-law stood up. He gave a blessing, and in the blessing he evoked the name of Jesus Christ. It shocked me. I felt so embarrassed. I still feel remorse when I think about it. A number of the wedding guests were Holocaust survivors. I wish it hadn't happened, but I have grown to know this man and love him as my father-in-law, and I know his intention was never to hurt. I think this is very important to understand. He was speaking from his heart, and it wasn't meant to make anyone feel uncomfortable. We never said anything to him about it because really I don't think he was wrong. We just weren't prepared to deal with it.

What my father-in-law's blessing shocked me into realizing was that we were really merging two cultures. Up until that point, I just hadn't looked at this as much of an issue. But it is an issue. That incident was a reminder to me that we can skim along the surface and believe everything is just fine, but we do all come from very distinct heritages and you can't pretend the differences aren't there.

I don't know exactly what we would have done if Eric hadn't agreed that the kids could be raised Jewish. I'm really not so crazy about the cafeteria plan, when you do a little bit of this and a little bit of that. I didn't want our children to be raised like that. To me, religion and culture aren't about experimentation. They are an important way to give kids a basis for who they are. It makes sense to me to decide on one religion and to stick to your decision. I do think it's easier for the Christian partner to raise a child Jewish than it is for a Jewish partner to raise a child Christian. I think that all of the elements of Judaism can be accepted by a person of Christian belief without conflict, but I don't think it works as well the other way because Christianity goes much farther. I don't think a Jewish person can accept a lot of the ideas in Christianity without having some problems and resentment. I know for myself that I couldn't have done it.

Eric and I have two children. We live in a fairly small city in Montana. I think that where you live is a big factor in this kind of situation. What has been difficult is not so much being married to Eric but living in a community and a place where there is simply no Jewish life. We've made what we can, but it's hard. I've always said that, in a small town, if you want to see a play, you have to put one on. If you want a synagogue, and if you want to have a Jewish community, you have to actively participate at a much higher level. Because Eric isn't Jewish, it really falls completely on me to develop whatever Jewish life we are going to have. I have to be responsible for the Jewish education of our kids because the community doesn't provide it.

At home, all of our religious observances are focused on Judaism. Occasionally we'll do a Shabbat dinner, and we usually go to services once a month. I sing at the synagogue. And we observe the major holidays. Our kids evidently have had enough exposure to Judaism to feel close to it and identify with it, because they definitely consider themselves to be completely Jewish. In fact, I think they have a stronger tie with their Jewishness because it isn't, so to speak, "in the water." It isn't in the environment. Our home is oriented towards Judaism, and we think about that and talk about it a lot. We have discussions about religion. Because Eric has read so much, he can give the kids an historical perspective about both Judaism and Christianity, and the development of each. So something we do in our family is that we have a lot of conversations about religions and the similarities and the differences between them. That's been good for all of us.

I know that my kids see themselves as different from their classmates much more so than I ever did, because the neighborhood I grew up in was so heavily Jewish and theirs isn't Jewish at all. I think that since we've worked a little harder at distinguishing them as Jews, they feel a stronger obligation to distinguish themselves among their peers. And then what happens is they get into fights, which are nonsensical. For instance, my daughter will say she's Jewish, and one of her friends will say, "If you don't believe in Christ, you're going to hell." That's the kind of conversation she'll come home with once in a while.

I do think the fact that we are bringing up our children to be Jewish has been somewhat hard on Eric's parents. We see his parents pretty often because they live only about an hour away. They know we have a home with a religious element in it, and they're happy that the children are growing up in a religious setting. But my mother-in-law in particular, who has been extremely gracious and loving and has tried within her own frame of reference to be supportive, has still expressed a number of times that she wishes more of Eric's Protestant background could have a place in our family. I think she is primarily concerned that Eric has given up something that is important to him. And I think she feels very strongly that by not having the children celebrate Christmas, we are somehow denying part of her family's culture.

Before we had kids, there was a certain amount of naughtiness associated for me in celebrating Christmas. It had to do with the whole experience of opening the Christmas presents and enjoying the tree. It's sort of the same feeling I have eating shellfish: "I'm not supposed to be doing this, but it's really fun." And when we were first married, we used to go with Eric's family to church services, just to be supportive of their traditions. But when we had our kids, I felt I had to be more consistent. We would still go over to see my in-laws on Christmas. We exchanged gifts with Eric's siblings and their families and with his parents. And we always join them for their Christmas dinner. But it is a very nonreligious observance.

There was a point of conflict that would arise each year because Eric's mom really wanted us to take the children to Christmas services. This was especially true when our kids were younger. I was uncomfortable taking them to church until they were old enough to understand more about their own identities. And once they were, I had no problem with their going. I think my daughter went a few years ago, when she was about ten. She thought the church was pretty with the music and so forth, but she knew that she had her own religion. I think that it's important for children to first be clear about their own identities, and then there are a lot of other things to experience that can enrich their lives.

What we've tried very hard to do is not let any of this be seen by our children as a competition. We didn't want to set it up with Santa Claus on one side and a potato pancake on the other. We don't want anyone competing for the children's attention by the size of the gift, with the holiday or the prettiness of the service, or even with the ease and comfort of being Christian, because it is easier. We want the context to be that different people celebrate different things, and we can share in celebrations that are different from our own.

I think our children have felt some of the pull between Eric and his parents over situations like having them go to church services. There have been a few other things. His mother has occasionally gotten one of the kids a book that looks okay at first but when you read it is clearly a Christian perspective or a Bible story. And the kids will look at me when their grandmother leaves the room and wrinkle up their noses. I say, "Just don't worry about it. Say thank you and put it away."

Given that Eric's side of the family didn't prevail, in a sense, I think that they've handled all this extremely well. I'm sure my mother-in-law is sorry that she never got to see her grandchildren wearing little angel costumes in the Christmas play, but at this point I think that she's overcome that feeling in a way that is incredibly admirable. She has done so many great things for us. She is sensitive about traditions and culture, she buys appropriate gifts on the holidays, and she even gives money to our temple. Every year or two she hands me $100 to give to the synagogue. About ten years ago, we started doing something, which we have kept up every year since. At Yom Kippur, when you have the names read at the memorial service, we always include the names of Eric's grandparents as well as mine. I think his parents appreciate that, and they always make a donation to the synagogue at that time as well.

Two of our most wonderful experiences have been the bar and bat mitzvahs of our kids. I coached the kids with their Hebrew to learn their Torah portions. Eric read through the English translation and researched to help them with understanding the portion. He would sit down with each child, along with different interpretations he'd found from various Jewish scholarly writings. Then he'd say, "Now here is the way this fellow perceives it, and this is what that one says. What do you think it means?" He helped each of the kids really understand what their portions meant. I have a wonderful image of seeing Eric sitting on the couch with each kid in turn helping them write the interpretation of their Torah portion. It practically brought tears to my eyes. He just has been so generous. And because he intellectualizes it, and because he finds it so interesting, I don't think he even sees it as sacrificing. I think he sees it as a real important piece of his fatherhood.

At both the bar and bat mitzvah, each set of grandparents was on the bema. Obviously, there were certain things that my parents could participate in that Eric's parents couldn't, because it involved the Torahs. But his parents did a special grandparents' prayer. We had them read it right at the beginning so that it would clearly be an integral part of the service. As I've said to my mother many times since, I really think both of these events were kind of restorative. They each took place many years after we were married. But they still served an incredibly important role. They brought together a lot of people from both families who hadn't been together since our wedding. And I think that because both celebrations were such wonderful experiences, they erased any discomfort that might have been left in anyone's mind from all those years ago.

Eric is a biologist. He has always enjoyed exploring issues in a very analytical way. The reading he has done on religion and the discussions he has participated in have helped make him feel comfortable and generous about sharing in the Jewish aspects of his household.

✖ ERIC (PRECEDED BY HIS WIFE, ELISE)

* * *

When I was in junior high school, there was a youth group at the church that I got involved in. Interestingly enough, one of the gentlemen who led the group was Jewish. It was right around Easter, and this man would put the whole experience of Easter into a kind of Jewish framework. He would connect it to Passover and talk about how the Last Supper was essentially a Passover meal. He explained it all to us in very Jewish terms rather than with the sort of adaptations that many Christians put into it.

* * *

My family went to church very regularly. I was brought up mostly as a Congregationalist, which is kind of the liberal end of Protestantism. I think that discussion about Easter and Passover was really a kind of watershed moment for me in a way. I began to get more interested in the Jewish roots of

Christianity. And I think from that point on I began to see Jesus simply as a very important historic figure, comparable to Moses and Mohammed and Buddha and so forth. This all happened when I was in about seventh or eighth grade. So I guess by the time I met Elise the notion of being around Jewish people was not foreign. I felt very comfortable with it. And the fact that she and I were raised in different religions didn't seem to me to be a horrible impediment.

I was twenty-seven when Elise and I got married. I'll be frank here and say that at that time in my life the general prospect of a long-term commitment of marriage to anyone was a little intimidating. But I really don't think my concern was compounded by Elise being Jewish. There is simply a kind of a trauma in getting married anyway, because it is such a major life event. Also, we had decided to have a Jewish wedding at a synagogue in Nashville, where her parents live. I guess the notion of having a ceremony that I wasn't completely familiar with, in a place I didn't really know, gave me a small amount of concern. I think that at least if we had a Jewish service in the town where we were living, where the surroundings were more familiar, it would have mitigated whatever uneasiness I felt.

I know that the religious issue has been harder in some ways for my folks. Once we had kids my mom would always say, "Why don't you come over to the church with us and watch the little Nativity pageant?" She would have loved for our kids to not only see it but also be in it. The pageant is something that is almost like Purim. The kids dress up and have a great time. I think there was in my mom's case a concern that our children were missing out on something and really almost deprived of something. I know we used to get into some fairly sharp discussions about why they couldn't be in the play. I think that sort of magical time when the kids were young was very hard on her. She couldn't go through the same old motions. It wasn't that she wanted to indoctrinate them into her way of thinking. It was more that she had things she wanted to share with them, but we really didn't feel it was appropriate.

Once we decided that we were going to raise our children as Jews, we made a really conscious effort to stick to that decision. I think it gets too schizophrenic to try to say they're both Christians and Jews, because in the strictest sense they can't be. We want them to be well grounded in Judaism and to have a solid point of reference. They know that I don't do things quite like they do, but they also certainly know that one is not better than the other. I go to church maybe a couple of times a year, just to keep contact. When it comes to things like Christmas and Easter, I don't feel horribly bad that the kids haven't gone on Easter egg hunts or that Santa Claus never came. I may have some sort of little twinges, but that's only because I think you like to see some of your own childhood events repeated.

Two occasions that I very much enjoyed were the bar and bat mitzvahs of our kids. I really wasn't uncomfortable with them in any way. As a matter of fact, I was almost as excited as I think Elise was. Certainly, I wasn't some sort of passive bystander, just kind of observing. I helped as much as I could. Again, these were very much family events. Granted, they're not the same family events that I grew up with, but they're important events and everyone shares in them. And really, for me, I think that's what it all comes down to: having a close and coherent family.

Nancy grew up on the West Coast. She is probably in her thirties. Nancy comes across as a strong and forthright individual who is not afraid of difficult situations. She seems ready to step in and take charge in order to get things done. But she wants her husband to be an equal partner. She doesn't want to have to take on responsibilities that she doesn't really consider hers.

✴ NANCY

* * *

I was raised Catholic. Until I went to college, most of my ideas about Judaism came from reading Judy Bloom books. This is going to sound so strange, but when I was about twelve I went through this period where it seemed to me that being Jewish and living on Long Island was the most exotic thing in the world. I developed this whole little fantasy world in which I was no longer a little Catholic schoolgirl on the West Coast. I was living someplace else, and I was Jewish.

* * *

During this time, I went on a food strike at home where I wouldn't eat ham or bacon. This went on for quite a while. My parents kept saying, "What's going on with you?" But it was a secret thing. I never told anybody why I was doing it. I just liked fantasizing that I was this other person. And for a long time that was really my only connection to what it meant to be Jewish.

My parents actually had a mixed marriage. My father was sort of fundamentalist Christian, and my mother was Catholic. They couldn't have been farther apart in terms of religion. We were raised Catholic. My father never converted, but he went to Mass with us occasionally and was supportive of my mother's wishes.

I was in Catholic schools for thirteen years. The high school I went to was really a very progressive place, and it attracted people from all different faiths and backgrounds. We learned about Judaism as well as Christianity, and we studied the Old Testament not as a Christian document but as a Jewish document. We also learned about Buddhism and Hinduism and studied Catholicism in relation to various other religions. So, by accident more than anything else, I was fairly well prepared at least intellectually to deal with an interfaith relationship.

I went to a college that was all the way across the country from where we lived. What does Jimmy Stewart say in one of his movies? "I'm shakin' the dust off these feet and I'm going to see the world." That was sort of my theory at the time. I wanted to break away from everything and have some new experiences. By this time I had very strong feelings about the Catholic Church. I found it to be extremely authoritarian. I had problems with the politics and the feminist aspects to the point where it made me really angry. I did go to the Catholic center at the university a couple of times, probably around Easter and Christmas. It's interesting. I had grown up in a very traditional parish with an old priest who was extremely sexist, and I hated it. At the university it was much more liberal. Some parts had been softened, other sections had been left out, and there was a lot of hugging. Even the priest hugged people. And strangely enough, I found the whole thing really irritating. I thought, "If I'm going to come here at all, it's for the ritual. I'm not doing it to be all lovey-dovey with a bunch of people I don't know." It just turned me off.

When I went home from college for breaks I did go to Mass with my mom, and the first year or so I was really bitchy about it. I would basically sulk and be kind of rude the whole time. I had a lot of mixed feelings about being there. My mother has always been able to separate the politics and feminist aspects from the spiritual parts. When she goes to church, those things don't enter her mind. She practices her faith because she has a personal relationship with God and her community, and that's fine for her. Finally I decided that out of respect for my mother I would behave better. And the truth is, there were things that I enjoyed when I went with her. I didn't feel a connection to the spiritual aspects of Catholicism, but I did like going through some of those rituals that were so familiar to me.

I met Harry when I was in graduate school. I was twenty-five at the time. Harry's father is somewhat religious. He goes to synagogue for all the holidays and feels an affinity with his Jewishness. His mother kind of had a reaction to growing up Orthodox that was similar to what I felt about Catholicism. She reacted negatively to a lot of the dogma and to what she perceived as sexism, and so she's always been kind of dismissive about Judaism. I think Harry's feelings are somewhere in between his two parents. Harry was bar mitzvahed and still says that was one of the most important days of his life.

When we decided to get married, we talked quite a bit about our feelings about religion. I told Harry, "I want you to understand going into this that I don't have any intention of raising our children to be Catholic." To me, that was never a question. It had nothing to do with Harry being Jewish. I wouldn't make that choice myself. Harry felt strongly that he wanted his children to be Jewish, but he was not very prepared to raise them in the faith because he didn't know much about it. Even to this day I tease him about that. We go to the High Holiday services and he can sing along, but he doesn't know the meaning of a lot of the rituals. He doesn't have a lot of background. So I said, "This is going to have to be your responsibility. You're going to have to teach me, and you're going to have to teach our children if you want them to have this. I will help you where I can, but you're going to need to be the one who is mainly responsible."

I do feel strongly that children need to have some religion. What I keep coming back to that is positive for me about the Catholic faith is the ritual. Not only do the rituals give a rhythm to the year, but somehow they also help to punctuate the year with this awareness of your faith and what connects you to other things in the world, as well as to other people. I've always enjoyed, and still do to this day, going to midnight Mass on Christmas and seeing all my friends and my mother's friends and that community of people who come together on that occasion. It is still very meaningful to me. I wanted our family to have something like that, and I knew I wasn't going to be able to provide it with the Catholic faith. So I said, "Fine. If we want to choose the Jewish faith for our children, I'm comfortable with that, and I will participate."

I was reluctant to commit to converting at that time, and still am, because I don't know that trading one set of doctrines for another is really going to solve my spiritual problems. But I have also said to Harry, "If at any point it became really essential to how we were going to raise our children, or if we come to a point where we feel like it is really going to make a difference for me to be converted, I would be willing to do the research and seriously consider it."

Before we got married, we also talked about this issue with our parents. My mom was a little worried. "Are you sure you can do this? What will you do about baptizing your children? Are you really ready to step away from Christianity?" I said to her that I appreciated her reasons for her faith. But I just had so many political and feminist issues with the Catholic Church that I couldn't raise my children the way I was raised.

Harry's mom and dad didn't seem to have any kind of a negative reaction about our marriage, but I was concerned that they might. I was in graduate school in Boston at the time. There was a Family Research Center that occasionally sponsored discussions about interfaith marriages. I went to a couple of those just to get a feel of what some of the issues were that I might expect from Harry's side of the family. And I was actually very surprised at the vehemence with which some of the Jewish women in the room spoke about their sons or daughters intermarrying. A couple of them felt that the Christians had persecuted their people, and so for a Jew to marry a Christian was really a betrayal. They also described the sense of loss that they felt when their children married out of their faith.

The next time I saw Harry's parents, I asked them about these things. I said, "I went to these discussions, and I want to talk to you about them. How do you really feel?" I was concerned. I wanted to know if this was a situation where their son was sort of leaving the fold and if they were having a lot of difficult emotions about it. Both of them reassured me that they really weren't. I'll never know whether they had secret feelings that they wouldn't share, but I took them at their word and said, "Okay." What else can you do? If they would have said, "Yes, we have problems about this," we still would have gotten married. It wouldn't have really changed anything for us, but there probably would have been different family issues that we would have tried to be aware of.

When we started planning the wedding, our first thought was to have an interfaith wedding that we would design ourselves. I went to a Catholic church in the area and talked to the priest. He basically told me that it's fine if I marry out of my faith, as long as our children will be raised Catholic. It was clear he wasn't going to be involved in our wedding unless that was going to happen. So I kind of walked away saying, "Well, thanks." Then we went to see Harry's rabbi, who is a wonderful man. And he said that he had an obligation to his congregants to only do Jewish weddings in their synagogue. He said, "That's sort of my boundary. If you want to have a Jewish wedding, you can have it here. I won't perform an interfaith ceremony for you but I'll be happy to bless your marriage."

So then we kind of started saying, "How are we really going to do this?" At that point the whole wedding planning was getting stressful for other reasons as well. We ended up deciding to go to Mexico and get married in a simple civil ceremony. And that's what we did. After we left Mexico, we went to my parents' place on the West Coast and had a party. The priest came and did some blessings and what was essentially the core section of a Catholic wedding. So that made the marriage official in the eyes of the Church. We signed all the papers, and then we flew home and had a similar kind of party here. But this time it was the rabbi who came in and did a blessing for us. So now I think we're covered on all sides.

When I look at Harry's relationship to his Jewishness, there is the cultural side and there is the religious side. And there seems to be a big gap between the two in a way that never was the case for my Catholicism. I mean, we were practicing Catholics. We went to church every Sunday. There was definitely a doctrine that went along with that and what you're supposed to believe. Culturally and religiously, everything was sort of combined. It's different for Harry. And learning the ropes about that has been a little bit confusing for me.

We have one son. He's almost eight months old. When our son was on his way, I felt a little bit of frustration with Harry. We didn't know if we were having a boy or a girl, and as we got closer to the birth, I said, "If this is a boy, you're going to have to get this bris arranged within eight days. If this is what you want, you need to start taking responsibility for it." He hemmed and hawed a little bit, and I was kind of surprised. I don't know if it was because there were a lot of other things going on in our lives at that time and he just didn't get organized or what, but I had to continually remind him. "Okay, the clock is winding down on this. If it's a boy, you're going to have this obligation. You're going to need to find a mohel. You need to take care of it." The conflict for me was that I felt like I didn't want to push this on him, but I wanted him to make a decision. He finally did get the bris arranged. But it seemed like it was the eleventh hour, which I had to admit I found to be a little disappointing from someone who had said so many times, "I really want my children to be raised Jewish."

My feeling with the bris was that it was not something I wanted to take responsibility for. I didn't want to have to be the one who had to make it happen. I wanted Harry to make some effort. I really feel that if he wants to raise his children as Jews, he needs to get in touch with his own faith and his own spirituality, because the children will absorb so much about Judaism through him. Like I said, I'm willing to participate in any way, even to the point of considering conversion, but I am not going to take it all on myself.

I think that it is good for children to be raised in a faithful community of people. I don't care which faith it is. When Harry and I decided to get married, we could have said, "Let's both convert and be Baha'i. We'll do it together." That would have been fine with me. But I feel it needs to be something. You know, it's really ironic that I was the one who was the practicing religious person almost all my life, and Harry was not. And yet here we are doing his thing because he said it was so important to him. But with the bris and other little things that come up, I'm the one who has to push to get the things he says he wants to happen. I start to think, "What's up with this man?" I want to say to him, "You really, really need to get your act together if you want to do this."

Norm grew up in the Midwest. He is an attorney and he is in his late forties. When Norm's daughter was born, he was completely taken aback by his strong need to have her be a part of the same religion as himself.

✖ NORM

* * *

I've always thought of myself as Jewish, but I had very little formal religious training. I did go to Sunday school for a while at a Reform temple. I used to have to take the bus to get there. I realized pretty quickly that if I got off the bus just one stop later, I could go to my grandmother's and she would make pancakes for me.

* * *

So that's what I did for an entire semester. I would get up in the morning, say that I was going to Sunday school, and go to my grandmother's. She'd make the pancakes and we would have a great time. At the end of the school year, I broke down and told my father what I was doing. I was crying, and I was really nervous about telling him. He couldn't stop laughing. And that was the end of my formal religious background.

Growing up, we did a lot more for Christmas than we ever did for Hanukkah. Christmas was really the main event. My exposure to the Jewish holidays was pretty much limited to a few major ones a year, like Passover, when I went to my cousin's house for dinner.

I don't remember thinking about whether or not I should be going out with Jewish girls. There was an early question that one of my relatives always asked: "Is she Jewish or not?" I had the sense that everyone would have approved if I was seeing someone who was Jewish. But I don't remember caring myself.

Even though I really knew so little about Judaism, and we did so little at home, I somehow connected to being Jewish. I went to a Quaker college, and I noticed that I always gravitated towards being around Jewish kids. The first week I was there, I remember calling home and saying, "These are my new friends," and their names were Sussman, Grubman, Newman, and Friedman. I gravitated towards that group despite the fact that I didn't have any of the religious training.

I was married once before. I met my current wife, Betty, when I was thirty-nine. It is quite amazing to me, but even to this day I can't exactly tell you what religion Betty's parents are. I don't really know what kind of church they belong to. Her mom is Catholic, and her dad is something else. Betty did go to a Catholic grammar school, but since I've known her she's never gone to church. As I thought about marrying Betty and having a family with her, I remembered a story that she told about her mother that had a big impact on me. Her mother had enrolled her in a Catholic school, and the day that she first brought Betty to the school, she told the nuns that if she ever heard her daughter come back and say that she was better than somebody else, or that her religion was better than somebody else's, she was going to pull her from the school. That was her mother's attitude, and that told me what I needed to know.

We were married by a judge. We knew that was someone that everybody would accept. I did want to do something traditional, so we had the breaking of the glass. I felt that I wanted it to be clear that some parts of the ceremony were grounded in Judaism.

Betty and I were both already a little older when we got married, so we started trying to get pregnant pretty quickly. During this period, and when Betty actually became pregnant, I thought a lot about what it would be like to have a child. I felt an extremely strong urge that I had never really been aware of before. I felt that I wanted to be sure that my kid would be raised as a Jew. Betty and I, of course, talked about different things we could do in terms of religion. In particular, I told her that I did not want this child to be baptized. That's something that probably would have happened pretty naturally because of Betty's background and family pressures. But despite my limited religious upbringing, the thought of having my child baptized to me was and still is the equivalent of saying, "It's not my child."

These were honestly feelings that I would have never expected to have. The most surprising part of all of this to me is how strongly I felt about it and how I really got angry and scared at the prospect of a child that was baptized. It's as if that child would be taken away from me, and I am someone who had wanted a child for a long, long time. The thought of that happening was just intolerable to me. I was extremely adamant about all of this. It was almost scary to me as to how strongly I felt, and in light of how little I had done growing up, it was very strange.

Betty told me she was comfortable about this, and I think that overall she has been. At any rate, she agreed. When Nicole was born, we took her to be named at the temple. I was insistent on that. I think Betty's parents were basically comfortable with everything, but I was worried about some of her sisters because they are pretty religious. There was a point where I worried that if my daughter were alone with her aunts, someone would go and secretly baptize her. I actually had that fear. I expressed what I was feeling and make it extremely clear that nothing like that was going to happen if I was going to continue to have a relationship with these people.

From the time Nicole was old enough, I've tried to get her to participate in some Jewish activities. She's gone over to the Jewish Community Center for some different things. In fact, that's where she went to nursery school. She took a little class there about Judaism, and we're trying to figure out another class for her to take. Also, we recently joined a temple, and I will begin to take her over there once in a while for different events. I'd like her to be aware of the temple as a regular part of her community. I want it to be a part of her life.

As a family, we are definitely observing the Jewish holidays more thoroughly than I did when I was growing up. For Hanukkah we make it a very clear point to light a candle every night. We also say a prayer, which I know I mangle, but nobody else knows. Betty bought some Jewish cookbooks so she could learn how to make latkes and some other traditional things. And I always tell a story. Unfortunately I tell the same story for Hanukkah that I tell for Passover, about Moses saying, "Let my people go." But it doesn't matter because it is still a story that Nicole can understand, and it's about the Jewish people. And then we discuss religion a little bit. We talk about "whose team she's on," which is how she puts it. I'm just trying to use as much of my limited education in this area as I can.

We also try to find places to go to for some of the other holidays. For Passover we will go to at least one seder. It's a little tricky because most of my family members don't do much. In fact, they almost laugh at the idea of going to these things. So I have to look for places to go to on the Jewish holidays. I really do. It's important to me because I want Nicole to have those traditions. I want her to realize that if she doesn't have them, it would be a loss.

I wish I had more of a background in Judaism so I could teach more to Nicole. And I am trying to learn as I go along. But I feel there is a limit to what I can do. There is a big group of us that goes skiing together. We are all Jewish, and we call ourselves "Jews on Skis." We even have a little web site, hats with emblems, and some other silly things like that. There are three of us in the group who never had a bar mitzvah. One of them said, "Why don't the three of us go back now and take the classes and get bar mitzvahed?" He was completely serious. I thought he was out of his mind. I don't have time to go to the bathroom, and now I'm going to start going to Hebrew school. That's something that's just not going to happen.

Recently Nicole happened to be at the bar and bat mitzvahs of two cousins. She liked going to those events. She talks about them and says that she wants to be bat mitzvahed too. But as soon as you tell her she'll have to go to Sunday school, she says, "Well, I can just go to other kids' bar mitzvahs." She definitely doesn't have the drive on her own to go to Sunday school, and I don't know if we'll end up sending her or not. I know it would be tough. I want her to go so she can get the education, but I also don't want her to be away on Sunday mornings. She happens to be a kid who doesn't easily join things. She doesn't like to go to gymnastics or ballet. And because Betty and I both end up being away a fair amount, Nicole likes to just be home with us when she can.

I know I should take every chance I can to get Nicole to do something to connect her to Judaism, and I want to do that. But forcing her to go to Sunday school wouldn't be good either. If I forced her to go, I would basically be saying, "I know we're sending you to a place you don't want to go, on a morning that is usually reserved for us as a family, but you still have to go because you need to learn about being Jewish." I'm afraid that if I did that, it would make her feel negatively about being Jewish. It will have defeated the whole purpose.

So far, Nicole does recognize and identify herself as Jewish. She has not, however, figured out that her mother isn't Jewish. And when she does, it will be an interesting test. Before she finds that out, I want her to have a pretty good grounding in Judaism and know that, no matter what religion her mother is, she herself is a Jew.

It looks like this is going to be it in terms of children for us, and I'm a little bothered by that. I don't want to be responsible for a permanent assimilation that ends another family line. That's why I feel it's so important for me to try to instill in Nicole a Jewish consciousness. I know that it will be very difficult unless she really does get a more formal Jewish education. Between her mother not being Jewish and Judaism not being a big part of my life, and the world today with the normal assimilation pressures, I know it's going to be tough.

I started thinking for the first time about whom Nicole might marry. I never really focused on this, but I very much want my daughter to marry someone who is Jewish. It's not only because of my feelings about assimilation. It's also because I feel that if she marries a person who is Jewish, it would be kind of like she picked my team, and she would be a little closer to me. But if she picks somebody who is Christian, somebody who goes to church, it would be taking her away from me a little more.

Kathy was born shortly after her parents moved to this country. She is in her forties and works as a massage therapist. Kathy does not practice the same religion as her husband and children. This has made her feel like an outsider at times, but eventually she did find her own way to feel connected to the holidays and religious events going on in her family members' lives.

❊ KATHY

* * *

My parents are from China. When they first came to the United States, they used to have visits from people who were basically missionaries. These people would come into my parents' home to help them with English, but they would always interject a few things about Christianity as well. All of my parents' friends who moved here were doing the same thing. And as my parents became more westernized, they embraced Christianity to a greater degree.

* * *

Our family owned a restaurant. Like a lot of other restaurants, ours was always closed on Easter and Christmas. So we just kind of called those days our holidays too. We would go to the Chinese/Christian Baptist church. We just began following the Christian traditions.

My parents were so focused on making a living for their four children and making the restaurant successful that they didn't worry much about religion. I was never baptized or anything like that. In high school I started going to various churches just to see what they were like. I never considered looking outside of Christianity. In fact, I really wasn't even aware of religions outside of Christianity. I was comfortable with my family and being our own little happy unit. I assumed my life would be very similar when I married and had my own family. I do remember just hoping and praying that I would be marrying a Christian Chinese boy.

I met Dean at college. I knew he was Jewish, but I didn't know anything about Judaism. I thought, "Okay, what is this supposed to mean?" I told my parents I had met someone Jewish, and they said, "Oh my God, you can't eat pork." Dean is Reform, and it didn't apply, but I really had no idea. And it was just through dating him and getting to know him that I kept learning a little more and a little more about Judaism.

Dean's background was Jewish, but he certainly didn't participate on a regular basis when I met him. We did go with his family to their synagogue for some of the holidays. The traditions were very foreign to me, and I would sit there not really understanding a thing. But then again, I'm American born, and my parents would take me to the Chinese Christian church where they spoke a different dialect than the one my parents spoke. So it felt like, "Okay, now I'm listening to something else I don't understand." I knew the service was important to Dean's family and I would sit politely and think, "It will be over in an hour."

When we decided to get married, my family was less focused on the fact that Dean was Jewish and more on the fact that he wasn't Chinese. His parents may have been somewhat upset, but there was never anything brutal said about it to either of us. Really, religion never became an issue for us until we had children.

We have two boys. And before they were born we started to think about what path we would want them to take in terms of religion. At that point, I did believe that there was a higher spirit. I didn't necessarily call it God. But I thought it would be good to have the kids grounded in some kind of religious foundation. We talked about it a little bit, and I felt that Dean had a firmer foundation with Judaism than I had in Christianity. Judaism seemed safe and healthy to me, and I felt that it would be fine. So we just kind of went in that direction. Also, Dean's parents were more involved with their synagogue than my parents were with the Chinese Christian church. I was fairly certain I was never going to convert. I felt quite strongly about that. So it felt reassuring to know that, between Dean and his parents, the kids could get the religious foundation I wanted them to have. It wouldn't have to come from me.

As my kids were growing up, what I did get involved with were just the chores of taking the boys to the synagogue for their classes and activities. I would volunteer occasionally at the religious school to help with one project or another. And I even took a few classes about Judaism and learned some Hebrew because I wanted to know more about what my children were learning. I kind of went through my own version of Sunday school and Hebrew school along with the boys.

One thing I would make sure of is that there were decorations up in our house for Hanukkah and all the different holidays throughout the year. I liked making everything look festive. I enjoyed the beauty of the decorations more than the religious factor. And it was good for the boys to see the holidays being carried into their home. Also, I would always go to the services for the holidays with Dean and the boys. I felt that if my children were going to be raised as Jews I needed to support them. Even though I didn't want to become a Jew myself, I felt that I had made a commitment to them and I wanted to help them. I wanted us to be cohesive as a family. The holiday services tend to be pretty long. I enjoy the music, but during the rest of the time I kind of daydream as opposed to getting very involved in the service.

I think the only time that I really felt a sense of separation and isolation from the rest of my family was when it came time for the bar mitzvah of my oldest son. We wanted it to be low-key, but gradually it turned into something bigger than we had originally planned. For months there were rumblings of, "Okay, we have to do this," "We need to plan that," or "We'd better get someone to help with that part." I felt that even though they were happy for me to be included, I really couldn't contribute because I didn't know what to do. And that's when I started to think, "What did I do to myself?"

I felt so bad. It was a real problem for me. Judaism was something I was just not integrally a part of. I had chosen not to be a part of it when I chose not to convert. I couldn't get past focusing on myself and how I felt, instead of on the fact that this was a joyous time. I felt isolated from what my kids were going through and what my family was going through. I thought, "I'm the mother. I gave birth to these children, and I feel so separate."

I started to feel more and more that I needed to validate my own upbringing and not just my husband's. I think that is something that always comes into your head when you're following one religion. We could have raised the boys with both Christianity and Judaism. Originally, that is something we talked about doing. But I chose in this household to not do both. I just felt I didn't want to do that. It was partly because I thought it would be too confusing and partly because of all the extra work. I feel like New Year's is bad enough. I have three New Years to deal with: the Chinese one, the Jewish one, and the one on December 31. I just didn't want to do it. So for the Christian holidays, we always just go to my family.

Probably the thing that would have helped me the most is if we had talked about this much more extensively before we had children. I don't think I gave it enough thought. I assumed everything would be fine. We talked about what religion the kids should follow, but we didn't try to think about the feelings and situations we might experience as we went along. I don't know if it would have changed anything, but I think that if we had talked more, the feelings I had at the time of my son's bar mitzvah might not have been so strong.

I know that for my husband, religion is more important to him as he gets older. And it is to me too. I'm someone who has always looked for spirituality in my own way. I feel very spiritual inside myself, but I don't feel that I need an organization in which to express that spirituality. I do care about communicating my values to the boys, and I think my values come out in what I say and do. The boys pick up on what I believe. I'm always searching for different things. At one point I got involved in a women's group that was very focused around God in nature. And I'd come home from the group and I'd share what we talked about with the boys. I've always gotten the sense from them that they know I'm just looking for my own thing, and it's okay no matter what it is. I believe they respect my feeling of wanting to find something that makes me happy. And it feels good. I appreciate that from my boys. I am very thankful to my husband because he is the same way. He has always supported my need to develop my spirituality on my own. Whenever I go off and try something different, he always says, "Fine, go and do it. Whatever you want." And I'm sure he's thankful to me for supporting Judaism.

I've discovered that the most comfortable way for me to feel that I am a part of Jewish life and the Jewish holidays is through the meals. Growing up in a restaurant, I really learned to enjoy cooking. So it has been just a pleasure for me to prepare all the different Jewish foods. I find it a lot of fun. I even did the seder for Passover a number of times. It was always a challenge but I enjoyed it. It was a way I could be involved and feel that I was really contributing something, instead of saying each time a holiday rolled around, "Oh, no, here we go again."

David is in his forties. He grew up in Chicago and worked for many years as an actor. David has become increasingly involved in religious activities. As his own involvement has grown, he has also found himself more willing and more able to understand the need of the people around him to do what they feel is right for themselves.

❊ DAVID (TO BE FOLLOWED BY HIS WIFE, ELIZABETH)

* * *

Both of my parents were Orthodox. Neither of them were fanatics, but they made sure that Judaism was deeply rooted in us. There were two synagogues in the city we lived in when I was growing up. One synagogue was Reform, and the other was Orthodox. My father felt that the Orthodox one was going to be too much for him so we joined the Reform synagogue. But then my parents decided that they missed some of the more traditional rituals, which did not exist in the Reform synagogue at that time. So we also joined the Orthodox place.

* * *

Each Friday night we went to the Reform synagogue, and every Saturday we'd go to the Orthodox one, which eventually became Conservative. Certainly, we observed all the holidays. And we observed the Sabbath.

When I started to date, because the pool from which to choose was relatively small, I don't think it was ever expected that I would date only Jewish women. But certainly I think it was expected, although it was unspoken, that I would marry someone who was Jewish.

By the time I got to college, I wanted to try some different things. I had bacon for the first time at my dormitory in my freshman year, and I absolutely loved it. I would still go to services once in awhile, but certainly I didn't do as much as we did at home. It's not that I ever left Judaism. I wasn't as observant, but it was always a part of me.

Elizabeth and I met when I was still in college here in Chicago, and she was in school in New York. It was summertime, and she was home on vacation. I wasn't looking for anyone to date seriously at that point. But we got together, and we went out during that summer. Then she went back east to school and I stayed here. We stayed in contact for three years until we finally came together after she finished school.

Elizabeth was born a Catholic but in a nonreligious family. The fact that we belonged to different religions was not much of an issue for her. And I'm sure that at first neither of us would have thought that we'd ever really be getting married. It just sort of jumped up on us that we were becoming very close. And then religion did become a big issue. In fact, Elizabeth claims that after a very romantic night I said to her, "You know, I'd love to marry you, but you're not Jewish so I can't." I don't think I was quite as tactless as that. There's no question, though, that this was a very serious conflict for me. And it's interesting. My parents were being very open. Before I first introduced Elizabeth to my mom and dad, I told them that I had met this great girl. And they said, "What's her name?" "Elizabeth Manderelli." There was a pause. When I finally brought her home they absolutely loved her. I remember I was in the car with my father and he said, "You know, I just have to tell you that Elizabeth is a wonderful woman. She is so bright and bubbly, and quite frankly, as far as your mother and I are concerned, conversion will be fine."

When push came to shove, the religious issue became very difficult for us. Even though we had been open about it from the beginning, there was a point where we would not even discuss it because it had become such a hot spot. We broke up over it for a time. It was really my struggle. I wasn't getting any pressure from my parents, and I was kind of surprised by that.

The real issue is that I very much did want Elizabeth to convert, and I was pressing for it. I didn't realize at the time how strongly I was doing it, but in retrospect I know I was pushing hard. I would keep coming up with "just one more thing" to try to convince her. I tried every tactic I could think of. I used the "5,000 years of history" card. I know African Americans who say, "We are living today, but we still feel the effects of slavery." I can understand that. I think that a people's history is ingrained in them. It was hard at first to explain this to Elizabeth because she is a person who always sees people as people. She doesn't focus on the differences.

I tried to explain to Elizabeth why it felt so important to me to carry on the Jewish tradition. I told her about how when I was growing up we lived very near a country club that didn't allow Jews as members. It's not that we wanted to join, but you always felt like an outsider in a way that was very clear to you. And when my parents were going to college, they both experienced quotas for the number of Jews that could be at their schools. Basically I felt that if I'm going to feel like an outsider anyway, I want to feel special because of it and be proud. I know it's confusing. I grew up with every freedom in the world, so why should these things bother me? To convey to her what was inside of me was difficult. It was hard to communicate.

Finally Elizabeth said she knew for sure that she did not want to convert at that time. Even though she understood what I was saying, she did not feel she could do something so major just for the sake of my convenience. At this point we were so much in love. I thought, "Well, okay, I have two options. I can lose her forever or I can go ahead and marry her." It was a struggle because I thought, "It is unprecedented as far as I know in my family to do something like this." But it felt obviously worth it to me. And as it turns out, we made an agreement before we got married that if we had kids, we would raise them as Jews and we would have a Jewish home. I was lucky because she was very, very flexible on this point.

I asked the rabbi who was at my parent's synagogue, with whom we were close, to perform the marriage. I think I kind of pressed him too, but he wouldn't do it. I understood and I respected him for his opinion. So we had to find somebody else. We found a rabbi who had made it part of his mission to be available to marry interfaith couples. At first we were planning to have the ceremony at the hotel where the reception was going to be, but Elizabeth's mom at the last minute got really upset about it. She wanted to see Elizabeth walking down an aisle of a church. Elizabeth was taking some classes at the university, and she said, "There's a chapel at the university. Let's get married there." My brother and I went to look. It wasn't terrible. There was no cross up on the altar, although when I looked around I noticed every single other cross in the room. I'd point to one on the doorway that was about half an inch high and say to my brother, "Do you see that cross? It's really bothering me." My brother in his wisdom convinced me that many Jews before me had been married in places other than a synagogue, so I wouldn't be the first. And I calmed down.

The plan was for the rabbi to come to the chapel to officiate. But the chaplain at the university was a minister. He said, "You know, I have never been part of a Jewish ceremony, and I'd be glad to help out if you need someone." We still weren't planning on having him, but we mentioned it to Elizabeth's mom and she loved the idea. It worked out fine. This minister was a very sensitive guy. I think he could tell I was feeling a little bit uneasy about things. The rabbi is the one who did most of the service, and the minister assisted him. The whole thing turned out beautifully. It was a lovely ceremony, and my relatives who came, many of whom were traditional, also loved it.

I think humor is really crucial to any relationship. Elizabeth has what I would call a very Jewish sense of humor. Because we are in sync there, it makes most other things pretty easy. There have been glaring cultural differences between us over things like food. We'll go to one of her family functions and there's always lots of macaroni salad. That's something we just don't see when we go to visit my family. But there haven't been any major problems over this issue since before we were married. The main thing was that we were going to raise the kids to be Jewish. It wasn't so important for me to have her be Jewish, but it was to have a Jewish home and Jewish kids.

Just after we were married, we went to my nephew's bris. Elizabeth had never seen one before, and she found it terrifying. She said, "Wait a minute. We have to agree that we're not going to do this." Seeing how upset she was, I felt it was not such a big deal. We could always have a son circumcised in the hospital. I said, "Okay, we'll do whatever you want." And before our first child was born, we did find out that we were having a boy. Elizabeth wavered up until maybe a month before he was born. Then she decided that she would be comfortable with a mohel. It was a very nice ceremony, and I think we were both glad we did it that way. And when my daughter was born, we had a naming ceremony. My in-laws really took part in both these events. If they had some objection to our marriage, it was never really seen by me. Her mother might have been a little slower to come around, but overall it's been fine.

In our family, we celebrate the Sabbath on Friday nights. We go to services together on all of the holidays. And I've brought the kids to synagogue with me on many, many Saturday mornings. We occasionally all go to services as a family on Friday night, but our schedules being what they are, most times we just can't do it. Elizabeth is trying to make that happen more often. She certainly takes a very, very active role. She participates a lot. I think she has really bent over backwards to be involved. Because she does so much, I probably only do about as much as I would be doing if both of us had been Jewish. I don't think that anything is different.

Every year at Christmas we take the kids and go to Elizabeth's parents' house to see the tree and exchange presents. It's interesting. In the spring I said to my daughter, "Do you know what holiday is coming up?" And she said, "Passover." Then I asked, "What's your favorite holiday?" And she said, "Christmas." Years ago I really would have been outraged by that. But I've come to terms with it. There was a pamphlet I saw at a synagogue I was visiting. It was around Christmas time, and the rabbi there had published this newsletter saying, "You live in the United States of America, and your kids are surrounded by Christmas. We know you all want to have a Jewish home, and have it free of those kinds of symbols. But there is no reason to try to convince your kids that Christmas does not exist, because it docs. And they can celebrate with other people." I thought that was surprisingly open-minded. After I read that I thought, "Oh, yeah, that makes a lot of sense." From then on, I was fine about the kids and Christmas.

One thing that has happened in our lives now is that I am studying to be a chazan, a cantor. I am really into it and the kids hear me practicing all the time. I'm doing it every spare moment. This has opened up the whole conversion issue again. But now it's very different. Practically speaking, in terms of looking for jobs and joining a congregation, it may make sense for Elizabeth to convert. I wouldn't want to press her on it, though. It really would make no difference to me at this point. It's interesting, because the more that I have been studying, the more open I become to the fact that everyone has to find their own way. If my kids for some reason left Judaism, it would hurt me initially I'm sure, but everyone has their own path, and Judaism is not the only way.

Elizabeth is a musician who grew up in the Midwest. As David has made changes in his life to become more active in Judaism, Elizabeth's life has necessarily changed as well. She seems comfortable about the decisions that led them to this point, as well as the direction their lives together seem to be taking.

✴ ELIZABETH (PRECEDED BY HER HUSBAND, DAVID)

* * *

I was raised Catholic, but I probably can count on one hand how many times we actually went to church. I would say my parents only made a halfhearted attempt to get us involved, and I really don't know why. I don't think it was because they weren't close to their religion. Maybe they just kept putting it off and never really got around to it. But we weren't big churchgoers even on Easter or Christmas. We really didn't start going to church much until I as a musician started playing a lot in church, and then I think my parents came mostly just to hear me play.

* * *

I lived in an area that didn't have much of a Jewish population, and as I grew up I didn't know any Jews. And I didn't really know anything about what Judaism was. All I remember is that every Friday night we used to go to my Italian grandparents' house. They were wonderful people, but I did have a great-uncle who was an extremely vocal, bigoted man, and he would be there too. And every Friday night we would sit around the table. The adults would be drinking the homemade wine. As a kid, I could sense that they were getting a little looser and a little looser. And eventually the conversation, which always was surrounding politics, would come around to who was to blame for this or that. It was always the Zionists who would get blamed. I remember it was 1973 and there was a gas shortage. And it was the Zionists' fault. Nobody actually used the word *Jews* or *Israelis* or anything like that. It was always just the Zionists.

As a little kid, I used to think that whoever these Zionists are, they must be just awful. They are responsible for high prices. They are responsible for crime. They're responsible for the gas shortage even. It was a mystery to me how one group of people could be so bad. I envisioned them as a really big grotesque mass causing all these problems. So that's the kind of background I come from. Again, it was just my uncle who would really talk this way, but he was a very verbal, very loud kind of guy and I was hearing it all the time.

I was from such a "white bread" area. It wasn't until I went to an arts academy for high school that I started meeting people not only of other religions but of other colors as well. My roommate there was Jewish. She was phenomenal, and she is the one who opened my eyes up. I learned a lot about her family and how they lived their lives. I realized very quickly that my uncle was just a guy full of a lot of hot air and that these Zionists weren't the awful people I'd heard about each week. I went to college in New York, and of course I had a lot of friends there who were Jewish. So by the time I met David, I knew at least something about Judaism and was comfortable with many Jewish people as well.

David and I met when I was home from college for the summer. This was not a time in my life when I was getting prepared to marry. At the same time, I didn't want to be wasting my time on a relationship that couldn't go anywhere, and I didn't want him to be wasting his time either. I knew religion might be an issue between us. And of course the closer we got, and the more we seemed to fall in love with each other, the more that it did become an issue. Also, I could sense that there was a little something with my parents, who weren't totally thrilled with our relationship, especially because there were other suitors around who were not Jewish. But since I hadn't been living at home since my mid-teens, I think they sort of felt that they could give me their opinions but then that was it. They weren't giving me any threats or ultimatums or anything like that.

When we were dating, David would come and visit me in New York, and we would go to synagogues together. He always liked to see the different synagogues and the people. Even in Chicago they didn't have quite the diverse types that there were in New York. So we would go, and I found it to be very interesting. I don't know if I was completely taken with it. I didn't feel, "Oh, I've found my spiritual home," or anything like that. But on one level it was something for us to do together. On another level it was a way to learn a little bit more about him.

It's not like it was great all the time. I did have problems when he wanted to go to an Orthodox synagogue. I think that what I tried to say when we first went in is, "Okay, they are just doing things differently." But some of it was repulsive to me. There have been times when I thought, "You can bring me over here so far, but beyond this point I'm not budging." The Orthodox community was perplexing to me. We had many, many discussions. How could somebody wear a wig? How could they live a life like this? Some things were perplexing to David too. It helped me to know that he didn't have all the answers to why people would go that route and why they would live their lives that way.

I did feel some pressure from David to convert. I would imagine that maybe a lot of people feel that converting is fine, but it's the reason you do it that's my issue. To do it for convenience' sake, to do it because somebody says, "You know, I'd like to marry you but you're not Jewish," seems wrong to me. I felt that if I had converted for that reason, it would sort have been an insult to both of us. It certainly is not like David was suggesting that I leave the Catholic faith, because I wasn't really in it anymore. So it wasn't like I had to turn my back on anything. But on the other hand, to join something in any kind of official paper-signing, taking-classes, and taking-the-bath type of way, just because it makes it more convenient to get married and find a rabbi, didn't seem to be my thing. I know many people who have done it, but it didn't seem to me to be the right thing to do. So I didn't.

We dated for quite a long time before we got married, and a lot of that was because we were trying to figure out how we would raise kids if in fact we ever had them. I read a number of books about whether it's good to expose a child to both religions. Based upon what I read, we decided that it wasn't something we wanted to do. The books all seemed to say that you should pick one religion and stick with it. If your kids ever want to reject it or go in a different direction, they can do that as they get older, but don't confuse them when they're young. Also, we did know that it puts a lot of stress on a marriage to have the child first and then go through the negotiating. So before we ever got married, we wanted to decide what we would do.

It was hard. There was no way that David was going to budge about wanting the children to be raised Jewish. I wasn't even sure what I was asking him to budge to, because I didn't have a religion that I was close to. And yet as far as the basic, fair thing to do was concerned, I had some problems with simply agreeing that the children should be Jewish. I would think, "Do I have to step all the way into his territory and he doesn't move at all?" He said that this is something he would have to do to be true to his heart and to his faith. It took me about two years, and I did a lot of reading about Judaism just to make sure that I would feel ultimately comfortable raising our kids to be Jews. And ultimately I did feel comfortable. At the end of two years I was thrilled with the decision. I was very happy about it. I didn't feel like it was any kind of a compromise or a sacrifice at all.

We were married at the chapel at the university. I did have some pressure from my mother and my grandmother to have a priest there. And also they felt that it had to take place in a church because they really cared about me being the bride and walking down the aisle of the church in a white dress. They didn't like the idea of having the ceremony downtown at some nice hotel. That's a very non-Catholic thing to do. It wouldn't have bothered me, but I thought, "Okay, my parents have done some great things for me, especially my mom, and if this is going to really make her happy, and David isn't objecting to it, we should do it."

The more I think about it, the more shocked I am that David ever agreed to get married in that chapel. There are tiny little crucifixes around it, which we didn't even notice at first. But I would have thought he would have been looking at this church with a fine-tooth comb. The whole place reeks of churchiness to me. There is no big Christ hanging up on the altar or anything like that, but there definitely is an altar. It's not like the bema that they have in a synagogue. But David said he was all right with it. So we settled on the chapel. And we were having a rabbi officiate, with the minister from the chapel assisting him. I then proceeded to lie to my grandmother, who was threatening to not attend my wedding if there wasn't a priest there. I asked the minister, if my grandmother ever went up to him and asked him what church he is from, to promise to tell her that he was Catholic. I mean, I was reduced to that. Now, fourteen years later, I would say, "Grandma, if you don't want to come, if you don't feel comfortable, I understand. I'm fine with it." But I was twenty-six, and I was trying to help everybody get over this and not cause too many ripples.

My father was great. He built the chuppah that we were married under. He was the one that put it together. I was very proud of him. I didn't ask him to do it. He volunteered. And he put some real thought into it. When my parents were married they had bought a beautiful tablecloth on their honeymoon, and he used that to cover the chuppah. Keep in mind that it was my father's uncle who was the anti-Zionist guy. And yet my father built that chuppah. That was a major stretch for my dad. I was real proud that he did that.

After we were married, we joined a synagogue. David was raised in a pretty observant home, and he has become much more observant as he has gotten older. He started going to services on Saturday mornings right after we were married. Sometimes it bothered me because I thought we could be just having a quiet Saturday morning at home or doing something fun together. But after a while I realized that this is something that is so dear to him. It is so important to him. And I thought, "You could have worse vices in this world than wanting to go to synagogue every Saturday morning." In retrospect, I think I have gotten myself quite a catch here. I go with him sometimes, but I really end up going pretty rarely. Most of the time it is because I am working now on Saturdays. Truthfully, if I wasn't working, I'm pretty sure I would be going a lot more. The time I really love going to synagogue is on Friday nights. I am much more comfortable going at that time. I like to look at it as a kind of way to end the week and begin to relax. We started doing that together when we first joined the synagogue, so we've been doing it for years. And now that we have kids, we go together as a family. Friday night is a shorter service, and if our kids are horrible, we just leave and try to go again the next week.

I think the best thing that we did was to take our time in making the religious decision beforehand. Of course, there is no guarantee that somebody is going to stick with whatever they decide to do. But for myself, when I made the decision, it never occurred to me that I could always change my mind and risk our marriage breaking up. I looked at it as a commitment that I planned to keep, and that's how I still feel. There are always going to be some parts of all this that are not easy. I think a lot of it has to do with how much you're going to let your family influence you and how much you're going to let them upset you. Because if they think they can upset you, I think they will try. Then you might begin to wonder if they are right and start to doubt yourself.

My mom is the one who has said some things over the past years that have really bothered me. It didn't happen so much before we had children, but now that we have kids, it's harder. Even as recently as this past Christmas Eve, she made a comment that upset me. My family has always made a big deal about the secular aspects of Christmas. We'd have the tree and presents and a big dinner. And Christmas is still very important to them. My parents never used to want to go to midnight Mass at Christmas, but in recent years they've been going. They don't go at any other time of the year, but at Christmas it's fun. I've usually been the one who takes them there because it is late at night, and it's hard for them to go on their own.

And actually on Christmas Eve our tradition is to have a big dinner here at our house. We do it here because we can accommodate more people. Both my parents and my grandparents live in much smaller places now. We don't put up one stitch of Christmas, and there are always Hanukkah decorations all over the place. There's even Hanukkah music going on in the background. My father recently passed away, but my mom and my grandfather still come, along with a couple of other family members. I couldn't live with my family not having a Christmas Eve dinner. It's quite odd, but they have never turned us down. We invite them every year, and they're here every year. And I do try to make it really beautiful. I'm not much of a cook, but I try to make it special for everybody involved. The way we explain it to our kids is that it happens to be Christmas Eve, and we're having my relatives over for a really nice dinner. But this is their holiday, not ours. And then the following day we go over to my mom's house or one of the other relatives, and we celebrate their holiday and see the decorations and exchange presents.

Two years ago, when my mom came into the house, she said, "Well, it is obvious who the Jews are in their neighborhood." I think if she had been Jewish that might have been funny, but she was saying it with a little bit of a snide edge to it. It bothered me. Or if she had never made any negative remarks to me before, I would have thought it was funny, because it's true. You drive through the neighborhood and it's Christmas Eve, and there are maybe five houses that don't have any lights up. They are probably either out of town, or they're Jewish.

But over the last five years since my oldest daughter was born, my mother has made a number of comments that I haven't liked. I know I'm sensitive to what she says. Maybe I have some deep-down desire to please her in some way, but I'm not sure. I'm still trying to figure that out. I remember the time that we told her we had decided to send our kids to a Jewish preschool. We visited tons of preschools and chose this particular one because we both just really liked it. At the time, it had little to do with the Jewish atmosphere because we knew we gave them plenty of that at home. We just liked the school. So for all kinds of reasons we decided to send our kids there. When I told my mom what we had decided, her comment was, "Well, they've won again." I think she just couldn't help herself. She doesn't say that kind of thing often, but when she does, it's quite a dig. I then remind her that it isn't a contest. We picked it after we went to all kinds of different places, and this is the one that we both really liked.

I think maybe my mother is a little better about this than she used to be. It really doesn't happen that often that she makes those kinds of remarks. Maybe she's learning by the way I react that when she says these things it doesn't really do any good anyway. It just upsets me and makes me angry. The interesting thing is that she is really a wonderful mom. This is a hard thing for her. And she happens to be extremely close to David's mom. They met through us. They didn't know each other before. They have become extremely close friends. And yet I think my mom still has a little bit of resentment that we went to "their side," and so that's why she makes a comment like "They've won again." She sees it in a different way than I see it.

It's just so different for the other half's family. I don't think that David's family ever had a problem with our marriage. On the other hand, they knew that I had agreed that we were going to have a Jewish home. They knew that their grandchildren were going to be raised as Jews. So they had nothing to complain about.

My daughter is a pretty together five-year-old, and she's asked me a lot of questions about all this. She's at the point where she is figuring out the connections between things and trying to understand what everything means. She has been very curious as to why the rest of my family celebrates Christmas but I don't. She has asked me many times, "Are you Jewish?" And my answer has always been, "Yes, I am." We live a very Jewish life, and we have a very Jewish home. Maybe this is the New Age approach, but I think you are defined by however you live your life and not by whatever papers you signed or whether or not you have been dipped in water. So yes, I personally consider myself Jewish. And if it ever comes up in conversation and people ask me, "Do you guys ever go to church?" I just say, "No, we go to synagogue, we're Jewish."

The biggest change in our lives over the last couple of years is that David's level of involvement in Judaism has really increased. He is now studying to become a cantor. In fact, I'm the one who brought it to his attention two years ago that this is something he might really want to do. I thought it was something he would really love. And he has definitely decided to go that route. We've talked about the fact that if David were ever to get a job in a Conservative synagogue, we would probably end up having a kosher home. We have a lot of friends who are kosher, and you know, as someone who likes lobster and shrimp and all kinds of things that lie on the bottom of the ocean, it's hard to imagine. I would certainly do it. I wouldn't be saying, "Hey, great." If it were just up to me, I would say, "No, I'm not interested in doing that." I can also see us maybe trying it and then just thinking, "This just isn't us." I would imagine that might happen. And if we did keep kosher, I'm sure I'd make a million mistakes and forget which pans go where. We'll see. I'm not closed to it, but I wouldn't be doing it because of any deep religious convictions. I would be doing it because David feels that it is something we need to do.

As for me, I am going to convert. I've taken some classes that interest me. I haven't done anything formal yet, but ultimately I will. At this point I am much more comfortable with the idea of converting. David isn't pressuring me at all. He could probably pursue his cantorial career and I wouldn't have to officially convert. Frankly, who would ever ask me if I had? But at the same time, it's not like I'm looking at any other faith or anything like that. We're committed to Judaism. We have a Jewish home, and we're leading a Jewish life.

2 Choosing a Christian Family Life

Of the interfaith couples I spoke to, far fewer are choosing Christianity instead of Judaism as the primary religion for their homes and families. The Jewish spouse often seems to be heavily encouraged by parents and other relatives to raise the children as Jews. That means the pressure on the couple to have a Jewish family life can be very strong. And although there are many aspects of Judaism that Christians may find hard to accept, couples have indicated that there seem to be more elements of Christianity that are harder for Jews to come to terms with. For example, many Jewish people are simply unwilling to accept the idea of having their children taught to believe in Jesus Christ or in concepts such as heaven and hell.

The couples in these stories are all raising their children primarily as Christians. There are some stories in which the Christian wives are far more active religiously than their Jewish spouses, and they regret that the husbands didn't teach their children much about their Jewish heritage. There is a story about a Jewish woman who decides that her children can be Christian because her husband seems to care so much more about his religion than she does about hers. And there is also a story in which a couple decides that their children will eventually be more receptive to learning about the "other" religion if they are raised as Christians rather than as Jews.

Meg is an artist who is in her early fifties. She grew up in a small town in Missouri. From the time she was very young, Christianity has been an important part of Meg's life. She finds the religious experiences she participates in to be extremely meaningful. At times she does have feelings of regret that she is not able to share those experiences with her husband.

✳ MEG

* * *

I grew up always knowing God. We went to church every Sunday as a family. My dad would sleep through the services sometimes, and I don't know if he ever opened a Bible, but he was a good man. He was an usher and a deacon in the church. My mom and aunt were the ones who put on the Christmas pageants, and they were also the choir directors. We were a big part of the church community.

* * *

We lived in a little town out in the middle of nowhere. Half of the people were Catholic, and the rest were the other Christian denominations. My family belonged to a Lutheran church. We didn't meet the Catholic kids until high school, because they all went to Catholic schools through eighth grade. There was one Jewish family that lived in the town. We knew who everybody was, and they all knew us. It was definitely a small-town atmosphere.

Being involved with the church was what I knew. And when I went through catechism in eighth grade, I finally began to feel a connection to the church other than just as a Sunday school attendee. I really got to know the Bible, and I came to this awareness about my relationship with the Lord. I truly felt that He was a part of my life.

I also felt a strong awareness about God when I first went away to college. I chose a school in a large city that was pretty far away. A lot of people told me I wasn't going to like it. I remember my parents driving away from the dorm, and of course my mom was crying. After they had gone I went out for a walk. I communicated with God through my thoughts, and I really felt not alone. I did not have fear because I knew I had Jesus with me, and He would take care of me.

When I first moved away from home I tried to find a Lutheran church to go to, but it was all old people. Then I found a great Presbyterian church that I could walk to on Sundays. The preacher was a wonderful guy. I stayed with that church for a long time. After college I kept living in the same area, and I found a job in advertising. That's where I met Richard. There was a definite attraction between us. It was funny because I had dated a lot of guys, and with each one I'd think, "He's a really nice person, but I know I won't be marrying him." Richard was the first one that I went out with and thought, "This guy has possibilities."

Richard is Jewish. The neighborhood he grew up in, and practically everyone he knew, was Jewish. His family didn't do much. They didn't celebrate the Friday evening rituals or attend temple on the Sabbath. Richard learned a little Hebrew when he had his bar mitzvah. I know he always thought he was Jewish more through his heritage than through his faith. When he was very young, his family celebrated Christmas. They didn't have a tree, but they had presents.

My parents completely accepted Richard. I think that because of the foundation they gave me, they trusted my values and never questioned whom I was dating. They were going to accept whomever I liked. They even told my grandparents all about Richard very early on, which I thought they wouldn't want to do. So there was no question that they liked him from the beginning.

The difference in our religious backgrounds is not something that was an issue for us, but it was something that was always of interest to me. I remember one of the first times we went to visit Richard's parents. Richard had an old girlfriend whom he was still good friends with. She was a very lovely Jewish girl. I remember that she called while we were there, and I heard his mother in the kitchen answering the phone. His mother was extremely amiable. "Oh, hi, how're you doing? It's good to talk to you. Just a minute, I'll get him." I knew right away it was this old girlfriend calling, and I thought, "Oh, I'm really not the one they want."

Even though they might have preferred Richard to marry someone Jewish, his parents have always treated me in an open and loving way. I never felt like they didn't accept me. And I remember that most of his friends were nice, except for one guy who was very religious. He was sort of crazy. He wrote horrible letters to Richard before we were getting married. I thought, "He is going to kill Richard so he doesn't marry me." He was that extreme. There were also some old friends of Richard who moved not far from us, and I think they were bothered by the fact that I'm not Jewish. They were nice to me but always only up to a point. Richard is so good about standing up to people. I remember him saying, "You don't include Meg in the conversation when we get together. You don't try to find out anything about her." He confronted them, and after that, the friendship was pretty much severed.

I always assumed that after Richard and I were married, I would just keep going to church. I would continue with my life, and Richard would continue with his. We wouldn't be together with religion, but we would be together in other ways. We were planning to be married in a nondenominational chapel, by a rabbi. It felt like a way to bring the two religions, and the two families, together. Before the wedding, we went to speak with the pastor at the Presbyterian church I had first joined. I just wanted to ask him, "What are we really getting into here?" And he was wonderful. He said, "Oh, Judaism is a beautiful religion. The Jews are wonderful people. But Meg, what are you going to do when you have kids? Will you be bringing them to church?" I said, "Well, they would be in the nursery because if I'm coming to church, they'll be coming too." To me, there was no question. He said, "I apologize for even asking. You're right. That's just a given. They will be a part of the church, as you are."

Richard and I talked a little about how we would raise our kids. We basically thought we would expose them to both of our religions. Everything would be shared. We'd celebrate Hanukkah and Passover along with the Christian holidays. We would each teach them about our own religion in whatever ways we could. And then when they were older, they could decide for themselves which religion they wanted to be a part of.

We have two children, and they were both baptized. Richard didn't question my wanting to have them baptized because that was a part of my religion and something I cared about. My parents came to the baptisms and brought gifts. I don't even know whether Richard bothered to tell his parents about these occasions. He might have said something like, "Oh, Meg's parents are coming because we are going to baptize Mathew this weekend." But there wasn't a feeling of, "Mom, you and Dad should really be here for this."

When the kids were little, we did light the menorah for Hanukkah, and the kids would say the Jewish prayer. But after six or seven years, it ended up that I was the only one still trying to make sure that we did anything to celebrate Hanukkah. I would buy the gifts. I would get the candles and set up the menorah. I felt that I was putting in a lot of effort, and it didn't seem to matter much to Richard. It was like he was just slacking off, not purposely, but because he didn't really care. And it wasn't only about Hanukkah. He really wasn't doing anything to teach the kids about Judaism. So I felt, "If he doesn't care, why should I bother?"

Richard will say he is Jewish, but he really doesn't do anything Jewish in terms of practice. Sometimes he starts to feel guilty, and then occasionally he'll go to a temple. He always takes the important Jewish holidays off from work. I'll say, "Why do you do that?" I don't know if it means anything to him, but I think it's something he feels he has to do because he doesn't want people at work to think he doesn't care about being Jewish.

One thing that happened recently is that his sister's son had a bar mitzvah, and I know that in some ways it made Richard feel a little bad. He definitely enjoyed the service. It brought back some of the things he had learned in Hebrew school, and he was singing along with the songs and repeating all the words. But afterwards he just seemed a little melancholy, and he said to me, "Oh, Mom didn't get to have this with Mathew." I guess he felt bad that his own son never had a bar mitzvah. A few months later, he told me that he had given money to a temple in the area. I think the bar mitzvah made him feel somehow disappointed in himself for not doing more in terms of Judaism, and he was trying to make up for it a little.

I know that our kids have been very much swayed by the fact that there has always been a constant from me in terms of practicing my religion, but there hasn't been from Richard. Mostly what they saw from him about being Jewish was indifference. And I think that as a result of what they got from me, and how little they got from Richard, both of our children are very definitely Christian. Mathew, our son, is eighteen. He has a very strong foundation in Christianity. It guides him. If you didn't know Mat was Christian, it wouldn't be particularly obvious. But with our daughter, Debra, it is. Debra is someone who very much walks her faith. She's sixteen. She does not party. She does not do beer. She does not date guys who are not Christian. She has a number of Christian friends, and they'll all pray together. She has devotions every day before she goes to bed, and she truly has a strong relationship with God. I think really that He is what gets her through her days. When she goes off to school on a day that she has a test, she sometimes will say, "I'm not ready for this. I don't have it yet." I'll tell her, "Say your prayers, and tell me what time your test is, and I'll pray for you too." For years Debra and Mat both went to a Christian camp in the summers. Debra in particular developed a wonderful group of friends that gives her support, and they help each other when they're having tough times or bad times.

The conflict for our children is that they are always wanting Richard to become a Christian. Debra, who is the worrier, is fearful she won't see her father in eternity. She's afraid that he's going to go to hell. Many Father's Days ago, she bought Richard a Bible. She is always trying to get him to go with her to youth groups or Bible study classes. I had a Sunday school teacher come up to me the other day and say, "I want you to know that I still pray for your husband, because of Debra wanting us to pray for her dad." I think she's asked a lot of people to do that. So I'm telling you, he is covered with prayer.

Richard's reaction is that he is totally uninterested in all of this. And the kids know it. Debra will say, "Dad, I'm going to pray for you." He'll say, "Well, that's good." Around the dinner table, it can get almost humorous. Mat will say things like, "Dad, why don't you come with us to this event over at the church?" Richard will answer, "Oh, I'd love to, but I think I'm going to sleep in." And they'll all laugh. The kids are old enough now to realize that this is not something they can hard-sell to Richard. They've got to have a more subtle approach. A while back, when Debra did keep pushing and pushing, I had to say, "Slack off, honey, you're going to drive him away more than pull him to you." I know that what the kids are feeling is that the church is a big part of their lives as well as mine, and it would be great if their dad could be a part of that too. The only times he's gone with us to church were when the kids were in programs, or at Christmas and Easter just because those are big family times.

I think that, for me, the hardest part has been the loneliness. This is an area that I wish we could have been together in. Where I was raised, the whole family would go to church and then we would come home and have chicken for dinner. And after that, we would go on a ride in the country or to visit friends. With Richard and me, Sundays have never been so great. The kids and I would leave for church on Sunday mornings, and Richard would be asleep in bed. If the kids were giving me a hard time, or I was running late, he would help me get them ready, and then he'd go back to bed. A lot of times we would come home and he would still be asleep. Somehow, that would set my mood the wrong way. It would be sort of a blue Sunday.

There is this one couple that I know from our church. They are so strong in their faith, and they have devotions together and pray together. I would love to have that with my husband, but I don't. I am always attending Bible study where couples might attend, but I'm by myself. So it's the aloneness, and not having my companion with me, that for me has been the hardest part.

Alice is in her thirties. She worked as an audiologist for a number of years before deciding to stay home with her children. Alice has always been much more involved in her religion than Gary has been in his. She has tried to give her husband plenty of time to become comfortable with the idea of educating their children in her faith. She doesn't want to rush him, but at a certain point she needs him to make a decision.

✖ ALICE (TO BE FOLLOWED BY HER HUSBAND, GARY)

* * *

When Gary and I met, he made it pretty clear from the beginning that even though he had been raised in a Jewish home in a somewhat observant manner, he wasn't doing much himself anymore. He kind of frowned upon organized religions. As for me, I was very much Catholic in my thinking. I had been raised in a very observant Catholic family. I went to almost twelve years of Catholic school. My family participated in all of the Catholic traditions and rituals during each of the holidays. There were advent candles at Christmas time, nativity scenes . . . that kind of thing.

* * *

I just always had the feeling from the start that Gary would think the way he was going to think and I would do what I needed to do. The fact that he wasn't religious made it easier to me. So in my mind marrying someone Jewish didn't present a problem. And things were fine, until we actually decided to get married.

I guess I always kind of compartmentalized my religion. I felt that it was something very private for me. And then when we decided to get married, I remember my mother trying to talk some sense into me. She would say, "Just keep in mind that religion becomes a very, very sensitive issue, and marriage is so difficult to begin with. You have so many issues that differences in religion kind of make everything harder." I just completely ignored her. Then we started planning the ceremony and had a real tough time trying to find someone to marry us. And that's when I really started getting very discouraged, very disillusioned.

The priest wouldn't marry us anywhere outside the church, and Gary wanted nothing to do with the church. Then we talked to a couple of different rabbis. We found one who would have married us on neutral ground, for a very large fee, of course. Ultimately, we became very disgusted and we ended up getting married by a justice of the peace at a chapel at Northwestern University. For me, it was a very cold, very unsatisfying experience, and I regret that.

We wanted to find some decent compromise that neither family would be offended by. One thing that happened was that there was this big, beautiful stained glass window at the front of the chapel. Gary's mother claims that a picture of Jesus was in there, but I never saw it. She found it, though. She was the only one who saw it, and she was very unhappy about that.

The only thing that could have helped is if one of us were willing to compromise. If Gary could have said, "Okay, let's get married in the Catholic church," of course that would have made everything easier. But he didn't want to make his family go into the church. His parents are both Holocaust survivors, and he couldn't do that. And I didn't want to get married in a synagogue because it felt hypocritical. Gary wasn't observant. Why should I make my whole family and myself go through a Jewish ceremony when it meant nothing to Gary? So we were kind of in a bind.

We really tried to make the whole thing as generic as possible. I had to write the entire ceremony myself, which was horrible because I had so many other things to do for the wedding. And we had to make very neutral psalms and nondenominational prayers and poems. It was just empty for me. I remember being so depressed on my wedding day. I was happy I was getting married, but the wedding itself was not a fulfilling experience. Gary had no problem with it, none. But then again, religion wasn't an important part of his life. For a long time I remember feeling that because I wasn't married in a Catholic church I had really missed something. It's kind of faded away now, but it was an empty experience for me.

Gary and I had tried to anticipate a lot of the issues we would be facing. We talked extensively about them before we got married. But you can't always know how you're going to feel. In retrospect, I wouldn't change anything really. I wasn't going to let religion stand in our way. We loved each other, and that's the point. Religion is not meant to separate, although it has separated people throughout history. Early on, we talked about my beliefs and I knew Gary thought everything was ridiculous, and that was hard. But he tried to be somewhat respectful of my beliefs, and he still does, because he knows I find peace in them.

I remember having this horrible existential crisis shortly after we got married. I would go to church by myself on Sunday, which I found extremely depressing. It was hard not having my husband with me and thinking that I was observing this religion that my husband was not a part of at all. And it was hard to accept that he didn't believe in Jesus and that ultimately Catholics believe that you're going to go to heaven if you believe in Jesus, and my husband wasn't going to heaven. It wasn't quite that cut-and-dry because I really didn't believe all of it anyway, but there were a lot of things that were not easy for me to reconcile.

At holiday time, it was particularly difficult. Gary would participate with me on a superficial level, but he couldn't really experience the joy of Christmas and Easter and all that. He would celebrate from an outsider kind of standpoint. He went to Mass with me and he would sit in the pew very irreverently, which is just not something you did in my family. We were always extremely reverent. He and I did always have a Christmas tree. I was lucky because Gary liked Christmas, in a secular way. We never had a menorah on Hanukkah until we had kids. We just always celebrated the Christian traditions because of me. He didn't care about celebrating the Jewish holidays, but he cares more now that we have children.

We never actually decided what we would do when we had children. That was always left up in the air. We addressed it but never came to a conclusion. Deep down, I knew I would probably get my way if there were a conflict because I cared a lot more than Gary did about religion. But basically we always thought we would raise them with both religions, and everything would be hunky-dory. We would have these wonderful, well-rounded children and we would celebrate Christmas and Hanukkah and all the other holidays, and oh, how lucky they would be.

Our children are four and seven. When they were born, there was no real problem. It did bother me that we were not baptizing them, but I got over it. It helped that my family never said a word. Everyone kind of denied everything. I didn't push too hard about baptizing them when they were born because I knew it was going to be a long, long struggle to get Gary to agree to that happening, and I knew it didn't have to be done right away.

We kept saying we were going to raise the kids with everything, but it wasn't happening. We were still doing the Christian holidays with my family, and that was it. I was the one who finally bought the menorah. I said, "Come on, let's get going here." We started celebrating Hanukkah. We lit the candles and played dreidel. We started going to Gary's brother's house for Passover and for some of the other holidays. My sister-in-law is an unbelievable cook, so I got her recipes for all the traditional Jewish foods. Gary never asks me to make those things, but if he did I would do it.

As time wore on, we kept thinking we were going to educate the kids at home in terms of religion, but that's a very difficult thing to do. We would talk a little about God and what was going on during holiday time. But we didn't really do much, and by the time my oldest daughter entered kindergarten, I thought, "This kid needs some religious training." Gary finally agreed to let her go to CCD at Sacred Heart Church. CCD is Sunday school, catechism classes. So last year I enrolled Beth in CCD. When she comes home from her class, she always has these little stories that we have to read to her about Jesus. Each story has a different lesson, and sometimes if I got caught up doing other things I'd say to Gary, "Would you just read her CCD thing tonight?" So he was reading these stories about Jesus. And then one time he said, "You know, Alice, I think you ought to be reading this. I think that what Jesus is teaching is great, and I think he is a good man and his lessons are very good for people, but I'm having a hard time with this." I said, "Okay, fine. It was a lot to ask of you. Of course you don't have to read it." And I'd never ask him to do that again because it bothered him.

It's the same thing with driving her to CCD. Gary won't drive her there. No matter what I'm doing, I am the one who has to drive her and pick her up from CCD and take her to church. It's only a three-minute drive, but he's very resentful if I ask him to do it. It's my baby. He probably feels like, "Come on, what more do you want from me?" And I can appreciate that, so I never push it. I go and get her. I work it out.

At the end of the year, the director of religious education from the school called me and asked, "Has Beth been baptized?" I said, "No, she hasn't." She wanted to meet with me and I was annoyed because I thought, "It's none of your business." But the reason she called is that in first grade they start getting the kids ready for First Communion. At that point, either you make a decision to go ahead with all of it or you get out, because the first sacrament is baptism and the second is First Communion. You have to do one before the other.

So at the end of last year I started saying to Gary, "We need to talk about this," and he would just kind of push it off. He didn't want to think about it. I explained to him why we had to talk about it now, and he kind of mulled it over the whole summer. Finally he agreed that the children do need religious education, and they do need to identify with some kind of religion. He said, "You're right, we will choose." It still took him about a year to decide that they could finally be baptized. Once in awhile I would press him: "What do you think, what do you think?"

Gary finally decided the kids could be baptized and that they could be Catholic, but he also wants Judaism to be a part of their lives. Of course, they know that their dad is Jewish. We celebrate a lot of the Jewish holidays now, usually with his family, and we always will. Gary feels very strongly about that, and I have no problem with it. And I think when the kids get older he's going to make sure that he introduces a degree of what I would call skepticism. He wants them to know that there is a whole world out there of people who don't believe in Jesus and that being Catholic is not the only option. But he'll wait until he thinks they are old enough to understand.

The kids are not completely clear about much of this yet. Beth used to say, "Well, I'm Catholic, and Brian is Jewish." Brian is her brother. She would just identify the male members of the family as Jewish. Or sometimes she tells everyone that she is Catholic and Jewish. She still doesn't fully understand that she is going to be just Catholic. I'm really not sure how she'll feel about the fact that we are all Catholic but daddy isn't. That was one of Gary's big things. "I don't want to have them Catholic because they're going to think daddy's different and they're going to reject me because I'm not Catholic." I said, "Well, I think that's our job to prevent that, and we will."

Gary will go to the baptism. He has asked me to keep it very small. He doesn't want to have a big christening party, and I wouldn't do that to him. It's just going to be the godparents and a few close friends. I won't even have my whole family there. We will let his parents know, but we're not going to throw it in their faces. I hate to hurt people. And we don't want to offend them. But ultimately the decision is ours, and I think that they both just want what is right for our kids. They want us all to be happy. Frankly, no one is going to be shocked.

I guess I thought this baptism issue was going to be more of a problem. It did take us several years to resolve it, but it was never an open conflict. It was just a very slow, loving decision. We both were very considerate of each other's feelings. I gave Gary lots of room, lots of space, and time to think about it. I appreciate the fact that it was a very hard decision for him to make. In fact, I feel like I owe him big time for letting me do this. It's funny, but I do kind of walk on eggshells with Gary around this issue. I don't even talk about when the baptism is going to be or any of the plans for that day. I don't want to make him any more uncomfortable with the whole thing than he already is.

One thing about interfaith marriage is that it makes you really evaluate your beliefs. It definitely makes you question what you think is important. If I had married someone who is Catholic, we would just be doing all this by rote. We would be going to Mass on Sundays, we would be baptizing our kids, and we would be going to First Communion. But I am forced to think about these things, and so is Gary. I need to evaluate why I am baptizing my children when they are four and seven years old. When you baptize your baby, you just do it without the same kind of thought.

The one thing I regret is that my religion is just mine. I miss being able to share it with Gary. I'll come home and he'll say, "How was Mass?" and I'll say, "Today was good, I feel good," knowing he has no idea what I am talking about. He can't relate at any level, but he accepts it. He just says, "Okay."

I think that if I had married someone at least who was Christian, or even someone who was devoutly Jewish, we could talk about religious issues in a deeper way. I have friends whose faith is very deep and they talk about it. If we talk about my faith, Gary will marvel at it but he can't relate to it. He really has no spiritual connection.

Gary is a physician. He grew up in a city in the Midwest. Gary's feelings about religions in general made it easier for him to agree to raise his children in another faith.

❈ GARY (PRECEDED BY HIS WIFE, ALICE)

* * *

I would say that the greatest factor that has helped us deal with this issue has been my apathy. If I felt strongly about this, it might be a problem, but I don't. The truth is if I felt strongly about it, I would never have married someone out of my faith. I would have seen that as being a real problem right up front.

* * *

I'm Jewish. Alice is Catholic. We really didn't talk about all this too much before we got married. I wasn't very concerned and I don't think she was either. We didn't worry about what to do with the kids because I wasn't even sure that I wanted to have kids when we first got married. We basically figured we would deal with it when the time came.

I would say the issue for us, from my point of view, has been why our children would need to be raised in any religion. I'm pretty much an agnostic more than anything. Don't get me wrong. I've had a very solid religious background. I went to Hebrew school until I was in eighth or ninth grade. I was bar mitzvahed. Then I went to Sunday school for another four or five years after that. So I certainly understand something about Judaism.

Alice and I finally did agree that it is probably a good thing for our kids to have some religious upbringing. It would be hard for me to teach them about Judaism because I'm not very observant. They wouldn't learn much. Alice participates in her religion more, so she can set better examples. I felt that her religion is as good as any other, so why not?

To me, religions are all pretty much the same. That really kind of summarizes it for me. They may have different ways of doing things, but all of them are a way to connect with God. They're basically the same, and if you think they're not, I think you're deluding yourself. And however you choose to do it, by being Catholic, being Jewish, being Buddhist, being nothing . . . if it makes you a good person, that's what's important. How you become that person doesn't really matter.

My kids are going to be baptized. They're going to be Catholic. I think a lot of people could be married to someone of a different religion and pretty much ignore it. But it's another thing to have your kids raised in another religion. That's a lot different. I had to think about that for a while before I agreed. The key for me is having an open mind. You have to know who you are and not feel threatened by people doing things differently from the way you do them. I did have a few moments when I wondered if my children would accept me and feel close to me in the same way if they really get immersed in another religion. But I believe they will.

Our kids are still young. They have questions about everything, including religion. There are questions about God. "Is God everywhere? Is he in my cereal?" They don't really understand yet that they are going to be just Catholic. Right now they would say they are both Catholic and Jewish. They know my family is Jewish and that I'm Jewish. My oldest daughter is probably as familiar with Judaism as some people who were brought up in the Reform movement. She knows about the holidays. She knows how to observe them, because we usually observe them with my family. She doesn't know any Hebrew, but most people don't read Hebrew or understand it. She knows as much as many contemporary Jews.

I definitely feel that as my children get older I will tell them more about my views on God and religion. I'm sure they'll pick up a lot of what I think on their own. As I said to my wife, "How could they be around me and not be exposed to other sides of all this?"

Of course, I can't predict what's going to happen. My guess would be that my kids will grow up in the Church so that they have a religion to observe, but they're going to know everything about Judaism because I'm here too. They know I'm not Catholic. I won't be going to most of their Catholic events. I'll continue to participate in some Jewish occasions, and they'll still be coming to all of those with me. Even though they're going to be Catholic, they'll see both religions and they'll know something about them. And as they get older, they'll know what their heritage is.

Gail grew up in a small town in the Midwest because that was where her father's business needed to be. Her story is unusual because Gail made a very untypical decision as to the religious upbringing of her children. She felt fairly comfortable with her decision before her children were born. But it became more difficult as the children were growing up and she saw them embracing holidays and traditions so different from her own.

❇ GAIL

* * *

I grew up in Wisconsin, in a little town of eight thousand people. There were five Jewish families living there. When we wanted to go to the synagogue, we had to travel over an hour away to Milwaukee, because our town didn't have one. That was real hard because it seemed like we were always going to synagogue.

* * *

We definitely went to services at the synagogue for all of the Jewish holidays. And we went to Sunday school each week from kindergarten on up. So we had to have that long drive there and back each time we went. Also, I didn't really enjoy Sunday school because all of the other kids lived near each other and went to school together, whereas I only saw them once a week. I felt like an outsider.

My dad's family was pretty Reform, but my mom's family was almost Orthodox. Being Jewish was always important to my mom. We would light the candles on Friday night. We did keep a kosher house, and again, it was hard because we had to go to the kosher butcher in Milwaukee to get all our stuff. We had family celebrations for all of the holidays. We used to have a seder with my mother's parents that lasted for about six hours, which was a lot of fun. And because we were the only Jewish family in town with kids, the teachers would always ask us to explain to everyone about the holidays. We'd bring books and food and whatever else went with the particular holiday to school and tell all about it.

I remember that the worst day of the year was Christmas, because our family didn't do anything for it at all, and we couldn't call anybody. But what was good is that the five Jewish families would always get together the night before, on Christmas Eve. We'd spend the evening at one of our houses. And Santa Claus always came, because a good friend of one of the families dressed up each year like Santa Claus, and he would come over and have a drink with us. It was pretty funny.

I had a steady boyfriend for three years during high school, and we stayed together for another couple of years even when I went away to college. I was home on break one time, and my mother said to me, "Don't you think it's time to end this? You know that Ron isn't Jewish. I think you should break up now since you'll never marry him, because you can only marry a Jewish boy." And she kind of made me agree to stop seeing him. I was pretty unhappy. This was a boy I loved, whom I had been with for a long time. We kept seeing each other for a short period without telling anyone, but I knew how upset my family would be if they found out. That wasn't something I thought I could deal with. And so I stopped seeing him.

Some of my aunts lived very near the college I was going to. As soon as my mother told the aunts that Ron and I were breaking up, they started setting me up on all these blind dates with Jewish boys. And I can tell you, one date was worse than the next. I do remember that out of all of them there was one particular Jewish dental student whom I really liked, but he didn't like me.

After college I moved to another town in Wisconsin. I started working, and I would occasionally go to these business conventions. That's where I met my husband. After one of the meetings, a bunch of us were in the bar having a drink, and my girlfriend introduced me to Phillip. We got to talking, and it turned out that I had just moved across the street from him. Phillip's father was Catholic, and his mother was Methodist. He had been raised Catholic, but for probably twenty years he hadn't been doing anything religious at all. He wasn't an atheist, but he just wasn't practicing anything. And this is the really weird thing. It just so happens that right about the time when I met him, something must have happened in his life, and he decided he needed to reconnect with his religion. So he had just kind of started up again with Catholicism right about when I met him.

We started dating. At this point, I still always went to be with my family for the Jewish holidays. I was really hoping to marry someone Jewish, because I had always thought that if I didn't marry somebody Jewish, I would have married Ron. But I was just coming off three years of these really bad blind dates. And I liked going out with Phillip. It was fun having him right across the street. He had a lot of money, and we went to all kinds of places together. Phillip was a thirty-seven-year-old bachelor when I met him. Everybody told me he would never get married. My friends would say to me, "You'll just have fun with him. Don't worry about it." And I really didn't.

I never thought our relationship was getting especially serious. And then all of a sudden, it did. I had met Phillip in May, and seven months later, on Christmas Eve, he gave me a ring and asked me to marry him. I was kind of shocked. Not that it really made a difference, but my ring is gorgeous. I was pretty young. I was twenty-five and I had had all these lousy blind dates, and here was this nice guy who wanted to marry me. So I said, "Yes."

The first thing I did was call my sister, who is married to a wonderful Jewish doctor. I didn't tell my mother right away. By the time I finally did tell her, she had already met Phillip a couple of times and kind of liked him. "Well," my mother said, "of course you know we would prefer that you would marry somebody Jewish, but if you really love him, that's fine. But you do know, don't you, that you have to raise your kids Jewish?" And I said, "Yes."

In reality, Phillip and I had already talked about this. He had been getting more and more into Catholicism. He wanted to raise our kids to be Catholic. I knew that religion mattered more to him than it did to me. And I said, "You know, Phillip, if your religion is that important to you, then if we have kids, and you want them to be Catholic, you will have to do everything. I will not do a thing."

I don't know if it was because I was young or what, but I really didn't worry much about any of this. I knew that Phillip had already strayed away once from his religion. I mean, he didn't go to church for twenty years right before I met him. So I didn't think he'd necessarily stick to being a practicing Catholic for very long. And even if he did, I didn't really think he would carry through with taking all the responsibility for giving the kids a religious education. I thought that if he did care enough to go through with it, fine. And if he didn't, the kids would automatically be Jewish anyways. This is something that my mom kept telling me over and over and over. "Kids born to a Jewish mom are considered Jewish." I kind of held on to that. And no matter which religion our kids ended up being, I figured that once they were old enough they were going to choose for themselves what they wanted to do. So I just kind of blew it off.

We decided to have a rabbi perform the wedding ceremony. First, though, we went to talk to the priest at Phillip's church, and the priest gave Phillip a dispensation to get married. But the priest said we had to be married in a house of worship. So that meant we couldn't be married outside or at a hotel. It would have to be in a synagogue. There was just one little synagogue in town that held maybe fifty people. And there was one rabbi in practically the whole state who would occasionally do mixed marriages. This rabbi happened to be good friends with my parents. He was about eighty years old. So he agreed to marry us. But we still couldn't get married at the synagogue because it was too small for all the guests. So then we went back to the priest, and the Catholic Church gave us a dispensation so that we could be married at the Marriott Hotel. We had a traditional Jewish ceremony. We were married under a chuppah. Phillip broke the glass. Even though we were being married by a rabbi, it was important to Phillip to just have the priest there. So the priest came to the ceremony, too. We told him he could say something, but he didn't want to. He just sat in the front row for the whole service. The rabbi married us, and then the very next week, he died.

One thing that was hard for me to get used to is that Phillip wears a cross. He never wears it out. It is always inside his shirt. You can't see it unless he is mowing the lawn and takes his shirt off or unless we are swimming or whatever. There are no crosses in our house. But Phillip does a lot of reading and likes to research things. So there are a lot of Catholic books around.

Phillip and I have two kids. They were both baptized. Baptisms and First Communions and confirmations are so important in the Catholic Church. People have these big parties, and the kids get all these gifts. When our kids went through any of these things, we kept it very simple. All we ever did for those times was have Phillip's parents and brother and sister come over. That was it. That made it easier.

Every Sunday morning Phillip would get up, and the kids would get up, and he would give them breakfast and take them to church. I never went with them. The kids knew that I wasn't comfortable going, and they never asked me. And Phillip never asked me either. They all really just knew that I am Jewish. They didn't say, "Oh, can't you come with us?" or, "I wish you would come." No one ever pushed me. And when the kids started going to CCD classes, which are the Catholic education classes, Phillip would always take them. Those classes met on Tuesday or Wednesday nights. And if Phillip was ever out of town for a meeting or whatever, the kids did not go. I wouldn't take them. I was willing to have them do it. But I could never take them.

It wasn't like we always had to negotiate what we would and wouldn't be doing. Everything was just sort of understood. I still always went to synagogue for the Jewish holidays, and sometimes the kids and Phillip would come with me. And we did do things for all of the holidays at home, which the kids loved. We did Hanukkah and Christmas. We did Easter and Passover. We always did a seder. We had books about the Jewish holidays, and we read about them and celebrated them. So even though my kids didn't go to Hebrew school, I feel they were exposed to both religions.

My daughter is nineteen now. She has never been confirmed in the Catholic church. She went through all the classes, but when it was time for her confirmation she decided she didn't want to go through with it. There were too many parts she didn't believe in. And she stopped going to church. My husband just about had a fit. I said, "Phillip, she doesn't believe it. If sometime later in her life she wants to be confirmed, she will be." To me, it was wonderful that Maya went through all these Catholic education classes and then didn't like it at all. She gave it a try, and that was fine. Really, I don't know if she believes in anything spiritual right now. She just has to find herself. She has always really loved the Jewish holidays. I don't know if she'll go to any religion at this point, but a part of me thinks that she might eventually turn to Judaism.

My son, on the other hand, did go through a Catholic confirmation. Probably the hardest thing for me has been having Adam really buy into

Catholicism. He is just very much into it. From the time he was pretty young, he volunteered at the Catholic church. He went on mission trips and did a lot of community service. He went to a Catholic high school and took theology classes, and he really kind of bought into the whole program. I think Adam will probably stay Catholic because he has really enjoyed the experiences he's had with it so far. There have actually been a few times that Adam has received some honor at the church, and at those times, I have gone to church with the rest of my family. But those were the only times.

Fortunately, I don't think Adam worries too much about my soul or my afterlife. He knows that I say my own prayers, and I go to synagogue and I'm a good Jew. And I think he knows that I'll be fine.

Overall, everything has worked out pretty well. As long as things are status quo, I'm a pretty easygoing person. I don't like confrontation, so there are probably a lot of things we haven't talked about all that openly. One thing that always did bother me was having a Christmas tree. We had the tree every single year. It's funny, because when I got married, of course I had no Christmas ornaments. Most people come into a marriage with some of their own ornaments, but I had nothing. One of my girlfriends gave me this gift, which was a huge box of handmade ornaments. I thanked her, but it really wasn't something I was thrilled about having. I don't do anything with the tree. Phillip gets it, and he puts the lights on. The kids decorate it. And I put all my little Hanukkah stuff out. But having the tree was hard for me.

And then, of course, we always had to be careful that my mom and dad didn't come to my house over the holidays, because my mom would have been really upset.

I had promised my mom that the kids would be raised Jewish, which of course they weren't. I know she figured it out. But we never talked about it. We never told her that the kids were being baptized. We never told her they did First Communion. We never told her about any of it. My mom and Phillip have always kind of had a love/hate relationship. I always knew that my mom would have preferred for him to be Jewish. Maybe if he were Jewish, I would be closer to her. I don't know.

The kids have learned to be careful in front of my mom. They know what to say and what not to say in front of her. They never talked about anything they were doing at church. And if we were out at a restaurant, they would never eat ham or pork in front of her. That's something they really don't even do with me. It's interesting. The one thing I have always done, besides going to synagogue, is that I keep up with some of the dietary laws I was raised with. I don't have separate dishes, but we never have milk and meat together at meals. I don't have ham or bacon or any of that stuff in my house. Since we used to keep kosher, that's just something I got used to and it's very ingrained in me. If we go out, my husband will order what he wants. But like I said, my kids really won't eat those things in front of me. And that's something I appreciate.

Ellen grew up primarily on the East Coast. She is in her twenties and is a graduate student in sociology. Ellen talked to me about how much she and Jim want to share each other's religious rituals and traditions just as they share other aspects of their lives together. Up until now they have been able to do that fairly easily. But recently they have started to plan for having children, and coming up with a way to handle the issue of religion has become more of a struggle.

❈ ELLEN (TO BE FOLLOWED BY HER HUSBAND, JIM)

* * *

One of my best friends when I was little was Jewish. Her family would invite us to share some of their holidays with them. We'd go over to their house for Passover. And then we would have them come with us for some of our events. I remember that we invited them to one of our church suppers. It worked out really well because they didn't eat bacon, and we didn't care as much about the pancakes. So we gave them our extra pancakes, and we got to eat all of the bacon. It worked out well for everybody.

* * *

I was raised Episcopalian. We went to church quite a bit. When we were little, we went almost every Sunday. I would say we were a pretty active family. My mom was in the choir. I was an "acolyte," which means I got to do things like help carry the candles and the cross during a ceremony and help the priest with Communion. Then as we got older it became harder to drag my sister and me out of bed on Sunday mornings, so we stopped going as often.

I went to an Episcopal college. I knew the college chapel would be just like the way I grew up, so I guess that was a plus, but it wasn't a major factor in my decision to go there. I did attend a couple of youth group meetings during my freshman year, but I didn't really pursue them after that. I would go to church maybe twice a year the whole time I was at college.

Jim and I were both enrolled at the same college, but he was spending a year studying in Israel and we didn't know each other. The story is that he was in Israel, and he logged on to his computer to see if he could find some-one back at the college to talk to. Because of the time difference, it was really late at night and all of his friends were asleep. But I was staying up late to work on a French paper. We became pen pals over the computer, and then we actually met when he came back to school. I think it's pretty funny that he had to go all the way to Israel to find a Christian girl back in the States.

At the beginning, Jim and I didn't talk much about religion because we were just so busy being in love and having fun. We did a few little things like light Hanukkah candles together that first year, and we both enjoyed that. When you're in that sort of fuzzy love stage, anything that the other person does is interesting. But it wasn't until we were serious and thinking about marriage that religion became not exactly an issue, but definitely something to talk about.

I was the one who pushed along our discussions on all this. I wanted Jim to focus on what his religion meant to him and how he saw Judaism fit-ting into his life. I was very concerned that he wasn't taking our differences seriously enough. I knew he loved me. I knew he was having a great time with me and that he wanted to stay with me. So I almost was like a mother about this. I would sit down with him and say, "Look, you're going on this path and you're making these decisions. What do you think your life is going to be like if you decide to stay with me? We need to figure this out before we go any further."

I was trying to understand how important Judaism was to him. I wanted some idea of how he wanted his children to be raised and whether he would expect me at some point to convert. I would have had a prob-lem if he had said, "Well, yes, I'm hoping that you will convert, and I haven't mentioned it because we are so much in love and we don't need to worry about it yet." I wanted to really understand what he was thinking and feeling. I needed to be very clear about what his expectations were. I also had to think about what I wanted for myself, because up until this point I hadn't really done that. You just grow up and assume that you're going to be like your parents and that everything is going to be sort of the same.

It's not like we were able to figure everything out before we got mar-ried. We've been married almost three years, and to this day I don't have a clear idea of exactly how it's all going to work. But at least we were able to decide that we could be together. We knew that neither of us wanted to give up our own religion and that we each wanted to share in the experi-ences of the other. We also found that what we had in common was a desire for our children to choose their own paths. We didn't want to pick for them. And we knew that we didn't want to choose one religion over the other. We both just wanted them to have some sort of religion, and some sort of faith, that we would practice in the home. And we think that eventually our children will make their own decisions. So those are the things we figured out before we got married, and we felt we could handle the specifics as we went along.

I think our wedding was really great. We decided not to try to have a rabbi involved in the service. We felt that the reason most rabbis don't officiate at interfaith marriages is because they honestly feel that type of marriage is not the best situation for a Jew to be a part of. It is not what they want to be doing. A rabbi is endowed with the honor of marrying a Jew to a Jew. I didn't want somebody participating in our ceremony who was not really comfortable with what we were doing. Also, a lot of rabbis ask that the children be clearly raised Jewish. And that wasn't something we were making a decision to do.

An Episcopal priest married us. We had to talk to him about how we wanted things to be done. First of all, most marriages are supposed to take place in the church, and that isn't what we wanted because we didn't want Jim or his family to be uncomfortable. So we decided to have the ceremony outside. There were a lot of parts within the service itself that we could modify. Basically, every time it said Jesus Christ we used the word Lord. We were both comfortable with that. Also, we wanted this to be a worship service for everybody who would be there, and we thought if we used the word Lord, people could put their own meaning into it. We also included the seven blessings from the Jewish wedding ceremony, instead of the benediction that the priest would normally have done at the end. I'm really proud of how it all worked out. I think the best compliment that we got was that many of the Jewish people said that it really felt like a Jewish ceremony. The Christian people said, "Oh, that was a very pretty ceremony, and I liked the blessings." So I think everybody felt included.

After we were married, we joined both a church and a synagogue. We haven't been to the synagogue in a while, though, because it just isn't that comfortable for us and we haven't found one yet that we like better. I feel bad about that, and I know Jim does too. We just don't feel like we really fit in there. It's a little cold compared with the church we joined. The way the Christians are is, "Oh, welcome. We're glad you're here." That's just not the feeling we get from the synagogue. It's different. I feel like an outsider if we get involved in social things at the synagogue. The synagogue experience is also difficult since I know very little Hebrew. I can remember the beginning of certain prayers if I hear them enough. But I think the Hebrew is a barrier for me.

So far, the church has been easier for us as a couple. Actually, the priest and his assistant both know Jim is Jewish and welcome him. I feel that they have been very respectful about his religion and have tried to include him to the extent that is appropriate. They understand the fact that he wants to learn and wants to participate up to a certain point. It's not like anyone is trying to get Jim to convert or anything like that. I would immediately leave the church if I felt that someone was trying to convert him.

The parts I've really been enjoying about Judaism are when we do things with our friends. I love going to celebrate the Sabbath at our friends' houses and doing some of the holidays together. It's also good because our friends know what our situation is, and there's no pressure to try to fit into something that isn't altogether comfortable. We haven't done the Sabbath rituals at our own house. Usually by the time Friday night comes around, we just go home and collapse or go out to our friends' houses. But I would like to start doing it at our house when we have kids.

There's one thing that I do regret. At times, Jim has had to go to Yom Kippur services and Rosh Hashanah services without me. That's because in the workplace everybody knows that I'm not Jewish, and I'm not entitled to getting those days off. If I want to take one of those days off, I have to take a personal day. That's often difficult to arrange.

I've really got a problem with that system because I feel that people should be given a certain number of religious holidays a year and be allowed to choose how they want to take them. For example, we always get two days off at Christmas, and most of the time we go to visit my parents at that time. But last year we stayed here. I could have gone and worked that second day after Christmas and then used that time off at Yom Kippur instead and spent the day at the synagogue with Jim. It really bothers me because I know he doesn't like to go by himself.

If Jim does end up going alone, I'll at least do the food preparation so he can come home and have that experience of a holiday meal. As a matter of fact, for Christmas this year I asked for Jewish cookbooks. I wanted to learn how to make a good kugel, a good matzo ball soup, and all those kinds of things. So that's what my family gave me. I got all these Jewish holiday cookbooks for Christmas. It was great.

Since Jim and I have been together, we have had several Christmas trees of our own. The first time we got one it was pretty funny. I think we were a little overly ambitious. Our apartment has very, very high ceilings. We thought that we might as well take advantage of the space, so we got this huge tree. And it wasn't just high; it was also extremely wide. With the angel on top, I think the tree went almost up to the ceiling. We had like maybe ten ornaments. Growing up, my dad always took care of setting up the tree. Now it was up to Jim. Jim tried to do it, and he didn't understand that the needles would go everywhere. In fact, they went every single place that they could possibly go. It was a real moment of discovery for us. I kept saying, "How could you not know about this?" and he kept saying, "Well, how do you think?" Between the needles and the size of that tree, it was too funny. We got a smaller tree the next year.

We don't have kids yet, but about a year ago Jim and I started talking more specifically about how we are going to raise children when we do have them. As a matter of fact, we went through a couple of months where that's all we talked about. It was difficult because religion isn't something that we usually think or talk about very much. We just kind of do our thing, which includes some aspects of Judaism and some parts of Christianity. But when it comes to kids, we want to really figure out what kind of identity we want to endow on them. Again, I wanted to make sure that we are at least somewhat clear on these things. So we tried to talk it all out.

We know that because I'm not Jewish, even the Reform tradition, which would be the most liberal of all of them, would say that our children are not Jewish. The children would have to convert in order to be considered Jewish. The only way that would be different is if we raised them to be Jewish from Day One, and then maybe some people would consider them to be Jews. But we weren't planning to do that because we wanted them to be learning about Christianity as well.

What we've decided so far is that when our children are born, they are not going to be baptized. If you do go ahead and have a christening and baptize them, part of what you're saying is that you will raise them in a Christian home, and they will be Christians. We don't want to decide that path for them. Also, as far as the baptism ceremony itself, I must have read it about ten times. There is really no way that Jim could say the words in that particular ceremony and feel comfortable. It doesn't matter so much because I know that you can always baptize somebody when they're older. So if our kids do choose Christianity, they can always be baptized later and become full members of the church.

We know that we will have some sort of naming ceremony when each of our kids is born. If we have a boy, we won't have a bris, but he will be circumcised in the hospital. That way, if he decides he wants to be Jewish, it will be easier. We'll do the Jewish holidays at home and teach our kids about Judaism. And then I guess we'll send them to Sunday school at the church. I don't want my children to ever feel, "You took my Jewish heritage away from me." I want them to be able to go into a synagogue and know enough Hebrew so they don't feel like an outsider. They are going to be outsiders to a certain extent. But if they choose at some point to really become Jewish, I want them to have enough tools to be successful in doing that, and to be able to marry a Jewish mate.

Jim feels that if we just educated our kids about Judaism, they wouldn't get a fair shake at Christianity because most Jewish people think Christianity is pretty hard to buy. They're very resistant to it. He thinks our kids will be more receptive to learning about Judaism if they're Christian than they would be trying to learn about Christianity if they were Jewish. He also said to me that if his children eventually choose to be Christians, he wants them to be educated Christians who know about Judaism and can speak from a position of authority and knowledge. And if that were the path they chose, it will be okay with him. I feel the same way about them becoming Jews. I want to be sure they would know something about Christianity as well.

I think we both feel that whatever our children choose, we want them to believe in God. I would be very upset if that didn't happen. How they choose to practice is up to them. It's not going to be easy. I mean, I know these aren't perfect solutions. I think Jim and I are doing okay with all of this now, but I think that things are going to be more difficult for us when we actually do have kids. Even though we talked about all these things and we are making decisions and choices, I know that for me it is going to be hard when we have a baby and we don't do the christening. And for Jim it is going to be difficult when there is no bar or bat mitzvah. Again, we don't want to send our children to Hebrew school and put them so specifically on a particular path. They can always choose to have a bar or bat mitzvah later if that is something they want.

A lot of people have great disdain for what we're doing, and it is definitely complicated. But I just think that when I'm an old lady and I'm on my deathbed, I will know that I have lived. I find it enriching that we are the type of people that we are. If I had married somebody who was the same as me, I know it would be easier because I would just do things without thinking about them. I think I picked the bumpier road. And to this day, I still don't have a clear idea of how it is all going to turn out.

Jim works for a software company and is also in his twenties. He and his family first lived in New Mexico and then moved east before Jim started high school. Jim realizes he will probably experience some conflicting feelings about raising his kids with an emphasis on Christianity rather than on Judaism. But after considering many of the different aspects of this issue, he still feels the choice is the right one for him to make.

⌘ JIM (PRECEDED BY HIS WIFE, ELLEN)

* * *

I come from a huge Jewish family on my mother's side. My mother's parents were Orthodox. My father, however, is Episcopalian. Before my parents got married, it was determined that my mother would be in charge of religion. They were married by a rabbi, and my mother raised us to be Jewish.

* * *

As far as Jewish education, it was for the most part influenced by where we were living. We spent time in many different communities. When we lived in Albuquerque, New Mexico, the Jewish education was pretty light. But when we moved to Cincinnati, we had a very active Jewish life. I went to Hebrew school. I was involved in a youth group all through high school. I was a counselor at a Jewish camp for several years. And my first serious girl-friend was Jewish.

Growing up, I never thought of myself as necessarily marrying a Jewish woman. The primary reason I felt that way was because of how my parents were coupled. And additionally, particularly in my elementary years and even through my high school years, I really didn't feel Jewish enough. What I mean by that is even though I participated in Jewish activities, my household upbringing wasn't Jewish enough. My family had a Jewish identity, but we still celebrated Christmas. We never really did a full Passover seder. Things like that bothered me. I felt that if I married a very Jewish woman who wanted a Jewish home and a Jewish life, I would not be prepared.

When I was a junior in college, I spent a semester studying in Israel. One night I ended up hooking into a computer chat room from the college I attended and started talking to Ellen, who was also a student there. We wrote back and forth a lot. And when I went back to college, we started spending time together.

At the beginning, religion wasn't an issue. First of all, I was familiar with Christianity and comfortable with it. And when we started getting serious, Ellen decided she needed to do some reading. She became very knowledgeable about early Christianity and what Judaism was like at the time of Jesus. She wanted to understand the two religions and how each developed. She wanted to see how they were the same and where they split from each other.

Ellen and I got married just a few years ago. I'd like to publish our wedding ceremony for people who are doing this now. We worked hard on it. An Episcopal priest officiated at the ceremony, but in lay clothing. He didn't wear a collar or anything like that. And ultimately, the Jews who were there felt it was a Jewish wedding, and the Christians who were there felt it was a Christian wedding. We had people in the congregation reading different parts, and we used elements from both religions. I think we pulled it off pretty well.

We belong to both a church and a synagogue. We each attend the other's house of worship. Whether we are going to the church or the synagogue, we go together, because we're a family. I don't want to send a message to Ellen's church community that I would send her alone. And she feels the same way when I want to go to synagogue. Really, we haven't gone to the shul since my dad died, a few months ago. I would say that the problem with our shul is that it's not the right one for us. It's Reform, it's very large, and it doesn't have a particularly Jewish feeling. We'll switch to a different one when we find a place that seems to fit us better.

I really think that if someone founded a shul that was based on mixed marriages, it would be great, because as an interfaith couple you don't feel much of a sense of community. As much as Reform synagogues try, they just don't make it. Partly that's because most of the outreach programs for interfaith couples are either passively or actively geared towards conversion. And couples pick up on that and think, "You know what? We're not changing. We want to be a part of something. We don't want to become something different." So if anyone ever established a shul welcoming mixed marriages, we'd be first in line to join. Right now, a lot of our relationship with the synagogue seems to be through the mail. "Now you owe this, and now that." In a church, you just give what you want, when you want to give it.

I'd say we go to church about once a month. I'm comfortable being in a church because I always feel it is a house of God. I find myself spending a lot of time looking at the stained glass. There are mostly Old Testament figures in the glass, and I can recognize a lot of them. And usually two or three of the readings are from the Old Testament. The thing I like most when I go to shul is the Torah reading. It's the same thing at church. I love to hear the readings. And I even like the sermon. When I sit there, I definitely have a feeling of being a part of something spiritual. Do I pray at church? I am definitely praying at church. It's different for me from praying at a synagogue. But it's like driving a minivan or a sports car. You're still driving. Whether you're in a synagogue or a church, you're in a community of people and you're talking to God.

I do have certain issues. I would not be comfortable going up for Communion. I don't think that is something I would ever want to do. They always have a part in the service for non-Christians to go up and get blessed, and I don't do that. One time I was sitting there during that part. I didn't get up, and this gentleman behind me starts tapping me on the shoulder saying, "You can go up now. It's for non-Christians." And I'm whispering, "I understand. I don't want to do it, but thanks."

I would never convert. In order to convert, you have to really believe so many of the things I have a hard time with. It would be nice to be able to buy into it all and to think, "Hey, they're right." But I always look and think, "You're wrong. There can't be a virgin birth." There are too many parts of it that seem to me to be wrong and completely implausible.

What's interesting is that because of how I look, I can be in either a church or a synagogue and nobody thinks anything of it. I don't look typically Jewish. I would say there are some people in the church whom I know and I like, and I'm always happy to see them. But I feel far more comfortable at the synagogue even though, like I said, I don't think this particular synagogue is the best place for us. We've not quite found the right spot. But hopefully, we will.

We don't have any kids yet, but we've thought a lot about what we want to teach them. We read one book on this subject that we really liked. Basically it says that when you have kids, you need to pick one religion. You can pick either religion, but you should pick one because the kids really want to know where they belong. So that's a big thing that we decided to follow.

Then the question is, which religion do we pick? We decided that our kids would have a Christian upbringing. We decided that for several reasons. First of all, the Jewish laws say that if the mother's Jewish, then the baby's Jewish. And if the mother's not Jewish, the baby's not Jewish. So we thought, "Okay, that's a pretty clear rule. We'll follow that." I know that some parts of Judaism do accept patrilineal descent. They say that if the father is Jewish, and you are leading a Jewish life, then you're Jewish. But then you get into the question of who is really a Jew and who isn't. Who will be accepted as a Jew in Israel? Would my kids be accepted as Jews by someone who is Orthodox? We're so exclusive. My feeling is that if someone wants to say they're Jewish, we ought to let them in. But that's not the way it is.

Also, I think that Christians can learn about Jews and have a respect for their religion. But it doesn't always work as well the other way around. There's more in Christianity that's harder for most Jews to understand and accept. There's all the stuff about Christ, the Second Coming, and original sin. But if the kids are Christian, I feel they can still learn about Judaism and be receptive to it.

If we have a boy, we decided that we are going to do a hospital circumcision. We'll do it partly for medical reasons and partly so that if he ever does decide he wants to convert, it will be easier. Also, we're not going to do a baptism. This is what we figured out. When you baptize a child, you're making a choice for that child. You are telling him he is Christian. And you're doing it at a point when the child can't even do or say anything on his own. He doesn't know his own feelings, and couldn't express them if he did.

We are intending that our children will be Christian, but at the same time we want them to accept Christianity on their own. They will be taught Christianity. They will be taught about Jesus. But we want them to arrive at Christianity when they are ready so that it will really feel like a part of them. We feel that process will actually be a gift that most people don't get.

We've thought about this a lot. And we understand the identity crisis part of all this for children. We do believe it's better to raise them in one religion. At the same time, we want to theologically educate them so that they can be comfortable around or in either religion. I think that is beneficial. So that's the decision we made. The kids will know they are Christian, but they will be exposed heavily to Judaism. They will have an understanding and knowledge about Jewish history. And we can still be involved with our children in a Jewish community. We can go to bar mitzvahs and brises and to the houses of friends to celebrate the holidays. If I can't give to the world Jewish children, I can at least give the world children who will be friends and appreciators of Judaism.

I'll tell you, when my children reach bar mitzvah age, it's going to be rough for me. I'm going to have to really figure out a way to get through that period. I'm going to know it's the time they would be studying and getting ready for their bar or bat mitzvahs. That will definitely be hard.

For every decision you make, I think you lose and you gain. You say to yourself, "Did I do the right thing?" It's something you say very quietly, in your own heart. And that can be true for any marriage. And if the positive things outweigh any negatives, as they definitely do in my case, I think you just have to get as comfortable as you can and say, "This is the decision I made, and I like it."

3   Finding a Way to Have Both

In these stories, both the husband and wife are interested in imparting aspects of their own religion to their children. Both of them want to teach the children about their unique heritage and traditions. Both want the children to be a part of the life-cycle events and holidays associated with the religion that they themselves are a part of. In some cases, a couple falls into this choice by never really deciding what to do, but more often a definite decision is made for the family to participate in both religions. In any case, this choice is not particularly common, but it no longer seems as unusual as it once did.

Debbie is a business professional who is in her early fifties. Her religion has always meant a great deal to her and she had absolutely no intention of becoming involved with a man who did not share her own beliefs. In their marriage, Debbie and Mark have been able to focus on the commonalities between them rather than on the differences.

✺ DEBBIE (TO BE FOLLOWED BY HER HUSBAND, MARK)

* * *

I was engaged once before to a Jewish guy, Brian, and we broke it off because of the religion. We went to see rabbis and priests and could never come to an agreement, and it was a heartbreak for both of us. This was a pretty long time ago. Nonetheless, I had been through it once before and I didn't want to go through it again.

* * *

I'm a Catholic. When I was growing up, we went to church every Sunday. We went to public school, but we also went to catechism classes.

Mark was brought up in a Conservative temple and had his bar mitzvah. I wouldn't say his parents are real involved, but they have always celebrated the holidays. He definitely feels Jewish. He is Jewish.

I met Mark on a blind date. I was on the phone with a friend in California, telling her I had just broken up with someone. Her neighbor happened to be over, who said, "Gosh, my husband has a friend in Chicago who is not dating anybody. You should fix them up."

Mark's last name is Cohen, which was the same name as my neighbors, who were Lutheran German. They spell it Koehn, but I assumed Mark was Lutheran German as well. Then about halfway through our first date, I found out he was Jewish. I thought, "Oh, no. Not again."

But you know, it really didn't matter. At first we were just sort of casually dating, so we kept going out. He was in graduate school and I traveled during the week. We had a really good time together, but we didn't think it was serious. So then, after about six months, we started becoming more exclusive, and then we started talking about it.

There were differences between this relationship and the one I had before. For one thing, I was older. Things are different when you are thirty-five than they are when you are twenty-five. My college roommate was Jewish. I had a lot of Jewish friends. I understood more things about the religion.

The main thing we both felt we had to decide was what was important about our religions to us. In the earlier relationship, I remember this conversation in which Brian said he could never live in a house that had any Christian symbols in it, such as a cross. Those were the kind of things that made him crazy. We could never come to an agreement about that. Mark didn't care about any of that. Nor did I care if he had a mezuzah on the door. Those symbol things didn't matter to us. Whatever the other wanted was fine with us.

What mattered to us about our own religions was that they enforce prayer and a hereafter. Brian didn't want to believe in a hereafter, whereas Mark believed that when you die, heaven is an option. That made a big difference to me. We both believed in prayer, we both believed in a hereafter, and we also both believed in the importance of community worship.

Actually, right before we decided to get married, when we were still trying to be sure we could really work everything out, we went to an outreach program at a temple. The program was for interfaith couples. It was around the holidays. It was, in my opinion, one of the most ludicrous nights I've ever spent with adults. We were there for two hours, and the group was talking about Hanukkah and Christmas and how these families dealt with it. Half the people were crying. They were saying things like, "My husband won't let me put up green and red in the house," or "I want to roast chestnuts over the open fire and my wife won't allow it." After we had been there for two hours, nobody had even mentioned the word *God*. When we left, Mark and I decided we would be okay. We weren't ever going to be crying about what colors to put up.

My dad actually was always pro-Jew. In fact, he told me when I was engaged to Brian, "You can marry a Jew, it's okay with me, but just don't marry an Italian." He was quite serious. He grew up in a Scandinavian neighborhood, and the Italians were the kind of underhanded mafioso type. So as long as I didn't marry an Italian it was all right with him.

It was a little rougher at first with Mark's family. Nobody in his family— his cousins, anybody—had ever married outside Judaism. So that was a little bit harder. I mean, they never said anything negative to me. They just sort of cautioned Mark. "Make sure you know what you're doing. This is really going to be difficult for you."

We did one ceremony for our wedding, with both a priest and a rabbi. It wasn't too difficult to find a priest to participate. The priests seemed more willing than the rabbis to do it. They won't go into a temple, but many of them will officiate at an interfaith marriage in a church or elsewhere. I did talk to one older priest who didn't want to be involved, but then we found a younger one who was willing. They still ask you to go through the Pre-Cana, which is basically a day of religious teaching, and Mark did that.

As for the rabbi, what actually happened was that Mark's brother-in-law's brother was a rabbi in the area. We called him, and he wouldn't do it. In fact, he was absolutely adamant that if you're marrying outside of Judaism, then you might as well not be a Jew anymore. Basically, that is what he said. So I got a list of rabbis from a friend, and we started making calls. We did find someone.

Before the wedding, both the priest and the rabbi asked us how we were planning to raise our children. When we met with the priest we told him Catholic, and when we met with the rabbi we told him Jewish.

We had set up different songs for the wedding ceremony, along with different prayers. Some of the prayers were in English, and some were in Hebrew. Plus, we were going to do one reading from the Old Testament and one reading from the New Testament. This particular rabbi had a bit of an entertainer in him, though, and he also added several pieces by Bob Dylan. So there was a whole other dimension—the Old Testament, the New Testament, and Dylan. We broke the glass. We also had a candle-lighting ceremony. It was what we wanted, except for the Dylan part.

I know that I would have a much harder time if I were married to someone who just wasn't spiritual at all. Part of it is that I personally like religions in general, and I certainly like the tradition. I think where many people get hung up is on not wanting to give up their own traditions. That's a lot of who you are. I didn't want Mark to give those up, nor did he want me to. In fact, we wanted to embellish them.

I love having Passover. I love Mark's holidays, and that one in particular. We had been dating for almost a year when Passover came. I had never been to a seder. He was working that whole day and wouldn't be able to get to his family's house, so I told him I would make him a seder. I bought a book and started reading about the traditions. Since I had never been to a seder, I studied it because I wanted to make it good for him. I had no trouble marching into that, just cooking everything and trying to figure it out and calling one of my Jewish friends every few minutes.

In fact, let me tell you about the charoseth. The first time I made it, I read the little history of why you do it, and all about the bricks and mortar. So I spent probably an hour cutting the apples into little bricks. I peeled them and cut them, and they were all like regulation size, sort of like Barbie doll-sized bricks. And then I made the nut mixture so that it was like mortar. You could have buildt an igloo with it. Mark came over and said, "What's that?" I said, "It's charoseth." He said, "That's not what charoseth is like. It's mashed apple." I said, "Don't tell me that." Now I make it in the Cuisinart like everybody else.

The point is that we support each other. We both try. I think at least on my part I have reinforced his holidays even more so than his family did. I go way out of my way. I mean, I make my own gefilte fish. I spend a lot of time preparing for him. And Mark spends a lot of time getting things ready for Christmas, certainly more than my parents did. The aspects of my holidays that he gets into are more often the secular parts, not really the religious ones. At Christmas, we put up a tree and we always have a good time with it. And I have a Nativity scene that I put up. I think that we not only accept that the other person has different holidays but also embrace them and really encourage them.

There are limits. Mark wants no lights outside the house. I had been decorating the house for several years, and I finally got around to buying lights for the outside, and he just was not happy about it. He doesn't want the outside of the house decorated at all. His perspective is that what we do inside our house is our business, but "I'm not trying to broadcast to the world that we're Christians." It is very emotional to him to put lights up on the outside. So that's fine. There have always been a few little things like that that just kind of push him over the edge. They come as a surprise to me sometimes. So before you venture into something new, make sure you talk about it.

It's sort of interesting. I think the Jewish side gets a lot more bothered about things like that than the Christian side. Having the menorah in the window certainly doesn't bother me. I'm the one who puts it there. Those things tend not to be an issue for me at all.

Before we got married, we talked about having children. We said we would raise them in both religions, with exposure to each, and that at some point when they were old enough we would let them decide what they want to do. And that is what we are doing. We have two children, an eight-year-old boy named Alex and a three-year-old girl named Laura. We did a bris for our son and a baby-naming at the temple for our daughter. And then we did a baptism for each.

When I teach prayers to my kids, I try to be careful so that Mark is comfortable with what is being said. If the word *Christ* is in a prayer, it has a whole different feel to Mark than if it says *God*. Christians use the words *Christ* and *God* fairly interchangeably. Praying to Christ is praying to God. But for Mark, Christ was a man who lived on earth, who was not God. So quite early on, I went through all of the prayers that are near and dear to my heart and took out the word *Christ* whenever it appeared and replaced it with *God*. I asked Mark to read the prayers and see if he liked them, and he was fine with all of them.

You know, there is no doubt I would love it if Mark and I were the same religion. Probably the main way it would be different is the way we pray. I pray to more of a vision that you can see. The Christ vision is something I can identify with, and having that to pray to is different. The way Mark prays, it's more to a power and not to a person. It doesn't have that personal figure in it. Also, there are certain prayers and areas I would like to spend more time on, that are uncomfortable for Mark. But there are enough other things that are comfortable, and that's what I concentrate on.

We're not trying to force-feed any of it. We're trying to expose our kids to both. We do have prayers we say at meals and before the kids go to bed. Actually, I've taught my son almost all of the Catholic prayers, so I say those with him when I put him to bed. At mealtime we hold hands, and we just say things from the heart. We don't say either a Catholic or a Jewish prayer. We just say thanks. The kids know the blessing over the bread and wine in Hebrew, and they also know the Catholic prayer before meals. So they know all of them, but as a family we sort of do an individualized version.

I began taking my son to church with me on Sundays when he was four. There was a class for kids his age. It was so much nicer to go to church and have him with me. I would drop him off in the class for an hour, and the rest of the time he'd be with me. I think it's pretty hard for kids to sit through any religious service for two or three hours. Then, when Alex was seven years old, he made Holy Communion. So he went to catechism classes all through this year.

Usually, after Communion, the next big step is confirmation. But we aren't going to prepare for that now. Instead, Alex has stopped catechism classes and started Hebrew school. He will have a bar mitzvah when he is thirteen. I think Hebrew school is a lot of work, and it would be too much to be going to all those classes. He still goes to church with me on Sundays.

By the time the bar mitzvah is over, quite frankly Alex will be old enough to decide which religion he is most comfortable with. Mark and I have talked about it. Either way he chooses will be fine.

I've actually studied this issue quite a bit. A lot of people said to me, "Your kids are really going to be screwed up." Then I read some interviews in a magazine with a girl who had been brought up with both, and she said "I'm so grateful because there is so much ignorance about both of my religions that is out there, and I don't have that." I feel that either our kids are going to be really screwed up (which I don't believe) or they are going to be much better educated when they make their decisions than most of us are.

Mark is a doctor. He thinks It probably would have been the breaking point in his relationship with Debbie if he had pushed her to be Jewish or if she had urged him to be Catholic. He doesn't think either of them could have accommodated the other to such a degree. It is clear that Mark appreciates the extent to which he and Debbie have been able to work together on this issue so they could both be comfortable.

✳ MARK (PRECEDED BY HIS WIFE, DEBBIE)

* * *

When we first started dating, we never thought it would go beyond that. We were very different. She was older, a different religion. She was successful and well into her career. I was still starting out. It was just a good time.

* * *

I think what happened is that we fell in love, and obviously you have to think about religion and what it all means. The way I looked at it was really quite simple. If you believe in God, which I do, how could you believe God would say that two people in love with each other who seem to be perfect for each other shouldn't be together simply because they have different religions? It didn't make any sense.

The reality is that there is just not that big a difference in a lot of the ways things are done in Catholicism and Judaism. If you take out Jesus, then the morals, the values, the upbringing, and the beliefs are almost the same. So as far as teaching and raising children is concerned, which obviously becomes an issue down the road, I think that if we believe the same things for the most part and have the same values, ethics, and morals, and if we believe in God and in heaven and in doing good things and in being good people, then that seems to be all right.

The symbols and traditions are special and important, but there is no reason why you can't participate and partake in both. We figured our kids would be extremely well versed because they would be both Catholic and Jewish, and they would have the opportunity to become fully involved in both religions.

We have belonged to a temple and a church for years. We all participate in the special times with both religions, whether it's Christmas, Easter, Passover, or Purim. In addition, we say prayers before every meal as a family. The prayers are not necessarily the typical Catholic prayer that my wife's family says when they all sit down for a meal where they mention the Father, the Son, and the Holy Spirit. It is a much more generic "Thank you God for this food" kind of prayer. Nevertheless, if we start to eat without saying a prayer, even our three-year-old will say something.

Having grown up Jewish, it's certainly different to deal with my kids praying to Jesus and that type of thing. But on the other hand, I take it for what it's worth. I know that religion in any sense of the word is good, and my kids are special because they are learning both. And I know it's important to my wife, so it's important to me. I try to be as reasonable and accommodating and understanding as I can and as I know that she is with me.

The most important thing is that you really have to love the person. The first part is the relationship. The relationship has to be right. If it is not right, this is just another issue that can get in the way and cause problems, and probably will.

We pretty much talked about everything beforehand and had a decent understanding of how we were going to do things. But it is sometimes hard, because obviously I probably skew things more towards the Judaism side and she skews more to the Catholic side.

Maybe it would also be different if I were Orthodox or even Conservative, or if Debbie were more like her sister who goes to church every day and is fairly "born again." I don't know how we would have done. But our levels are compatible. We are both very deeply religious in our own ways, and we are similar in how we share our traditions and values.

Some subtle issues are there. Judaism is a little bit different from Catholicism in that I don't feel I need to go to temple every week, but I know deep down inside I am still very much Jewish. On the other hand, most Catholics do go to church every week, not because they feel that they have to but because they want to. There is sort of a difference and it's a hard difference to explain, especially when you are trying to teach your kids about how to participate in your religion. It could sometimes seem that if you look at the Catholic side of the coin, there are things happening all the time. It has a much more active religious participation, especially compared with the participation level of a Reform Jew. Yet that doesn't mean that there is less feeling on the Judaism side. It's just different. It's just very innate. So from the kid's standpoint it can be confusing if he goes to church every week and goes to Jewish events only a few times a year.

Our kids feel lucky. I've heard other kids in our car say to my kids, "Boy, you guys are so lucky. You're Catholic and Jewish." And my kids will say, "Yeah, we get to do it all."

I don't know if our kids will ever make a choice on their own about one religion or the other, at least not for a long time. I think what they understand is that their dad is Jewish, their mom is Catholic, and they are Jewish and Catholic. And you know what? I'm sure that they will each develop their own religion as they get older. I would imagine that what will happen is that they will continue to celebrate both religions with us. We'll continue to have our Christmas tree each year and decorate it in blue and silver, which is what we always do. We have our own traditions and they will have their own traditions. They will probably meet someone, and depending on who that person is, if it's someone who is Jewish or someone who is Christian or Catholic, maybe they'll gravitate in some direction. But hopefully they'll continue to keep and take part in pieces of the religion that matter to them. The bottom line is helping them to become good people and teaching them to have good morals, good ethics, good understanding, and love for each other and God.

Ruth is an artist and a teacher. She was not raised with much of a religious background, so she felt it would be easy for her to be flexible about incorporating two religions into the household. When it came to her children, though, there were some lines that Ruth found she was simply not able to cross.

✽ RUTH (TO BE FOLLOWED BY HER HUSBAND, CHRIS)

* * *

I would call my background ultra-Reform. I once heard a rabbi refer to the "revolving-door Jew," who would go into the temple on Rosh Hashanah and go right back out again after Yom Kippur. That's how my family was. Those days were the only times of the year we were ever in a temple.

* * *

I'm one of four girls. It was a big deal in our household for my mom to get us all dressed for the holidays. Each year we would get a new outfit. My mother would always make us get wool because the holidays are in the fall. And it seemed that almost every year it would turn out to be at least 75 degrees, but of course we still had to wear our new clothes. I went to Sunday school, and I had a confirmation. I didn't go to Hebrew school. The possibility of getting bat mitzvahed is something that was never even discussed. I know that my mother was raised doing more than we did in terms of Jewish practices, and when my grandmother came over, she always used to hide the bacon.

In December, we used to do both Hanukkah and Christmas. I remember sitting at the dinner table, and my parents would have the four of us kids take a vote about when we wanted to get our gifts. We could have them all on the first night of Hanukkah, one for every night of Hanukkah, all on the last night of Hanukkah, or all of them on Christmas morning. We always chose Christmas morning.

I got a lot of reinforcement in my family for not looking particularly Jewish. My parents would say, in what they meant to be a very complimentary way, "Oh, she looks just like a little shiksa." They thought that was great. At the same time, there were a lot of jokes about marrying a nice

Jewish boy. They would tell me to go to college to get my "Mrs." degree and then marry a Jewish doctor or lawyer. But it was just joking. When I started dating and did go out with people who weren't Jewish, it wasn't really an issue for my parents or anybody else.

Chris and I met when I was thirty-five. He had been raised very traditionally Catholic, but he wasn't doing much by the time we got together. When our relationship began to get serious, we talked just a little about how we might raise our kids. I wasn't willing to have them be Catholic, and he wasn't real interested in raising them Jewish. I wasn't strong enough to say to him, "It's either Jewish or nothing." When you're raised the way I was, it's hard to know how much you even wanted to be doing. Anyhow, we just sort of went blindly ahead and decided to get married.

We had our wedding at a university chapel. The first time I walked in, I saw that it had the Old Testament on one wall and the New Testament on the other. I said, "This will work." And then when I took my mother back to see it, there was a huge cross right up in the front. Even for my family, it was a little too much. I was thinking, "This is so strange. I'm sure that cross wasn't here the last time I came." Well, it turns out that this chapel has a removable cross. It just comes and goes. So they took it down for us, and it was perfect.

At our wedding ceremony, we had both a priest and a rabbi. We found a priest without much trouble, but we searched pretty hard before we found a rabbi. We had to pay him quite a bit, and we had to be sure to do it before the ceremony because he was in such a hurry to leave right when ours was over so he could get on to the next one. We met with the priest and rabbi separately, and they said the same thing everyone we know had already been telling us. They all said, "You should choose one religion or the other. Don't raise your children in both." So what are we doing? We're raising our children as both.

Chris and I have two daughters and a son. Before our oldest daughter was born, the subject of baptism came up. That's one thing I knew I didn't want to do. So I just said, "No." I told Chris that even though I'm not that Jewish, I knew I could never have a child of mine baptized. We barely talked about it, and Chris didn't push for it. So none of our kids were baptized. Also, our son didn't have a bris. He just got circumcised in the hospital without any ceremony.

The way we do things in our family, everything is very equal. All of the kids have my name as a middle name. We try to do everything half and half. We have Hanukkah and Christmas. We have Easter and Passover. The way we celebrate all of the holidays is pretty much based around meals and gifts and families and being together. It makes me pretty nuts when Hanukkah is right on top of Christmas. We end up lighting the candles and going to a family party on my side and then heading over the next day to have a big holiday dinner with Chris's family and doing Christmas with them. For Passover, there's always a seder. And for Easter, there's always a family dinner and an egg hunt. So the kids have done it all.

Over the years, we've all sometimes gone to midnight Mass. Chris really likes to go. The kids are older now, and they don't always want to go with him, but I still go. The kids are at the age where they complain about going to church, and they complain about going to temple. For years I took everyone to the family service at the temple for the High Holidays. Now the kids are old enough that if we go, they should go to the regular adult part. It's tricky. We never had to join the synagogue to go to the family service, but we'd have to now if we want to go to the main service. It's very expensive, and I'm cheap about doing it. If I do keep going, it will be partly for my mother. She likes to go with us, and it's something she wouldn't do on her own.

There's one particular thing that Chris and I have been very delinquent about. We haven't done our wills or decided what to do with our children if something happens to us. We haven't done it because we don't know what to do. The logical thing is for the kids to live with someone in one of our families. But by doing that, we would really be choosing for them to have a life that is only Catholic or only Jewish. It would be very hard for me to have a Catholic person raise my child. I feel that there is just too much that they do with going to church and all the rituals and all the properness. It's just not my style. And Chris isn't really comfortable with the prospect of his children being in a family where they would be raised as Jews. This is a discussion we've had over and over, especially every time we get on an airplane. We just can't decide.

I don't know. I'm such a lower-end Jew. For me, the biggest issue is really the guilt I feel about my children. Even though I wasn't raised with much of a Jewish home life myself, I still feel guilty about not giving more to my kids. Actually, I feel that this is one area we are not doing very well with as parents. I think we should be doing a better job teaching them about both religions, because what they're getting is a minimal job for each. They've never gone to Sunday school. They've never had any formal religious education of any kind. I look at other families and I get insecure and think, "They're doing it better than we are when it comes to teaching their kids about their religion and their identity and their place in life."

I never had a strong enough incentive to really do more. But when I look at those other families, it does make me think of trying. I have heard that there is a group in our area that meets to talk about these kinds of issues, and I am thinking of going to one of their meetings. Even though we've been married for eighteen years, I still have questions. I'd like to talk about some of this with people in my situation to see what they are doing. I obviously am not totally comfortable with what I've been doing so far.

Chris is in his fifties. He grew up living in a suburb of Chicago not very far from where he lives now. On an intellectual level, Chris can understand why his wife is uncomfortable about having their children go through rituals that are a part of his religion. But on a different level, he still has a strong need for those rituals to take place.

✸ CHRIS (PRECEDED BY HIS WIFE, RUTH)

* * *

I am the oldest of six children. Both my father and mother were very religious Catholics. I remember going to Sunday morning church every week and usually joining my grandfather there. Most weeks, one of us kids would go back with him to his house for breakfast, which was always kind of nice.

* * *

My parents gave each of their kids a private parochial school education for both elementary school and high school. At the high school, there were frequent masses, which I would always attend. I took a class on religion every semester. When I went to college, I chose to go to another Jesuit institute, and I continued taking theology courses whenever I could because I enjoyed them. When I went home for vacations, there was still the mandatory Sunday church time with my family.

My first job when I left the university was to teach at a Catholic all-boys school. I spent a year doing that. They also had regular Sunday masses, but I don't remember going to too many. This was the point where I was probably moving away from the normal Sunday religious experience. It's not so much that I actually disliked it. But I realized that going to church wasn't anything that gave me tremendous satisfaction. It wasn't filling any void. And just going for the sake of going wasn't for me.

Even though my parents were so religious, they were also very open and accepting. They never really told me whom I should and shouldn't go out with. I dated a lot of Jewish girls. There was one Jewish girl I had met when I was in high school, and when I was probably twenty-six or twenty-seven, she called me up out of the blue. We ended up having a very strong relationship for about eight months. We were basically living together. Then she went on a trip to Israel. When she came back, she said she had decided she wanted to be with somebody Jewish. So she left me. But that relationship, along with several others that were deep and long, helped clarify in my own mind what I wanted to find in a person.

I think that for my brothers and sisters, one of their main criteria in looking for a spouse was to find someone Catholic. And in fact each of them did marry a Catholic, and they are all fairly religious. I knew that for me, finding someone Catholic wasn't an issue. If it happened that way, fine. If it didn't, that was okay too. There were other things that mattered more to me than religion.

Ruth and I met at a party when I was about thirty. I knew almost on the first date that I was going to marry this girl. Ruth is Jewish, but she has never been at all religious. She went to Sunday school, and she always gets together with her family to celebrate the holidays. Even when we decided to get married, religion was not something we talked about much. There was no pressure about what to do from either of our families. The only thing I can remember kind of talking about was that in terms of kids, we'd figure it out later. But, you know, that really didn't work.

It's very easy, I think, to approach this issue and basically say, "Let's not make any hard decisions and let's just sort of feel our way through," or "We'll figure it out later. The kids are little now, and we've got time." What can end up happening is that you never make the decision because you're never really confronted with a point where you have to decide. And as a result, the two- or three- or four-year-old becomes ten or eleven or twelve. And if you finally decide then that you want them to know something about their religion, it's not that it's absolutely too late. But oftentimes, if you're going to get a ritual process started, it is very hard to get a teenager suddenly interested in going to Mass or Sunday school or whatever. It's just a lot harder.

We have three kids. When they were born, none of them were baptized. I would have liked them to be. But basically, Ruth wouldn't let that happen. It was something she just didn't want to do. Baptism is a fairly strong demarcation, certainly in Ruth's mind and probably in reality, between being a Christian and being a non-Christian. I actually think Ruth harbors the belief that our children are automatically Jewish, because that is the religion of their mother. Anyhow, I can see why she didn't want a baptism.

The problem was that after twenty years of Catholic education, I felt like I had to do something. So there was a time shortly after each of the kids was born, and Ruth wasn't around, when I just did the baptism ritual myself.

I remembered the basic words you're supposed to say, and I remembered that at times like this you could use regular water instead of holy water. Did it count? Who knows? But it made me feel better. It's not something that I really planned. It's just that when you're holding a little baby in your hands, there is this tremendous sense of empathy and love and emotion. In that situation, I kind of just felt it was the right thing to do.

Ruth and I could never agree that our children should be baptized. We also didn't agree that they could be Jewish. Ruth mentioned that idea to me at one point, and I said, "No." Looking back from where I am now, I think that some religion would probably have been better than no religion. It's not that I felt anything was inherently wrong with the Jewish religion. But at the time I wasn't comfortable with the idea.

What we've basically done is teach our children about our religious backgrounds by celebrating all of the holidays on both sides. And that's as far as we've gone. The kids have had no formal religious training of any kind. They've never gone to Sunday school or taken any theology courses. I think that this is an area in which Ruth and I could have found a way to compromise, in order to give our kids a lot more than we did. And in that respect, I do kind of feel that I've failed.

I know that all of our children are fairly ethical individuals. But what mainly bothers me is that I don't see them as having a strong base in terms of doing things for others. I don't see in them a whole lot of desire to donate their time. Those are the kinds of things that you focus on constantly when you are brought up in a religious environment. "If you have something, you should give something back." Ruth and I set examples in this area to a certain extent. We each do a fair amount of volunteer work. But I just think that in a religious environment, you pick up those concepts about helping others a lot more thoroughly.

I know that if I had married a Catholic woman, I would be going to Sunday Mass probably every week. We would be bringing our kids up Catholic, and going to church each week is just one of the things you do. But much as I'd like my kids to have more knowledge about religion, I wouldn't really want them to have the same kind of training I did. I think that there are a lot of different perceptions about the same fundamental force, about God. And I don't believe that there is only one right way to look at everything. Forcing my kids into one very structured approach is not something I want to do. What I'd really like is to find a way to expose them to different modes of thinking about religion. I'm not sure exactly how to do that. I think it may make sense to get them into a Sunday school class where at least they can learn something about religion and methodology and just pick up some of the basic 101 concepts.

Even though things have come up around this issue that are not always easy to figure out, I still don't think that Ruth and I should have necessarily tried to work all of these things out before getting married. If we couldn't have worked them out, the implication would have been, "Well, then we're not going to get married." I think that if two people are in love, and they have found their mate, most other aspects are secondary. I don't think religion is something that should get in the middle when two people love each other.

Susan is a landscape architect. She is in her thirties. Susan and her husband are interested in customizing each of their religious holidays and events to reflect their separate back-grounds as well as the values they share as a couple. This is something they have been talking about for a long time, but they are not yet sure how they are going to work everything out.

✷ SUSAN

* * *

I guess when I was growing up I figured I would marry someone Jewish, and I always had it in the back of my head that my parents would prefer me to marry somebody Jewish. But I never felt like I had to.

* * *

I grew up in the Reconstructionist part of Judaism. For about as long as I can remember, I went to Hebrew school. I had a bat mitzvah. My family was pretty involved in the synagogue. We didn't go to services every week, but we celebrated all the major holidays.

Terry and I met at grad school. He was in the same program that I was in. Terry was raised sort of generally Christian. His family celebrated Christmas, and that's about it. At the time we started dating, Terry was getting involved in a Bible study group. He went every week, so we would discuss the things they talked about. And actually it made me think about Judaism a lot more. We had a lot of religious discussions when we first started dating. It was kind of frustrating because our basic ideologies are the same, but we had a lot of points where we just couldn't get any further. We saw some things too differently.

We talked about our religions a lot more when we were dating than we did once we were married. We talked about whether we would have kids and how we would raise them. We came up with a lot of different ideas about what we could do. Once we talked about raising our children Jewish until they got to be a certain age, then teaching them how Christianity came from Judaism, and from then on basically teaching both religions. That's one idea that we liked.

I remember when we were starting to date seriously, and I was telling my parents about some of our discussions on religion and how to raise kids. My dad wrote me a letter giving me his thoughts and some ideas of how it could be done. Both sets of parents were very open and welcoming. Before we were married, Terry came to a couple of Passover seders at my parents' house, and I celebrated Christmas with his family. I don't think either family ever said anything negative. So things could have been a lot more difficult on that level.

For our wedding, we had a judge and a civil ceremony. We incorporated some Jewish elements by having a chuppah and breaking the glass. Plus, we had some readings from both religions. We felt like we both put it together, and it felt satisfying to each of us.

One thing I wasn't prepared for is that I think it's pretty easy for Terry to get involved in Jewish holidays, but I have a hard time being open-minded about Christian holidays. It's not too bad with Terry's family because they aren't very religious. The first couple of years we only celebrated Christmas at his parents' house. We didn't celebrate Christmas at home. I have always been against getting a tree at our own house. It just didn't feel right to me to have one. But when our baby was born a few months ago, it was right around Christmas, on December 23. Terry's parents came up and they brought a tree and decorated it. I was pretty tired when we came home from the hospital so at first I wasn't really even that aware of everything. Gradually I decided that celebrating Christmas in our home wasn't as bad as I thought, because I realized that for Terry and his parents it's just a special family time more than anything else.

Our son's name is Brian. We didn't know we were going to have a boy, but as the time got closer I started looking into what would be involved in having a bris and talking to Terry about whether we wanted to have one or not. Terry was fine with the idea. We pretty much decided that when it came to any Jewish ceremony, he had no problem with it as long as I did all the research, put things together, and made sure he's included. I talked to a Reconstructionist rabbi who explained the parts of the ceremony to me and gave me a bunch of booklets. I went through the booklets and put together my own ideas. I went over all of it with Terry to make sure he felt comfortable with everything. We ended up making it a little less Jewish and more of a spiritual ceremony. Some family members from my side came. Terry's family was invited, but they had just been up the weekend before over Christmas. They would have been welcome, but I think they wanted to let my family do their thing. I really enjoyed putting together the bris and kind of creating a type of Judaism that fits us. I'd like to continue doing things like that.

When Brian was first born we started talking again about how we were going to raise him in terms of religion. We didn't come up with any definite plan. He's three months old now, and we still don't have a set idea of what we are going to do. We're just trying to think it out. We're beginning to talk about a very family-oriented religion. It is important to each of us that we get together with both families for celebrations. Family matters a great deal to us, and we want Brian to know that. So I think we'll do all of the holidays, and Brian will learn something about both religions in that way, at least.

Also, for a while, Terry and I were having Shabbat dinners on Friday nights, and when Brian gets older and more aware, I'd like to start doing that again. I'd like to send him to Hebrew school, and that would probably mean getting involved in a synagogue. Terry's not really interested in going to church, so I don't think he'd want Brian to do that either. There are certain things that both Terry and I feel strongly about. We both find a spiritual element in land-oriented experiences. For example, one year for Yom Kippur we were out of town and not able to get home. So we gathered a bunch of readings and went out to a beautiful spot in the woods and made a fire and kind of reflected on the past year and talked about next year. We like adapting some of the holidays to fit our mutual spirituality. We'd like to teach Brian about that type of thing as well.

I want Brian to be grounded and have a sense of belonging to something, but I'm not really sure yet if it's going to be Judaism or a sort of religion that is based on shared family experiences and celebrations. It's funny. When I first started realizing I was getting serious with somebody who wasn't Jewish, it was very hard for me to think about raising kids who weren't strictly Jewish. It was almost impossible for me to believe that might happen. But now it doesn't seem so difficult to imagine. One thing that has made it really easy for me is that Terry is interested in religion in general. He enjoys learning about Judaism and participating. I think it helps tremendously if you are both pretty open-minded and accepting of the idea that you each have a lot to learn from the other.

I also think it really helps if you know what your religion means to you and what kind of adaptations you're willing to make. Terry and I hashed a lot of things out before we even decided to get married. Again, you can't think of everything. But for us, having all those discussions and talking honestly about everything really helped a lot. I guess it's just another part of making your marriage work.

Murray works in real estate. He is in his late fifties. Murray and his wife stressed tolerance and emphasized family as they exposed their children to both of their religions. And now the children are old enough for Murray to have some idea of how it has all turned out.

✖ MURRAY

* * *

I'm the youngest child of three. My parents had me late in life. There is a ten-year gap between my twin sisters and myself. Clearly, there was a great deal of expectation in my household for the Jewish son to marry a Jewish girl and have a Jewish life. From the time I was very young, this was always understood. It was not merely insinuated. It was something that was spoken about.

* * *

I come from a Conservative Jewish background. My father was born in Russia, and my mother is from here in the States. The neighborhood I grew up in was basically a Gentile environment without much of a strong Jewish influence. But we made up for it at home. We were a very Jewish family in terms of cultures and customs. We celebrated every holiday. I was bar mitzvahed. And we went each summer to South Haven, Michigan, which was very Jewish.

When I was in high school I played a lot of sports. My school had strong teams. There were four thousand kids at the school, but probably no more than five or six of the kids were Jewish. My mother was concerned about this and pressured me to transfer to a different school with a much larger Jewish population. But because I was entrenched in sports, I wanted to stay where I was.

I met Amanda when I was a sophomore in high school. We saw each other in the halls and became infatuated and went out on a date. She knew I was Jewish. I knew she was Catholic. We went out once, twice. We were just kids. I couldn't even drive yet. We attended a party together just prior to our junior year, and there was a very strong feeling on my part and on her part. We were very attracted to each other. That's the last I knew. Now it's thirty-eight years later, and that's really as simple as how it started.

If you believe in fate, I think that's what this was. We came from two totally different families and from completely different worlds. Amanda was raised to be a very strict Catholic girl. She was a churchgoing person. And my family was very much Jewish. We were fifteen years old, and already people were telling us that we're different and that we shouldn't be together. But we just didn't see it. It didn't come across to us. We were somewhat offended that religion was looking to separate us rather than give us a means to unite. Religion was a barrier. And we recognized at an early age that for us, it didn't matter. The more each of our religions told us that it was wrong for us to be together, the less interested and involved we became in organized religion.

Amanda's father worked for Jewish people for twenty-five years. He had a wonderful relationship with them. But when we had been dating for three and a half years, he all of a sudden decided that we were getting serious, and he did not want his daughter to be serious with someone who was Jewish. He put pressure on her to stop dating me. Well, we were already very much in love and were moving forward. I was in college. So what happened is that a year later Amanda left home. She left the home she had never really ventured beyond. You have to understand, this is an extraordinarily conservative person. This is a person who had been structured by the Catholic Church. She never did anything wrong. She was a good student. She was a perfect white canvas.

My sister took her in, and Amanda lived in a room in her basement and worked downtown. But we wanted to be together. After six months it was becoming frustrating; it was becoming difficult. We spoke on a Sunday afternoon, and she said, "Why don't we just get married?" And I went to my father and said, "Dad, I'm going to do this."

By the time we decided to get married, we had been dating for about five years. We were twenty. My father was always pretty respectful of who and what I was. He knew I was kind of a strong-willed person, and he was always supportive. He had to sign for me to get married because I wasn't of legal age. And he did do that, even though it wasn't what he necessarily wanted.

At this point, Amanda had moved out of her parents' house. Her father is not speaking to her. And her mother is just torn between the two of them. Amanda's father, who had always been a very quiet, austere person, is saying things like, "I'm the man of the house. What I say goes." He doesn't know how to deal with the fact that his daughter, who absolutely has never given him any grief and who has been a perfect child, has all of a sudden chosen a path he doesn't like.

We went and bought rings and got an apartment. And the following Sunday we got married. Our wedding ceremony was performed by a Reform rabbi, in his study. The only family that we were in touch with at this time was on my side. The wedding guests were my parents, my sister and brother-in-law, and my niece.

So we were married. I became a schoolteacher, and Amanda was already working. We lived our own lives. I'm sure that because we got married at twenty, with not a pot in the world, nobody expected it to last. We really grew together and made our lives together, independent of everything else.

Probably one of the biggest differences between us was that Amanda and I didn't eat the same. She was what I call a Gentile eater, not a good eater. Beyond that, we were just two people who seemed to have found each other and had a great deal of respect for each other. Within our own religions, we were now pretty much at the same level. I probably never went into a temple unless I was invited to a bar mitzvah. I didn't have a burning desire to lead more of a Jewish life. I didn't feel like a close member of the clan. Church had been an important part of Amanda's life. But by the time we got married, she stopped going to church except for family weddings and things like that.

The difficulties with Amanda's father went on for five years. Amanda did talk to her mother, and we would have dinner with her every now and then. Amanda's brother died, and even at the funeral her father wouldn't speak to us. What finally changed things is that her mother became ill. She developed cancer, and at this point her mother said, "This has gone on too long. It has to stop." It was near Thanksgiving. Amanda and I went to their house on Thanksgiving Day. We walked through that door and it was like nothing had ever happened. Her father said hello to us, and everything was fine from that day on. It took some time, but eventually everyone just put it aside and moved forward. It was never spoken of again. It was like those five years didn't exist.

My mother of course had problems with our marriage. She had wanted her Jewish son to marry a Jewish girl, and she wanted a Jewish daughter-in-law with all the trimmings. She didn't get that, and it was very difficult. My wife would wear a cross, and my mother was very offended by that and would say things to her. It was strained at best. My mother's biggest cry was, "The children will always follow the religion of the mother." Her worst fear was that she would have grandchildren who were Christians. That was a mortal sin to her. She was just mortified by the thought. It was irrelevant to me.

At first, my mother's attitude bothered me a great deal. Finally, at one point I told her, "You're my mother. I love you. If you're not happy with my choice of a wife, I can't do anything about that. I'm going to come and see you. And if you want to get along with Amanda and with me, it's up to you." I wasn't going to let her beat me over the head about this anymore. If she wanted to be unhappy, she could be unhappy by herself. I'm going to be what I am.

Amanda and I have always spent a lot of time talking about all kinds of subjects. We were not a couple, even as children, who went out with many other people. We were very much into ourselves and our own world, and that was our strength. And as we talked about things, I never looked at her with even an inkling of what my mother and father wanted, which is for her to convert. That was never a thought in my mind. Nor was it in hers. We were two different people. She had blond hair, and I had dark hair. I didn't ask her to change her hair color. I could accept who and what she was. Even to this day, I don't know another human being who is an innately finer person. The fact that she believes in Jesus or Catholicism was always secondary to me. And she felt the same way towards me and Judaism.

We have two daughters. When it came to children, our approach was that we were going to give them everything. We were going to have half-breeds. When our children were born, we went to temple to give them a Jewish name. And then they were each baptized in the Catholic church. Both ceremonies felt comfortable to us.

The girls never went to any kind of religious school. They learned about their backgrounds at home and from friends. They realized from the time they could talk that they came from two parents who had different religious backgrounds. And we explained to them the differences between the religions and the respect we have for them both. I think that helped make them who they are today. Both girls have a great deal of respect and understanding for all kinds of people. And when it comes to tolerance of differences, especially religion, they are very tolerant and very well grounded as to who and what they are. There is no ambiguity. The duplicity of who they are sits well with them. When they went to school and someone asked, "Who celebrates Christmas?" they raised their hands. "Who celebrates Hanukkah?" They raised their hands. These were the kids who wore both a chai and a cross to school. That was their own little "red badge of courage." They loved that branding that made them a little different. At different points over the years, we asked both girls if they wanted to have a more formal education in either religion and their response was, "No, thank you. We're learning enough with what you're showing us."

Since my oldest child was born, we have always celebrated every holiday, Jewish and Christian, in our home. And everyone came. We'd have a lot of family and friends over. I lost both my parents when the girls were very young, but the rest of my relatives would come. So a Gentile girl had every Jewish holiday in my family for twenty-eight years. We did Christmas, Hanukkah, Easter, Passover, Rosh Hashanah. Everything. We were fun holiday people. We always had lots of decorations. We would have little ceremonies. Rabbis would die if they saw what I do for the Jewish holidays, but I always made them fun times. I made sure there were games. We still play games. We play penny pitch at Rosh Hashanah. There are games I've had for twenty years. We do these silly things. The main thing is that there is a family gathering and a time of importance, and we enjoy it. Our home is the center of our family. And so what we accentuated more than Judaism or Catholicism was family. That was the strength of what we did.

I think that at first my wife went through a long struggle of learning to participate in this very overly aggressive and loud Jewish environment when she was with my family, having come from a quiet, more sedate, less intrusive Polish Catholic upbringing. And yet I believe in my mind that she took the best of both worlds. She is who she is. You couldn't change her. But there are things she looked at and liked, and she incorporated them into who she is. For instance, she grew up in a family that didn't say "I love you" very often. They weren't as huggy or kissy as a lot of my relatives are. They were much more reserved. When we had our children, Amanda consciously raised them in an environment that was more openly loving and caring than her own family had been.

Now one of my daughters is twenty-eight, and the other is twenty-four. I think it's interesting because, the way it's turned out at least so far, the younger one has always been less associated with Judaism than the older one. Clearly, if there is a scale, she is more to the Gentile or Christian side. They were both exposed to the same things. But you know, when you have two children, sometimes one is a little bit more like the father, and one is more like the mother.

The younger girl, Robin, has never been very comfortable in the Jewish world. Even when she was in high school, she always dated Gentile people and would go with them to church. She was more comfortable going to a church than she was being in a temple and being around Jewish people. There is one situation that I think exemplifies exactly how she feels.

Both girls were great athletes. Not good, but great. That was our life. That's what we spent all our time doing. Somebody had approached Robin about playing in the Junior Maccabi games, which are basically the Jewish Junior Olympics. She was going to be the star pitcher. It was going to be in Baltimore. We put down a deposit, and she went to a couple of practices. It was a big deal. We were going to bring a group of twelve people with us to watch the games. We went to a meeting about it, and all the parents of the girls were there along with the team. We were the only family that wasn't completely Jewish. The coaches went off on a long tangent about the importance of "playing for your people" and "doing it for the Jews." I could just see my daughter sitting and thinking, "What are you talking about? I'm here to play softball." She did not feel this association.

In the car she told us how uncomfortable she had felt, and the bottom line is she no longer wanted to play. This was a girl who loved to play ball. There was too much Jewish pressure for her, and she didn't want that. How do you go back to these coaches and say, "My daughter doesn't want to play because it's too Jewish for her"? But that's sort of what I had to say. It's not that she didn't want to play sports. She just didn't fit into this environment. She had Jewish friends and socialized and did the bar and bat mitzvah circuits. But in the case of the Maccabi games, the coaches were making it like a special club, and she didn't see herself as belonging to this club.

Robin's in a relationship now with a Christian man, and I'm sure they'll wind up together. I will be shocked if they don't. I would be shocked if she met a Jewish man and started dating him. I could never see her being married to someone Jewish. I don't think there is any comfort for her there.

My oldest daughter, Lucy, married somebody Jewish. They had a Jewish wedding ceremony. Even though she got married by a rabbi, she still celebrates every Gentile holiday the way she was raised. She has a Christmas tree, she puts up all the tinsel, and she told her Jewish mother-in-law from the beginning that this was how it was going to be. Her husband is very comfortable with that because he is Jewish but not very active. She's been married for four years. I'm not sure what she'll do with her own children. The way she sounds, I think she might have them go to Hebrew school.

Lucy's in-laws work for a temple and are very involved in Jewish life. We get together with her in-laws on a lot of the holidays. We might have the first night of Rosh Hashanah at our house, and then the second night we'll go to theirs. They are very tolerant of the fact that we're not as religious as they are. Nobody pushes anybody to be anything more. So now more tolerance has been extended.

Religion never really entered into anything except in a positive way. It gave us an opportunity to celebrate our religions. It taught us respect. Instead of being a problem, it wound up being a wonderful tool for teaching our children tolerance and understanding. We're very proud of our girls because they have those things.

I think that what helped Amanda and me is that I never had a yearning for her to be somebody different. I always accepted her, and she always accepted me for who and what I am. That part never changed, and that's where we as a couple are very lucky. That's why we are going to be celebrating our thirty-third wedding anniversary at the end of this month. Even when the kids came along, there was never a feeling of, "Maybe I should have married somebody else." If we ever had harsh words over the years, nothing has ever come up in our lives where I have ever had the sense that she was unhappy or that I was unhappy with religion. It was never an issue.

Jessica grew up in a large city in the Midwest. She is in her early fifties and works in the field of social services. When Jessica met Peter, the values they shared helped make them both feel that the differences between them could be overcome. And in some ways, that has been true. But as they get older, their shared values are more easily overshadowed by each individual's needs and desires.

❂ JESSICA (TO BE FOLLOWED BY HER HUSBAND, PETER)

* * *

I grew up in a pretty Conservative Jewish household. My father had been raised in an Orthodox environment. My mother didn't grow up with any kind of religious background. Her parents were from Europe and were very Jewish culturally but were more like Socialists than Jewish in any religious way.

* * *

My sisters and brother and I all went to Hebrew school. My brother was of course bar mitzvahed, but the girls weren't. I went to services with my dad for all the holidays. We always celebrated at home as well, and we usually included a lot of relatives from my father's extended family. I liked it all very much.

Passover is one holiday that I used to have a lot of questions about. I never liked the parts of the seder that I felt were inhumane, like the plagues and the killing of the firstborn. I would think, "What kind of nonsense is this?" I remember there was a period in college that whenever God was brought up, I would say "She" instead of "He." I gave that up because I figured that a God that dealt with so much destruction and anger couldn't have been a woman.

I went to a college that didn't have many Jewish students. My mother had really encouraged me to go to a school where there would be a larger Jewish population, but I chose otherwise. I remember that the first year when the High Holidays came around, I was very homesick, very lonely. There was a bus trip that took students to another town to the closest synagogue, and I did that for Rosh Hashanah. But the synagogue was Reform, so it didn't have the same sort of flavor that I was used to. It was very different, and I didn't like that. I talked to one of the religious studies professors about it, and he said he had all the prayer books in his office and I could come and study in the Religious Studies building. On Yom Kippur, that's what I did. I just did it on my own. So it was very important to me to celebrate the holidays at that point.

I went east to graduate school, thinking that I would meet more Jews. I definitely wanted to marry a Jewish boy, and my expectation was that I would, but it didn't work out that way. I pursued Jewish boys, but they never pursued me. It wasn't as if I said to myself, "I'm never going to date anybody who isn't Jewish." I did go out with different kinds of people. But my preference certainly would have been to be with somebody who was Jewish. It was always an issue for me, but obviously not enough.

After graduate school, I came back home and started to work. That's when I met my future husband. Peter would probably call himself a Methodist, and when I met him he was not at all religious. I probably could not have dated somebody who was very religious, nor could they have dated me. One thing that made it very comfortable is that my parents really liked him. They absolutely would have preferred me to marry someone Jewish. My mother had suggested that strongly over the years. But she was ill by the time I got married, and it didn't make as much difference to her at that point. And my father really liked him as a person, as a human being. So he overlooked the religious differences. If my father hadn't liked Peter as much, I don't know if we would have gotten married. We probably would have, but it certainly helped that my father was so encouraging. There were no family problems on either side at all. His parents liked me very much. They thought he was lucky to have me.

Peter used to go to services with my family and me at that point. We talked about him converting, but there was no way he possibly could have done it. Just like I could never become a Christian, he could never become a Jew. It was very clear that neither of us would ever convert. But when we decided to get married, I told him we had to have a Jewish service, and he went along with that. He had no problems with it.

My parents were affiliated with a Conservative synagogue, but I knew a Conservative rabbi wasn't going to marry us. I started looking for a Reform rabbi to do the wedding ceremony. I called a number of people that I knew for recommendations and was told no by several rabbis. I was also told by several people that what I was doing was a terrible thing. And at one point when I called a rabbi's secretary, she told me that I was worse than the Holocaust and that people like me were causing the death of the Jewish community. I got off the phone in tears.

I was quite disturbed by this whole process, but we finally found a rabbi. He did insist that we meet with him to talk about how we would raise our children. He asked Peter to think more about conversion and about making a commitment to raising the children Jewish. Peter said he would think about it.

After we were married, we continued to celebrate all the Jewish holidays with my family. I would go to services with my dad. We had most of the holiday dinners at our house. Peter never went to church. There was no Christian element in our life whatsoever. The only thing we would do is go to see his family at Christmastime. I bought gifts for them, but we never went to any kind of religious services. Peter was somewhat interested in having a Christmas tree, but I said no to that. It wasn't something I thought I could have in our home.

We were married two years before our son Alex was born. Alex never was circumcised. That wasn't something I wanted done to him at all. I didn't worry much about his future Jewish education and whether or not he would go to Hebrew school or things like that. We weren't living anywhere near a synagogue at that point. The only thing that I remember feeling differently about when Alex was born is that I didn't want to celebrate Christmas with Peter's family anymore. I didn't want Alex involved in all that. And for a couple of years, we didn't go to see his family during the holidays.

By the time Alex was old enough for Hebrew school, we had moved to an area where there were some synagogues. I looked around for one to join. What I liked was the old traditional synagogue I always had gone to with my father. I still had the same problem with the Reform ones. They didn't give me the same feeling as the one I had gone to growing up. I liked the more Conservative shuls, but I felt they would be too much for me without the support of a Jewish husband. We eventually joined a Reform synagogue, and Alex did go to Hebrew school for a couple years.

One thing that's interesting is that you don't pay to go to church or Sunday school, but you pay to go to Hebrew school. Belonging to a synagogue was very expensive. That became a major issue, because we couldn't really afford it. We probably could have pursued some kind of financial aid, but we didn't. It was just a problem to Peter. He felt that it was very strange that you would have to pay to go to services on the High Holidays. When I was working and had my own money, I felt like I could justify sending Alex to Hebrew school. But when I had another child and started staying home with the kids, I felt like I really couldn't.

My father died when my kids were still small. That changed the whole Jewish environment for me. I guess being Jewish was really a connection with my family. I had still been going to services with my father on the holidays, and without him it wasn't the same. My brother and I went together to the synagogue for a couple of years, but it just didn't give us the same feeling.

I keep thinking that if my father had been alive while the children were growing up, a lot of things might have been different. In the first place, he probably would have paid for Hebrew school. Also, I think Peter would have been much more supportive of and involved in the Jewish experiences that we do have, because he had such a good relationship with my dad. The way it is now, I have the seders and all the other holiday dinners at our house, but Peter's participation is extremely minimal. He will agree to be there, and that's about it. There's never any interest or enthusiasm.

My mother died a couple years after my father. Peter's parents are both dead as well. I think when you lose your parents it really changes things around. The earlier you lose them, the more important your heritage becomes. I think that you begin to look backwards a lot more. You begin to have regrets and wish that you could go back to some of your childhood experiences and preserve some of them for your own family. And so that becomes very difficult. If you each find comfort from different directions, that is very hard.

At this point in his life, I don't think Peter is sure exactly what he wants in terms of religion. When he was growing up, he went to church every Sunday. Both of his parents were Sunday school teachers, and church was an important part of his life. He even played the organ at church, so for a time church music became very important to him. Now he has started listening to church music a lot of the time at home. It's not something I like to listen to, but he finds a great deal of comfort in that kind of music.

Life is full of compromises, including compromises about religion. We started having a tree at Christmas. This began after our parents had died. It simply became much more important for Peter to have the tree. I felt he really needed it. I decided that this was something I could give him that didn't have to take anything away from me. And so I said, "Okay." I even had a whole bunch of ornaments, because I have always collected little things. I didn't buy them as Christmas ornaments. I bought them because they were little things that I liked. But it made it easier to have the tree, because we used all my things as ornaments. Peter loves it. It's something we can share with his brothers and sister. It makes him happy. It makes the kids happy. And it's fun. So having the tree feels all right.

The last couple years, Peter has wanted us all to watch certain television programs together on Christmas and Easter. They have mostly been stories about Jesus Christ. One of the reasons I am probably not a strong practicing Jew is that I don't believe in a lot of the Biblical stuff. I don't feel it has any real relevance to my life. And a lot of the Bible stories are very violent. I just find that they are not helpful at all. I'm culturally Jewish, but I certainly don't believe in a lot of the religious parts. And that's how I feel about Christianity. I have a very hard time understanding or accepting the religious aspects of Christianity. It doesn't make sense to me. The kids will watch these shows, and it doesn't make sense to them either. I know that bothers Peter.

Peter and I do have a lot of things in common. Our basic values are very similar, and that's probably what brought us together in the first place. We both believe in honesty and bringing the children up right. Those things have nothing to do with religion. They have to do with what kind of people we are. But if you come from very different backgrounds, there are things that are going to come up. It's hard sometimes for Peter and me to show a united front for the kids, because on some big issues we just aren't united. The kids are very aware that there are differences between us and that we don't look at things the same way when it comes to religion. I think that when you are raised in a Christian household, there is sometimes a real God-fearing aspect. The children grow up being scared about the whole idea of going to hell. They think that if they don't do certain things, they won't just be in trouble with their parents, but they'll be in hell. Jews don't grow up with any of that fear at all. Those kinds of teachings have absolutely stuck with Peter. They have left him with an underlying feeling of disquiet. It has affected his outlook on life. And in that way, we're very different.

Over the last few years, it has really bothered Peter when he hears our kids describe themselves as Jewish. I've always defined them as Jewish, and that's how they define themselves as well. My oldest daughter recently started college, and last Friday she went to a Shabbat dinner. I don't think she'll go every week. But it was one place she felt comfortable. Peter continually reminds the children that they're only partly Jewish. He wants them to remember that they have another background.

I guess I'm pretty comfortable with the way we have done things. There are times that I feel sorry the kids didn't go to Hebrew school, but I also know it wasn't really an option. I have three children, and they have each asked me why they didn't go to Hebrew school. This has come up especially at the times when their friends are getting bar or bat mitzvahed. That's another thing. I knew we would never be able to pay for a bar mitzvah party. I feel bad, but I tell them that if they want to go to Hebrew school later, they can. I tell them that a lot of adults are getting bar mitzvahed and they can do it at any time, and it can be very meaningful that way.

I think that if I had married a man who was Jewish, some things would be very different. We would have been involved with a synagogue. It would have been easier to belong to the kind of synagogue I would feel comfortable in if my husband were Jewish. We live near two different synagogues, and even though we don't belong I get their bulletins each month and read them religiously. I read a lot of Jewish publications and a lot of books about modern Judaism. And sometimes I think about taking a class at a synagogue. I would find that of interest.

I think that sometimes religious differences in a marriage don't become important until much later. When you are first starting out and you're in love, you don't usually worry much about religion. You're concerned about pairing up with someone and developing a relationship. You're caught up in the romantic aspects of marriage, and you're willing to give almost entirely to the other person. It's a selfless kind of love. And then as you get older, you begin to think about what your own needs are. I think that's true for Peter and me. Both of us spend more time now looking back to our own family traditions. They seem a lot more important than they were in the beginning when we were first learning about each other and developing as a couple.

Peter is also in his early fifties. He grew up in a city in Illinois and is a business manager. At this point in his life, Peter is hoping that it is not too late to teach his children more about his own background and the traditions he grew up with. It has become important to him to expose the children not just to the values that he and Jessica share, but to some of the differences between them as well.

✖ PETER (PRECEDED BY HIS WIFE, JESSICA)

* * *

I was born in Denmark, into a family that was very much a part of the Lutheran Church. My great-great-grandfather and five generations before him were all pastors in the Danish Lutheran church. People in Denmark seemed to have a very different relationship with the church than they do here. People primarily went to church for the major holidays and when they were, as they say, hatched, matched, and dispatched.

* * *

My parents immigrated to the United States, and we became active in the mainstream Protestant Church. That conformed more to what people are used to in this country, which means we started going to church on a weekly basis. Mostly what I enjoyed was celebrating the holidays, such as Christmas. I liked knowing what to expect when each holiday came around. Children especially, I think, like that kind of repetition.

When Jessica and I met, I was comfortable with the fact that she is Jewish. We had neighbors when I was growing up who were Jewish, and I had learned a little from them. More importantly, we felt the same way about a lot of issues. I think it would be much more difficult to marry someone with very different values. If you were a liberal Democrat and somehow married a person who was a member of the John Birch Society, there would be a lot more conflict than you would have between two religions, and two people, that in essence share a great deal.

I think the fact that our values were so similar took a lot of the sting out of any differences between us. Certainly it's true that we were raised very differently. For Jessica, other religions are sort of exotic, like maybe they came from another planet. She was raised in a way that left her with an attitude of "us versus them." For example, she felt it was perfectly normal for me to go to New Year's services with her on Rosh Hashanah, but the thought of stepping into a church is just terrifying for her. And when someone has these deep-seated feelings, you really can't rationally talk about it, so there is no point in pushing the issue.

I don't think it's reasonable to assume that just because you have a particular background or because you were educated in a certain way, all other people should think and behave and react just like you. Because then in a way there's a tendency to think someone must be moronic if they can't agree with you. You have to be able to step back and say, "Okay, their experience is different from mine, but it can be just as positive." I used to try to explain this to Jessica. I said, "You didn't meet me until I was twenty-six years old, but I led a whole part of my life before that. I am Christian. I grew up going to church. You have to understand that obviously it is going to have a substantial effect on me. It is going to have an impact on how I deal with raising the kids and all sorts of things."

We were married by a rabbi. It was important to Jessica, and I had no problem with it. One thing we really didn't do is talk much about kids ahead of time, and that's probably the thing I most regret. We didn't think carefully about how we would handle the religious education of our children. It's interesting because if my parents had never come to the United States, my children would have learned about religion in the schools. In Denmark, religion was considered a scholarly subject like any other subject. So they would have been educated in that regard. Here in this country, obviously you have to separate the church and the state. Public schools have to be clear of religion altogether. So that means the parents have to step in if this is something they want their children to learn about.

The only real difficulty we had in terms of religion was with the children. It's been more important to Jessica for the children to identify themselves as Jews than it was for me to have them be Christian. Different aspects of a religion matter more for different individuals. There is the cultural aspect, the traditional aspect, what you could call almost the home-comfort aspect, and then the religious aspect. People pick up on different parts of the religion depending on their wants and needs. For example, Jessica's view of celebrating the major Jewish holidays is mainly based on the fact that this was something that was done in her family as a child, and therefore it is important to her. It is important to her siblings and to her extended family. And she wants her children to have the same experiences. So we have all the holiday dinners at our house, and her whole family comes. But she doesn't really connect with Judaism in a religious sense.

Over the years, Jessica has felt uncomfortable in some cases when the kids would do things with me that had even a somewhat Christian overtone. I've taken them to a number of events at Danish organizations, and they've also gone to some Danish language camps. A lot of the events, and particularly the camps, have a Lutheran as well as a Danish context. There is often an invocation by a Lutheran pastor. And that's the kind of thing that I can see makes Jessica a little uncomfortable.

One issue we had early on was about a Christmas tree. When we first got married, Jessica wasn't comfortable with the idea of having a tree. But for a Dane, a Christmas tree is the life that allows you to survive the winter. Initially I accepted what she wanted. But after a few years I said, "If you're going to have a Passover seder, I'm going to have a Christmas tree." So we started getting a Christmas tree each year, and I've really enjoyed it. It's something that I remember having all the years I was growing up, and I like having it to look forward to again. You just don't always realize at first which aspects from your religion and your childhood are going to be the most important to you. It took me a while to realize how much I wanted my children to share that Christmas experience with me, in the same way Jessica wants the kids to partake in the Jewish experiences she grew up with.

What I try to explain to Jessica is that our children need to understand both of our religious traditions, because both traditions are a part of their heritage. And it's not that hard because they are so closely related. In a way, it's sad because my children are absolutely illiterate on the subject of both religions, and that's not right. I wish I would have given more thought to this and had more discussions on religion and children and what that means. I would have tried to impress upon Jessica that we needed to give them a firmer footing in both Judaism and Christianity.

What I am trying to do at this late date (my youngest child is thirteen) is talk more to my children about the history of these religions and why they have evolved the way they have. I want them to understand that some of the extraordinary things about religion are its constancy and its resilience and its capacity for change. These are all things I grew up learning about, and they are things I wish my children could identify with and have a deeper understanding of. Also, I want them to know that only by learning more will they eventually be able to decide for themselves what their own beliefs are.

Joy grew up in the South. She is in her late thirties and has known Scott since she was twenty-five. Joy and Scott felt they needed information and support to deal with the many issues that began to come up as they considered incorporating two religions into one household. They were bothered by the lack of resources their city offered for intermarried couples. Eventually, they decided that if they wanted something more in their community, they would have to create it themselves.

✖ JOY (TO BE FOLLOWED BY HER HUSBAND, SCOTT)

* * *

The most important thing to me about the church we belonged to when I was growing up was that many of the people who led the educational programs there, including the minister, were very scholarly in their approach. They didn't have a lot of dogmatic rules or viewpoints. I was comfortable there because I felt that they always encouraged questioning. That attitude sort of became the hallmark of my faith, and I do really tend to be a questioner.

* * *

I'm from a fairly small town in Mississippi. My parents were both from that area, so I always had lots of extended family around. My family belonged to the Presbyterian Church, which provided what I would say was a fairly moderate Christian environment.

There were exactly two families in our town who were Jewish. I think that because the town was so small, assimilation was really important. Neither family seemed to go out of their way to let people know they were Jewish or to do anything obviously connected with Judaism. There were no kids my age in either family, so my exposure to them was fairly limited and I really didn't know them very well.

I left Mississippi when I was eighteen to go to college in Memphis. After I moved, I began attending the church I still go to off and on during the year. It's an Episcopal church, and it is a very liberal environment. It's located in downtown Memphis, and it's involved in a lot of urban ministry, community projects, and those sorts of things. It really fits in well with my sense of what being a Christian is.

I was part of a big group of people in college, including a number of Jewish people. One of them happened to be a girl who is Scott's cousin, and she set us up. I actually had never given much thought as to whether or not I would marry someone outside the Christian faith. But as soon as I met Scott, before we even had our first date, I knew that we would be together. I had this sort of instant realization that my ability to make this relationship work would be based on whether or not I could really live my beliefs. I knew I wanted to maintain my Christianity. And I knew he was Jewish and wasn't about to change. So right from the beginning, these issues started going through my head. I started off thinking about them on my own, but we were talking about them together fairly early in the relationship, after about a month or so.

What made sense to me, and what I was just really trying to feel out from Scott, was whether or not it would be acceptable to him for us to live a dual-faith existence. I knew that of all the choices we could make, that's by far one of the hardest. But it seemed right to me. It was clear that we both felt strongly about our backgrounds. I think we're both fairly nontraditional in the way we view religion, but we still each maintain a strong connection. So there was really never any chance from my perspective that either of us would convert.

In some ways I think that because this was a situation where I didn't know anything, I really didn't have sense enough to understand what I was getting into. The whole concept of raising kids was completely foreign to me at that time, so that was something I didn't even deal with much at first. I was concerned at the beginning about things like, "What sort of Christmas china am I going to have if I marry a Jewish person?" I'm someone who loves to entertain, and Christmas china was just the first thing on my mind. So within about the first month or two, I said to Scott, "Okay, so how do you feel about Christmas china?" He said, "Well, I don't care so much if you want to have it, but does it have to have crosses? I mean, what exactly is Christmas china?" Now of course it seems completely trivial, but that was ten years ago. I was just trying to figure out how to incorporate the little things that mattered to each of us into our lives.

I remember that in the early days, a lot of our discussions about the differences between us centered on food. We would talk about what constituted an acceptable bagel and that sort of thing. When we thought about a life together, we always planned to invite lots of people over for meals and to celebrate holidays. I was completely fearless about trying to cook the traditional Jewish foods, and when the Jewish holidays came around we just started making things. Scott's mom is not a cook, and she was just floored that we would go through all this trouble. But we both really enjoyed it.

I do think that one of the most difficult stages for an interfaith couple is when you've decided to get married and you're trying to work everything out. It depends partly on where you live and what your community is like, but planning the wedding can be very hard. Leading up to the time of our wedding, Scott and I had no interaction whatsoever with other interfaith couples because we simply didn't know any. It would have been good to be able to talk things over with people who were in similar situations.

What we wanted for our wedding was to have a dual-faith ceremony. We wanted both a minister and a rabbi to conduct the ceremony, and we wanted those people to be individuals that we had a connection with. Certainly, our families were very supportive. They had a lot of logistical questions like, "What do you do about this or that?" but there was never any doubt on either side that this was a good thing for both of us. What made it very hard despite the support of our families was that the people in the community and the clergy we approached would say, "You can't do this" or "We can't help you to do that." Planning a wedding when your community is saying, "This is not possible," is very difficult.

What we ended up with was a minister who was a close friend of mine and a judge who was Jewish and was a friend of Scott's family. We couldn't find a rabbi that Scott felt comfortable with who would do it. We really struggled with how to incorporate the Jewish elements into the ceremony. It worked out fine, but it was a difficult time. And after we got through it, and after we were married, we said, "Okay, clearly if we are going to have any sort of network of interfaith couples, we're going to have to create it, because there is nothing here and everybody is deaf, dumb, and blind when you ask a question or want some help." So the process of planning our wedding was sort of the catalyst for our starting an interfaith group.

It wasn't so much that we had specific things we were having problems with. It's more that we felt very alone. It would have been easier if we had been living in cities like Washington, D.C., or Los Angeles or Chicago because they already had resources and groups in place. In Memphis, we were definitely isolated. And it really wasn't the same to talk over some of our issues with friends who were in same-faith marriages. We tried. Once we said, "We're having a problem deciding where to put our Christmas tree." They just looked at us. "What's the problem?" Our problem was that Scott had agreed to have the tree, but he didn't want it to be in the front of the house. I grew up with it in the living room. That was part of the whole point, so that people could see it from the street. But he wasn't comfortable with that. And so, it was a matter of compromise. "Where do you put the tree if it's not going to be in the living room?" It wasn't a big issue. It wasn't like we were fighting about it, but we just didn't have anybody that we could sort of knock it around with until our interfaith group. And I'll never forget the first time we brought up this question in our interfaith group several years later. "Where do you put the Christmas tree?" Everybody in the room started laughing. "Oh, thank God. Here are some people who actually know what we're talking about."

What happened is that soon after we got married, we put the word out to all our friends that we wanted to start an interfaith group. We ended up with three other couples who were friends of friends. We just called them and said, "We want to start this group. Would you come over for dinner and talk to us about it?" And they did, sort of reluctantly. We told everybody, "We are looking to create friendships with people in similar relationships. You don't have to tell us your problems. You don't have to bare your souls. We'd just like to be friends with you. We want to have a community." And that's how it started. We were all either newly married or about to be married. It sort of stopped and started a few times at the beginning, but now it's been going along continuously for about five years, and we've grown to twelve families. We all have kids now, and we do primarily kid-centered events. A major focus is to give our kids a community of peers.

Scott and I have three children. They are all still very young. The oldest is barely five. Our goal is to maintain a dual-faith household, and that means practicing both of our religions and teaching our kids about both. I've learned that being a practicing Christian is very different from being a practicing Jew. For example, a practicing Christian is typically going to go to church on a fairly regular basis. But people might consider themselves practicing Jews even if they go to synagogue only twice a year or not even that. They might do more things at home. That's pretty much how Scott is. For example, we try any Friday night when we're at home to have a Sabbath dinner. We light the candles and say the prayers. We also try to say grace every night at dinner, and we rotate a variety of different prayers. The prayers might be Jewish, Christian, or just sort of basically secular. So I think for me the goal is to have a presence of spirit, which we can find in a variety of ways.

I don't think it really works when the Jewish parent is the one who teaches the children about Judaism and the Christian parent teaches them about Christianity. What Scott and I are doing is trying to learn about each other's religion and work together to teach the kids about both. I don't think there has been anything I'm particularly uncomfortable with about Judaism. But it's taken a lot of education because I really hadn't been exposed to it. I have a really compulsive personality, and when I'm feeling anxious because I don't understand something, one of the ways I cope is that I read obsessively. I just sort of immerse myself and take in as much information as I can find so that I can be comfortable. And that's what I've been doing in this case, because I really want the kids to see me comfortable with Judaism.

Scott is not quite as comfortable with Christianity. There have been parts that have been harder for him to get used to, like Christmas. That has been a big one. Easter is sort of a tricky time as well, because, as Scott says, "As a Jew you can ignore a lot, but the whole celebration of Easter is a little hard to reconcile." I wouldn't say that we've really gotten to a point where we are completely comfortable with that one yet. But one of the nice things is that, as a couple, we have a really good relationship for communicating, and we both work at it. So we've gotten to the point now where we can just say, "You know, I'm still not there on this one."

One thing that could have been tricky is figuring out what to do about any kind of formal religious education for our kids. It turns out that some people in the Chicago area have developed a dual-faith curriculum that teaches kids about both faiths. Our plan is to start out using that curriculum at home with our children. It begins at the kindergarten level, which is where our daughter will be next fall. It's set up so that you do twenty-four or twenty-six classes throughout the year. It teaches about both religions in a very respectful way. It does a lot of comparing and contrasting. It doesn't really ignore the differences, but it certainly emphasizes the similarities. We're actually very excited about this, because the curriculum looks very good to us.

My hope for our kids is that they will find a way to a meaningful relationship with God. I think it's entirely possible that they will eventually choose one religion or the other, but I don't think it is absolutely necessary for their sense of spiritual well-being. I hope that being raised in a dual-faith household will make them compassionate and tolerant of other people's choices. I hope they'll see that there are many choices that can be good choices.

By marrying someone who is a different religion, I think you give up the ease of raising children. It's sort of a double-edged sword. If I were in a same-faith relationship, it would be easier to find a spiritual home that I could plug my family into, and we wouldn't have to provide our children with a religious education at home. On the other hand, my faith has really grown as a result of having to be mindful about these issues.

I've felt pretty well prepared for most things so far, I guess. I always sort of look at any issue I'm dealing with as just sort of a detail along the way. My feelings about my marriage are so strong that they override everything else. There are times when I think, "Okay, well here is another thing that we've got to figure out." But I don't ever think of it as insurmountable. I don't ever think that it is something we can't handle, because so far we have managed. We try to take things as they come and we do what we can. I think neither of us is particularly the type of person who believes that God is in the details. We just sort of figure that God is probably happy that we're doing as much as we are.

Scott is just a few years older than Joy. He seems to still feel a little awkward about some of the aspects of their dual-faith household. But overall he clearly finds the religious experiences he and Joy share to be far more satisfying than the ones he had with his own family when he was growing up.

❊ SCOTT (PRECEDED BY HIS WIFE, JOY)

* * *

I grew up here in Memphis. My mother was president of the local chapter of Hadassah. My father was very involved with the Conservative synagogue that we belonged to. I went to Sunday school and Hebrew school. When I was about to go into fourth grade, they started having bussing in Memphis. At that point, my parents decided to put me into a private Jewish elementary school that was almost a hundred percent Orthodox. I really didn't belong there, and I never felt welcome. I was teased a lot because I didn't fit in. I was there for only a few years, and then I transferred back into the public school.

* * *

When I turned thirteen, I had a big bar mitzvah. Right about this time, my friendships began to change. I moved away from having primarily Jewish friends to having mostly non-Jewish friends. I still had a few Jewish friends in high school, but I was leaning towards another group. And when I started to date, it was mainly with non-Jewish girls. I've probably had only two or three dates with Jewish girls in my life.

Even though my mother and father participated in a lot of Jewish groups, we didn't do as much at home as I would have liked. We rarely had any of the holiday celebrations at our house. We tended to go to the home of one particular uncle, whom I really disliked. That always gave an unpleasant tone to the holidays. I would have liked to do more in our own house, and I can tell you that my wife and I do more Jewish things in our home now than I ever did when I was growing up.

Joy and I were together about three years before we got married. I wasn't sure at first if I would really marry her or not. We had a lot of discussions about intermarriage. It helped that Joy was finding books and doing research, because she really learned a lot and exposed me to different ideas that I hadn't really considered. Once I knew I really did want to marry her, my major concern was about how to mollify my parents. They were open to our relationship, but they still had a number of things they wanted to discuss. So there were a lot of questions to be answered and a lot that I had to develop in my own mind as to how I was going to describe our plans to them.

The biggest thing was that Joy would not be converting. That is something I had to get across to my parents, and especially to my father. I knew that it would be hard for him to accept. I guess there was a little hope inside me early on that one of these days maybe she would convert. I think my father held on to that hope a lot longer than I did. So I had to get it across to my parents that, "No, she is not going to convert, and no, we are not going to be raising our kids exclusively one way or the other." And as time went on, I got more used to the idea of having a dual-faith life. I felt that it would be a shame for our kids if we didn't teach them about Joy's upbringing as well as mine. It wouldn't be fair to her, and it wouldn't be fair to our kids.

Creating the wedding ceremony was hard. We went into it with naiveté and thought that ultimately we would be able to have what we wanted. I first met privately with a Conservative rabbi at the synagogue where I grew up, and then Joy and I went together to meet with another rabbi in the area. Both of them put out the company line, which was, "We can't do anything for you, but also we wish you would decide on one religion or the other." The Conservative rabbi tried to talk me out of the marriage completely. That really disappointed me. I respected his reasoning, but it still hurt. This was the synagogue where I grew up, and I expected something more. So we had a minister, and a judge who is Jewish. It was a little weird for the judge because we were really asking him to represent the Jewish side. It wasn't something he was particularly comfortable with, but it all worked out. We could have found a rabbi from another community who would have officiated, but it didn't make sense to me to fly in a rabbi that I had never met just to perform a ceremony. It would have had no meaning to me.

We have three children, two girls and a boy. When each of our kids was born, we did a sort of naming ceremony. We created it ourselves and did it in our home with everybody in the family participating. When our son was born, we didn't try to do a full-blown bris. I just decided to do what was meaningful to me, and so I got my father and my brother and my son, and the four of us went down to the office of an OB/GYN I know, who also works as a mohel. He performed a bris in his office, with enough ceremony that it felt very right to us.

Even though we are planning to raise the kids dual-faith, right now I feel like we mostly bring Judaism into our home. We do the Sabbath dinners and light the candles and have the wine and the challah almost every Friday night. We do big celebrations with our interfaith group for Passover and Hanukkah. If I had married someone Jewish, I would almost guarantee that we would be doing fewer Jewish events and celebrations in our home than Joy and I do right now, because we would have relied on the institutions instead of knowing that it is up to us to create everything ourselves. We would have said, "Okay, the kids are going to start Sunday school when they're five or six and we don't have to do anything else." For me, I know I'm a much more involved Jew than I would have been otherwise.

I'll pretty much go along with whatever Joy wants to do for the Christian holidays. Joy is unbelievably great on the Jewish side. She helps tremendously. She can make a matzo ball soup that would kill you. But unfortunately, I'm not so good on the other side. There are times when I feel uncomfortable with some of the Christian elements, although I try to get that feeling out of the way because I know how much she does for me. The problem is that even when you know something intellectually, sometimes it's still hard to get past certain feelings. Joy knows that, and it's okay. We do have the tree for Christmas. I'll participate in Christmas and I don't do it grudgingly or anything like that because most of it is a lot of fun. But each year, I hope she doesn't want to put the tree up more than a week before Christmas. And each year, I'm still ready the day right after Christmas to take that damn tree down and get it out of the house.

4 Looking for Alternatives

These stories are about interfaith couples that have had to look for their own unique ways to handle the issue of religion. There is a story about a husband and wife who can't find enough to share in either of their own religions, so they turn to something else altogether. There is a Christian wife who is still hoping to find a way to incorporate either of their religions into her family in a way that her Jewish husband might accept. There are some stories in which the couples decide they can be very comfortable having little or no religious aspect to their lives. And there is even a couple that wants to raise their sons and daughter in different ways so that the needs of both parents can be better met. The choices that are made in these stories are genuine attempts to deal honestly with this issue in a way that will have real meaning for the individuals involved.

Lynn is in her late forties. She grew up on the East Coast and works in the field of video production. Lynn and her husband have made a series of choices about religion that feel right to them as a couple. The only times problems seem to occur are when other people are offended by those choices.

✳ LYNN

* * *

For my parents, belonging to a synagogue was mostly a social thing. We attended a Reform Jewish congregation. My parents participated in the men's club and the women's club, and there was also a drama club that they liked. The synagogue gave them a means of getting together with other people.

* * *

My sister and I went through Sunday school. I never liked it, and I never got anything out of it. We didn't do too much else. We would celebrate Passover, and we would also go to the High Holiday services. Once in a while, we did go to Friday night services with my parents. Our rabbi was pretty liberal and progressive. During the Vietnam War he would frequently talk about the war and the wrongness of it. I used to be stirred by his sermons. I liked that part of the service, but nothing else really ever resonated with me.

My grandparents on my mother's side were very assimilated. They never belonged to a synagogue or did much in terms of Jewish traditions or rituals. But my grandmother on my father's side was Orthodox. She always used to light the Sabbath candles. Even though I was very close to her, we never discussed religion. She died when I was thirteen, and when she died I decided in what was obviously a pretty sophomoric way that there was no God. He let my grandmother die, he didn't hear my prayers, and from then on I was just really disassociated from the whole thing.

For as long as I can remember, my parents had this viewpoint that Jewish men are better. They believed that I would have a better life if I married a Jewish man. My father even went so far as to say that non-Jewish men have the reputation of beating their wives and fooling around on them in a way that Jewish men don't. "Jewish men honor their wives more. They put their wives up on a pedestal. And if you marry a Jewish man, the Jewish woman becomes the focal point of the family, and that doesn't happen with a non-Jewish man."

My mother, interestingly enough, went out with a non-Jewish man all through high school and the early part of college. It was a very serious relationship, and I think that even though her parents were not religious, they dissuaded her from continuing it. So she didn't go as far as my father when she talked about this. All she really had to say about my seeing non-Jewish men was that it would create problems further down the road. "You may be young. You don't see any problems now. But when you raise children, or later if you decide you want to practice your religion and it differs from his, it will be a problem."

I thought my parents were kind of ridiculous. As it turned out, when I was quite young I did marry a man who was Jewish. We had met in high school and then went on to college together. We had a Jewish marriage ceremony performed by a rabbi, under a chuppah. The Jewish part of the ceremony didn't mean much to me, but that's how we both were raised and that's what our parents wanted, so we did it. That marriage only lasted a short time.

By the time I met Craig, I was in the throes of left-wing philosophy. I was a political science major, and I really did see religion as more divisive than anything else. The problems in the Mideast disturbed me. I didn't think the Palestinians were being treated fairly. All of the human rights issues and all of the religious issues sort of got tied up together in my mind. When I met Craig, having any feeling about practicing my own religion was right away not anything to be considered.

Craig was raised Catholic in a very religious family. He has aunts and uncles who are priests and nuns. He went to church every Sunday and to a private Catholic school. When he went away to college, he started to absorb a lot of knowledge about other issues and do independent reading and studying. He just quickly fell away from believing anything about Catholicism.

Craig and I both knew that we were each basically agnostic. The only thing that used to worry me is that our friends would tell us that once we had kids, we would need to do more in terms of religion. "It's important to the kids. The kids need to have some moral upbringing." They also would tell us that as we get older, there was a good chance we'd each turn back to our own religion. So sometimes I would say to Craig, "Do you think you will ever turn back to Catholicism? And how would that affect us if that happens?" He was pretty firm that it wasn't going to happen, and I felt the same way about the possibility of me getting more involved in Judaism. We each really felt that religion would continue to be a nonissue.

I was thirty and finished with law school by the time Craig and I got married. Our wedding was sort of interesting. It was at Craig's mother's house, and it was very small. A judge performed the civil ceremony, and then

Craig's uncle, who is a priest, stood up and said some very generic Old Testament words about marriage and love and that he hoped we would go forth and multiply. At one point, he also made the sign of the cross. I was a little bit uncomfortable with that, and interestingly enough so was Craig. It wasn't what we were planning on. I do like his uncle. He is very open-minded, and I could tell he was just trying to appease everybody. Craig's mother wanted some sign made that our marriage was being blessed by Jesus, and Craig's grandmother was sitting there with her eyes closed and pressing her palms together the whole time. So I knew he did it for them a little bit, and I knew that the Old Testament portion was something he did for my parents. I was worried about how my parents would react to that cross, but they were really very understanding about it. They said, "We know this is a part of who Craig is, and a part of his family." They liked Craig. He may not have been what they had imagined for me, but they could see that we did well together and that I was happy.

There is no question that Craig and I have been affected by the very different backgrounds we come from. I feel Craig has been influenced by some of the ideas he grew up with. One is that you should deny yourself things and make sacrifices here on earth so that you will later be rewarded with a wonderful afterlife. Whether Craig will admit it or not, I think he sometimes views life that way. I see it in the way he chooses to live his life and the decisions that he makes. He denies himself a lot of things. He lives in a pretty modest way compared to the way he could live. I think somehow he does believe that maybe there is a payback, whereas I feel that I live much more in the present, and I want things now because this is the only life I'm aware of.

Religion really doesn't come up as an issue between the two of us. It does come up around us and we address it, and sometimes we get a little bit heated as we are addressing it. For instance, there have been times when I felt he didn't understand why I'm sensitive to a particular comment. We used to have this discussion about how I never liked it when somebody referred to someone as a Jew. Craig would say, "Well, what's the difficulty with saying that?" I tell him it is just a derogatory way of describing a person. You wouldn't say, "So and so is a Christian from New York." When you add the word Jew in that way, it all of a sudden has this kind of negative connotation to me, because it's been used that way throughout history.

Even though I don't feel drawn to the religious part of Judaism, I absolutely feel connected to it culturally and historically. I grew up knowing all about the Holocaust and reading Anne Frank. And of course Craig never had any of that. There is a book Craig was given when he graduated from high school. It was written by Churchill about World War II, and it was one of Craig's favorites for years. And when I look at this book, I see it really is all about World War II, but there is maybe only a page and a half on the concentration camps. There is a lot on Hitler and the Nazis but hardly anything about the extermination of the Jews. I find that very interesting because my whole childhood was steeped in that, and Craig had a very different perspective.

When we go together to see movies about the Holocaust, we are both affected. But I think I am moved in a different way. Something strikes a chord in me and it's not the same chord in Craig. So there are subtle differences between us. But they don't affect our day-to-day life, and they don't make me feel like he doesn't understand who I am or where I come from or what the issues are about.

Craig and I have two sons. Joey is almost thirteen, and Dan is ten. Neither of our boys was circumcised. When Joey was born, we had just come back from living in Europe. It seemed as though nobody had their sons circumcised in Europe anymore. And at the time, the College of Pediatrics was saying there was no reason to do a circumcision other than religious reasons. I felt strongly that I didn't want my child circumcised. There wasn't enough of a reason for us to have it done, so we just decided not to.

My parents were astounded. "Aren't we coming to Pittsburgh for a bris? How can we tell our friends you had a son?" And I told them, "Well, we're not doing it. It's just who we are. We're different from you and your friends. This is our son." It just didn't feel wrong to me at all. It actually felt very natural, like I was really doing what I needed to do. It would have felt very artificial to go through with a circumcision and the religious ceremony of a bris when it wasn't what we wanted.

One thing that's been very good for the boys is that my sister and her family live in the same city that we do, and Craig's mom lives nearby as well. We are able to join each of them for the different holidays, so our kids have exposure to some of the traditions and rituals of both religions. My sister's family always celebrates Passover and Hanukkah. She'll light the candles, and we'll have potato pancakes. And at Christmastime we go over to see Craig's mom. She always has a tree and makes a big Christmas dinner. And for Easter we'll go out with her for Easter dinner. But in every case, the focus is on eating and gifts, and nothing else. We don't bring in any religious elements.

There have been times when I know things have been confusing, especially when the boys were little. I remember that when Joey was in kindergarten, he came home and said he wanted to ask me something. This was around the holidays, and since he had just started school, it was the first time he was really hearing so many people talking about Christmas and Hanukkah. He was five years old. And he said, "What are we? Are we Christmas or are we Hanukkah?" I said, "Well, you're a little bit of both. Your father was born Christian and your mother was born Jewish, so you're half and half." He looked down at his body and he said, "Well, which half is which?" He was looking for a physical line, and he thought there was some way he could define who he was by looking at himself and seeing that one half was one thing and one half was something else, which I thought was very cute.

It was hard to explain all this to the boys when they were really young. But the older they've become, the more we have tried to talk to them about how we feel. We'll say, "Your dad and I don't really believe in this, but we know lots of people who do. If you're interested in pursuing it, we'll help you. If you want to go to temple, you can go with your aunt and uncle. If you're interested in seeing what church is about, you can go with your grandmother. We're not telling you that you shouldn't believe. We're just telling you that we can't help you with this because your father and I don't believe."

I know that sometimes I impose my own views on the boys without really wanting to. I'll be watching the news, and there will be some other ethnic war breaking out somewhere or other, and I'll make a comment in front of them that I later regret. I'll say something like, "That's what religion does." My own views do come out. I realize that I am influencing them, but then I think families who do take their little kids to temple or to church are influencing them in the ways they believe as well. The children aren't old enough to come to their own decisions. They're doing what their parents do. I don't want to impose too much on my kids, but I think it's natural that I am going to influence them with my views and perspectives. And the same is true with Craig. So these children are going to know how mommy and daddy feel.

Both sides of the family are somewhat accepting of what Craig and I believe, but that's not to say they don't have issues with the way we're raising our children. I think Craig's mother would prefer to see us raise our kids in a religion, particularly in her religion, although frankly I think she would feel more comfortable with us picking either one rather than having none. She has pretty much said that at times. But I think at this point she knows it's not a possibility, so she doesn't mention it anymore.

As far as my family goes, there has been some difficulty with my sister and her husband. I know that when my sister moved to this city, she envisioned our families celebrating the High Holidays and Passover together and doing all the food preparation, and it didn't happen like that. My sister married someone who was raised Orthodox, and especially early on when they first moved here, he and I had some conflicts. One issue was the fact that Craig and I had started the tradition of having a tree in our house for the holidays. Craig was sort of excited by the idea of having a tree, and I guess I was too. I never had one, and I thought they were pretty. I always felt a little bit excluded with my Christian friends who grew up with a tree. So initially I thought, "It sounds fun. And it's something I would have wanted as a kid. Let's do it." And of course it was something Craig always had as a child. I was a little bit uncomfortable with the idea. But we went ahead and did it.

At first we called it a solstice tree. That's a pagan term celebrating the changing of light and the season. We tried to explain it to our kids. "We're bringing this tree into the house in the middle of winter, and we're putting lights on it to symbolize that even though it is cold and dark now and there's not much greenery or flowers around, spring will be coming soon." Nobody let us get away with calling it a solstice tree for very long. People would say, "Oh, your kids don't understand what solstice is. It's a Christmas tree."

My sister's husband was very offended by the tree. He said, "You know, you're Jewish. How come you're letting this Christian symbol in the house?" I would go into the history of what the tree was and its pagan origins, and it didn't matter to him. He thought this was a betrayal. And my sister had problems with the fact that we had a Christmas tree but we didn't have a Hanukkah menorah. She would say, "You're celebrating Craig's traditions. Why do you let him dominate?" But to me the Hanukkah menorah was much more of a religious symbol. It has to do with faith in God and the miracle of the lights and the oil, and I couldn't deal with any of that. With the tree, I didn't connect it to a deity. I was able to make the distinction more.

I got the sense that my sister and her husband were sitting in judgment of Craig and me. It wasn't pleasant, and what made it even harder is that her husband had gone a step further by saying that because of the Holocaust, it was more incumbent upon Jewish people to preserve their traditions. He said we owed it to the people who perished to continue the Jewish traditions. That's a real low blow. I can care just as much and I have been committed to working on Holocaust projects, and I'm very much politically aware of what happened back then. I've also made sure my children know about the Holocaust. We have read a number of books about it. I've told them that if they had been living in particular places in Europe at that time, they would have been exterminated. I know that sounds harsh, but I think it's important for them to really understand what happened.

Some people think that the only way to teach morality is to have your kids belong to a religion and adopt a certain set of religious beliefs. I believe that you can teach morals, and about what's good or bad, without the framework of a religion. Craig and I are trying to raise our children with humanistic values. Our kids know about right and wrong. The only grounding they don't have really is that there is a God. They know that some people do believe in God and that He or She accepts a lot of religions. But they know their mom and dad don't really believe that.

Craig and I do feel sort of alone sometimes. We're the only people we know that don't subscribe to a set of religious beliefs. There are no other couples we know of who have children and who have decided to do the same thing that we're doing, which is basically nothing. When our kids were younger, I sometimes struggled with the lack of a sense of community. I think for a lot of people that is what religion offers them, and in the beginning I felt left out of that. The schools in our area are all closed on the Jewish High Holidays. I would see families walking to temple with each other and having someplace to go. And of course that's what I did as a child. So it stirred up all those memories. I think at the beginning I felt left out, sort of lost and a bit adrift. I've been a parent for almost thirteen years now, and that feeling has lessened. I am more comfortable with the insecurity and the vagueness of not having a defined spiritual path.

I don't know if this will change, but so far my kids haven't really expressed a need for anything further in terms of religious participation. It might be different as they get older. It remains to be seen how they are going to handle all this. But I think that because they are exposed a little bit to both traditions, and because we've talked so much about it, they don't really feel too lost. One thing I do know is that I would never say the kinds of things to my kids that my parents said to me, about how it is better to marry certain kinds of people. I think I would feel pretty comfortable with whomever they choose, because I view people as people. I really do. I don't think there are that many important differences deep down between us. I think we are all basically good people and we all share a lot of common traits, and I guess that's what I always look for. At the same time, I'm aware of the differences, but I think that's what makes things interesting.

Allan and his wife are both therapists. When he was growing up, religion was not a big part of Allan's life. But as part of an interfaith marriage he felt a need to define himself more in terms of his religion. Allan realized that if he wanted his children to learn something about their heritage on his side of the family, they were going to have to learn it from him.

✖ ALLAN

* * *

My father was Jewish. His family two generations earlier came over from Russia, and a number of my great uncles and aunts spoke Yiddish in heavy Eastern European accents. My father, being born here in the States and trying to succeed in business, did his best I think to distance himself from observance.

* * *

He married somebody from a mixed background. My mother's mother was Jewish and her father was Italian-Catholic. My mother technically would be called Jewish and at one point had a Jewish confirmation, although her family was hardly practicing. And yet in a different period her parents sent her to a Lutheran Sunday school. So, in reality, her family did all manner of things.

When I was growing up, I had no real religious identity. We always had a tree for Christmas. I was not bar mitzvahed, so I got to stay out after school and play football with all the Catholic boys while my other friends were off going to Hebrew school. My aunts would take responsibility for Passover, and we would go to a seder each year at one of their houses. We did a minimal amount of celebrating of the High Holidays, and we did that much only because at one time in first grade I came home from school and said, "Boy, those Jews really have it easy. They get Christmas off, and they get to take these other holidays off too." My father said, "You're Jewish, and from now on, you're taking those holidays off too." And that was my awakening to the fact that I was one religion or the other.

I've been married twice. My first wife was Jewish. I was divorced from her after six years. I met Judy at work after my first marriage broke up, over twenty years ago. Judy is Catholic but not practicing. Religion was pretty much a nonissue for us. We probably talked briefly about kids and kind of said, "We'll deal with that when the time comes." Our two daughters are now fourteen and sixteen. When they were born, I really wasn't that invested in having them be one religion or the other. I felt willing to be pretty open and flexible up to a point. But there was a line that I always knew I wasn't going to cross, which is that I couldn't let my kids be raised as Christians. I wasn't willing to go that far. Judy had her own line, and it was, "Okay, they won't be Christian, but they won't be raised Jewish either."

We tried dabbling around with a few things. We sent the girls to an Ethical Humanist Sunday school for a while. Politically, that was pretty acceptable to both of us, but my wife felt they weren't really getting much in the way of religious instruction, so after about a year and a half we gave that up. Then we tried a Unitarian Fellowship. We were looking for a compromise position. The reason we wanted to do anything at all is that we both kind of wanted to give our kids more of a background and more of a sense of cultural heritage. We were looking for some connection with a culture, with a people, and with a history that extended beyond our two hundred years here in the United States.

About ten or eleven years ago, my dad died. Probably as a result of that, it kind of dawned on me that if my kids were going to connect to anything and feel like a part of anything, I couldn't rely on someone else to make it happen. I was the senior male of the family now. I guess I had to grow up and say, "If I want this to happen, I'm going to have to do it for myself."

I started going to High Holiday services at different synagogues. Judy and the kids would occasionally go with me. I wasn't trying to impose anything on them. We would go together, but it was really for me. I wanted to have more of a grounding in Judaism so that I could be more available to give our daughters information about their heritage and answer their questions. When they said, "Dad, tell me about this," I didn't want to have to keep saying, "I don't know."

I looked for a synagogue that I liked. A friend tried to hook me into a Reconstructionist synagogue, but despite the fact that I liked its political leanings, it was way too conservative for me. It was also very hard for me to take my wife there, since a lot of the service is done in Hebrew. I ultimately found a Reform synagogue that I have started going to. I haven't joined it yet, but I do contribute to it. I've taken a couple of classes there. I've also done a ton of reading. I have a shelf that is basically filled with books about Jewish history and culture, and those were all accumulated and read in the last five years.

Being in an interfaith marriage, if anything, has forced me to find myself. In my previous marriage, I didn't have to define myself as a Jew. People did it for me. I was a part of a Jewish marriage. I was a part of a Jewish family. I would go visit my in-laws and we would celebrate Jewish things. But it wasn't until I said I wanted to be more Jewish that I was really able to do it.

The major issue for Judy and me is that we kind of grew together in a very enmeshed relationship. We are both professors. From the time we met, we have done the same things, believed in a lot of the same ideas, and had the same politics. I think there was an unspoken fear that if one of us explored some place that the other one didn't want to go, it would be hard on us as a couple. This was clearly something Judy wasn't going to join in. But I ventured out, and it didn't become threatening to her. Our relationship remained stable. If I had become more interested in Conservative Judaism, it might have been harder. As it is, she feels very comfortable going with me to the Reform synagogue on the High Holidays.

So far, all I really do is go to High Holiday services. I haven't done too much else yet. It's not that I won't. It's just that I haven't. We started for a while actually celebrating Shabbat, but the kids were already at that age where Friday night was sacrosanct for them. One daughter is in high school, and the other is about to be. Friday night is when they meet with their friends. It was hard to maintain Shabbat, and I didn't feel that it was enough a part of who we were as a family that I was going to force the issue. But we still do pick up a loaf of challah on Friday to have with dinner.

There are other things I'd like to do. I'd like to do some more studying. If I were better at languages, I'd like to learn some Hebrew. And sometime in the next few years, I'd like to go to Israel with my family. I went there twice when I was in college. Part of the reason I'd like to go is to see what's changed in thirty years. And part of it is that there is heritage there for all of us.

I know my younger daughter in particular is very interested in her Jewish history. She studied the Holocaust this year, and I know she's been doing a lot of thinking about it. I can see her, when she is ready, picking up the pieces of her heritage so that she can begin to learn from them.

Jenny is a nurse/midwife. She grew up in one of Chicago's ethnic neighborhoods. Jenny and her husband Bruce both wanted a chance to share aspects of their own religious backgrounds with their children. At the same time, they really did not want to raise their kids to be a part of two religions. So eventually Jenny came up with a unique idea, which they decided to try.

✴ JENNY (TO BE FOLLOWED BY HER HUSBAND, BRUCE)

* * *

As a child, Catholicism was somewhat of a comfort to me. My home life was kind of screwed up. My mother was an alcoholic. It was not an easy time, so one of the ways I could really feel better about myself was to be a good Catholic girl. I could go to daily Mass and do the kinds of things that were pretty much universally regarded as good things. Being a good Catholic was a way in which I could feel more positively about myself, and it is something I felt very, very connected to.

* * *

Up until the time I went to college, my religion and my life were totally intertwined. There wasn't any demarcation between one and the other. I grew up in a neighborhood that was almost entirely Catholic. My friends were almost entirely Catholic. I attended Catholic schools all the way through high school. All of my teachers during my formative years were nuns. And as it happened, I had very good teachers. They were wonderful, strong, bright women, and so that was a big piece of me. I went to a Catholic university, but at that point I started to cut back on going to church. And in college I began meeting all kinds of people. I was definitely somewhat intrigued by people who were different from me.

I met Bruce at a college graduation party. Bruce was raised Jewish in a pretty Conservative home. Was he involved in a synagogue? Not at all. Did he go to services? Three times a year. But did he celebrate Shabbat? Every single Friday. His family always had Shabbat dinner at home. There is no question that he very much identified himself as Jewish.

I had no idea Bruce was Jewish until we had gone out a couple of times. I said something about a ring he had on, and he told me he had gotten it for his bar mitzvah. I guess I just assumed he was Catholic, or at least Christian. His name isn't obviously Jewish, and nothing about his appearance is either. So it's not like there were any hints.

Even in the first couple of months, we began to get pretty serious about each other. And then Bruce one day in the course of discussion said, "Well, I would never marry somebody who was not Jewish." I was really pissed. "What the hell do you think you're doing here? Why would you even date me? It's not that I'm necessarily interested in marrying you. It's just . . . why would you even do this?" I thought it was the most inconsistent thing I had ever heard of, and I thought it was very disrespectful to me. So that was a pretty hard moment.

It was also kind of a wake-up call. This was my first indication that even though Bruce and I seemed to have similar feelings about our religions, the way he thought about things and the way I thought about things were somewhat different. My attitude was, "What difference does it really make?" At the time, I had very little appreciation of what kind of family and social pressure he was under about all this.

We still kept seeing each other. Bruce spent some time talking to people about our relationship and gradually began to rethink his position on marrying someone who wasn't Jewish. I was reassessing things myself, and there was even a time when I thought I could possibly consider the idea of conversion. I had way more spiritual curiosity than Bruce did, and I was open to trying something different. We actually went to see a rabbi. But there wasn't enough to motivate me to make a change. Bruce wasn't interested in learning more about Judaism or becoming more active. He basically said, "This is who I am." So if I went through a conversion process, it wasn't something we would be thinking about together. I would have to do everything on my own. Besides, even though Bruce seemed to want me to convert, I honestly couldn't figure out why. His feelings didn't seem to come from any kind of real belief system. So I just decided not to pursue it.

We finally decided to get married. Even at this point, we didn't actually talk about kids. We were more just thinking about ourselves and what we would do for a wedding and things like that. We never really did talk about kids in any great depth.

Bruce really wanted to get married by a rabbi, so I said, "Fine." It didn't make any difference to me. We did go through the Catholic Church to get a dispensation in order to be married. I definitely still felt Catholic, and that was something I wanted to do. And we found one of those fly-by-night rabbis to marry us, whom I wasn't crazy about. I had gotten a copy of the *Jewish Catalogue*, and I kind of followed that to plan the wedding. I pretty much wrote the service myself. There was nothing from Catholicism that was incorporated, because what I didn't want to end up with was kind of a mishmash of parts that didn't really go together. The one thing I wanted to do on the morning of my wedding was to go to church with my dad. We went to Mass together. That was something I cared about doing on the day of my wedding, and I was glad I did it. It felt right to go.

Religion was pretty much a nonissue when we first were married. And then I got pregnant. And of course it became much more of an issue because we started thinking, "What are we going to do when we have this kid?" Bruce was still very uninterested in doing all that much in terms of Judaism, and so I felt it was grossly unfair for him to have such strong opinions, which he definitely did have, regarding the religion of children. He wanted our children to be Jewish. Period. And meanwhile, I was beginning to look at myself a little bit more and think, "You know, even though I did consider conversion at one point, I'm really not sure that I am capable of changing this part of me. My beliefs are kind of diffuse, but culturally I'm very much a Catholic." That part of me wasn't something that I was sure I could change or wanted to change. It seemed like it was so much a part of me that if I changed it, I wasn't sure what else would change along with it.

So then Simon was born, and because he was a boy, it kind of put the issue right there on the table. "Do we do a bris or not?" And Bruce said, "Well, we're planning to circumcise him anyway. We've only got one eighth day, and if we don't do it then, the decision is made. But if we do it on the eighth day, the decision may or may not be made." So I said, "Okay." There wasn't any question of a mohel doing it. I barely knew there was such a thing at the time. Bruce's dad is a doctor, so he just arranged for one of the urologists at the hospital to do it. We had a rabbi who came to the hospital and said some prayers, and that seemed fine.

There was no question of having Simon baptized. That was something I knew Bruce would not even consider. One of my concerns about this was that I had a brother who died of crib death in the '50s. He died prior to being baptized. This was a huge issue at the time because the feeling was that if babies aren't baptized, they don't go to heaven. They go instead to this place called *limbo*. So the fact that my brother died without being baptized was a very big deal. It was so upsetting that when my parents found the baby blue in the crib, the first thing my father did was baptize him. The second thing he did was call the fire department. I mean, that's how important a thing it was.

I actually thought it would bother me more that we didn't have Simon baptized, but somehow doing the little religious ceremony for the bris was enough for the time being. I figured we could always have him baptized at a later time. Besides, my sister baby-sat for Simon once, and when I picked him up she said, "You don't have to worry anymore. I baptized him." I said, "Give me a break. You can't baptize him if I don't want you to." I'm sure she did it, but in my mind it didn't really count because it wasn't something I wanted her to do.

I assumed that even if Simon didn't have any formal Catholic education, the Catholicism would just come through because it's so much a part of who I am. I thought he would just sort of get it. I decided I had more of a responsibility to kind of buff up the Judaism side. We joined a temple, and I got involved with Hadassah and started doing some volunteer things. Simon was in a local nursery school, and at Hanukkah we would bring in dreidels and I would make latkes for everyone. Simon seemed to become more and more convinced that he was Jewish.

We just kept going along, and periodically we did talk about religion. We still weren't sure what we were going to do as Simon got older, or how we were going to handle things. Then when Simon was two and a half, we had a set of twins, a boy and a girl. Because Simon had been circumcised on the eighth day, our son Gary was too. We did it the same way. The rabbi came to the hospital. So Gary had a bris. But we didn't do anything at all with Julie, our daughter.

By the time the twins were born, I knew my husband a lot better. I understood more of his feelings about Judaism. A movie had been on about the Holocaust and after watching that he said to me, "This is why it feels so important to me for my kids to be Jewish. It's just that I feel a responsibility to continue things." I knew what he was saying. But at this same time I was realizing that what my spiritual searching over the years had kind of led me to was a feeling of very much wanting to reconfirm the value of my own upbringing, and what it meant to me, and my own cultural identity.

I certainly didn't believe in a lot of the dogma of Catholicism. But I didn't think that culturally it was something that I wanted to give up or change. It kind of became apparent to me that there was still something in me that couldn't say, "Okay, go ahead and raise the kids Jewish." Maybe it was just a kind of selfishness on my part, but I wanted to be able to pass down a lot of the good things that I had gotten from my own religion. I wasn't sure that I could let my kids be Jewish and act like a good person about it. And I think that is probably the bottom line. I did not want to do something in my life that would make me angry and resentful. I was afraid it would lead to real problems in my marriage. My mother was a resentful, angry woman, and I didn't want to be like her. So I wasn't sure what to do.

I was very comfortable raising Simon Jewish, because it seemed like he was already going so much in that direction. But I wasn't comfortable saying, "Okay, all the kids can be Jewish." So then I asked Bruce, "What if the boys are Jewish and Julie is Catholic?" Well, Bruce thought about it and decided it was something he could live with. So that was the solution we settled on.

Both of the boys had already had brises. So what we did was, we had Julie baptized. The boys went through Jewish religious schools. They both had bar mitzvahs and they both have been confirmed. Julie went through the catechism programs and had a Catholic education all the way through high school. She did First Communion, confirmation—all of it.

Even though our sons and our daughter had different religious training, at home everything was very blended. There were no boundaries inside of our house. For instance, all of our holidays have always been done in a very family way, and I think the kids connected to every holiday equally. We have a Christmas tree, and we also do Hanukkah. Everybody got Hanukkah presents, and everybody got Christmas presents. At Passover there is no bread in the house. Easter always falls around the same time as Passover, and of course Easter is one of my family's holidays. So when my relatives come for Easter, I have a large variety of menus. I have Passover menus that can also work for Easter. On Fridays during Lent we don't eat meat. And on Fridays during Lent when it's Passover, we don't eat bread or meat. So we observe things together.

Julie's First Communion was a big deal. It was no bar mitzvah. The bar mitzvahs were huge events. But nonetheless we made it a big deal. And because Julie and Gary are twins, at Gary's bar mitzvah we allowed Julie to pick out something special for herself that we called "a jealousy present," because Gary was getting so many gifts.

We all do the same thing. We all go together to the temple or the church for the holidays. And there has never been a time where we have said, "Well, Julie, you have to go to school, but the boys can be off." They've all done everything together. They all have the same opportunities. They're now in college or beyond, and they all have the same opportunities to come home for holidays, regardless of what the holiday is.

I have to say that both Bruce and I participated in the religious education of our children. That wasn't true at first. When the kids were still little, I had started going to church again on a fairly regular basis. Simon was in about first or second grade, and I was taking him to religious school at the temple every Sunday morning and then trying to get to church myself. But lots of times there would be some activity at his Sunday school, and I would stay to help. Bruce would be home reading the paper. I finally said, "Excuse me, this is going to change. You want this, and you better make sure you're there." So he started taking Simon to Sunday school each week. He actually became very involved in the synagogue and was even treasurer, and then president, for a couple of terms. He became a part of the community. And a door opened to him that I'm not sure would have opened if he had married somebody who was Jewish and hadn't been forced to get more involved.

Julie and Gary are twenty now, and Simon is twenty-three. The one with probably the stronger Jewish development is Gary. Simon is a little bit more ambivalent. All of Simon's girlfriends have been Catholic. Julie is very divided. She most often calls herself half Catholic and half Jewish. Julie's boyfriend is Jewish. She has often talked about what would happen if she were to marry someone Catholic. Because we have always done everything together as a family, she has grown to enjoy the Jewish holidays as much as the Christian ones. She feels she would lose a lot if she didn't have Judaism along with Catholicism in her life. When she was only about ten, and we were on our way to a Rosh Hashanah service, she said to me, "Wait a minute. What happens if I marry somebody who is not Jewish? Will I still be able to celebrate Rosh Hashanah?" I said, "Well, you know, you'll always have your brothers and your dad."

I think my kids are all somewhat confused about their identity. I really don't think Bruce and I accomplished what we set out to do. Looking at it now, I think what we both wanted was to bring to our kids that treasured part of our childhood that says, "This is who you are. There is no doubt about it. This is who you are, lock, stock, and barrel. You are connected to this. It is who you are." We wanted to give to each child a strong religious and cultural identity. We could give them the theological part, but we couldn't give them a really pure cultural experience because it just wasn't there. I could not raise Julie with the same Catholic upbringing that I received. I couldn't even give her that sense of identity because it is not as pure around her. Both Bruce and I are too present in this family for the kids to get only one culture or the other. Everything is too blended. There is just no way around it. So instead of a message that said to them, "This is who you are," they came out with the message, "This is who you are, but you're also this." That isn't what either of us was trying to do. Each of our children ended up with something totally different than we had anticipated. It's something that I think is valuable and worthwhile, but it wasn't what I think either of us intended.

Bruce is a design engineer. He also grew up in the Chicago area, but in one of the suburbs. Bruce told me he would not necessarily recommend that other couples raise their kids the way he and Jenny did. But still, in some ways he does seem comfortable with how things turned out.

染 BRUCE (PRECEDED BY HIS WIFE, JENNY)

* * *

I think there is value in having a religious component in a family. It adds something to your life. It gives you something to hold on to. It is one thing that is pretty constant. So with that said, I think it is better if everybody is marching to the same tune. Because if you're hoping to reduce conflict and reduce ambiguity, having a family in which everybody is the same religion means there is one less thing to worry about.

* * *

I grew up in a neighborhood that was sixty or seventy percent Jewish. My friends were predominantly Jewish. My father said Kiddish every Friday night, and my mother was president of the sisterhood at the synagogue. We all went to Hebrew school. We celebrated the holidays with family and friends.

Possibly the only oddity in our life as a Jewish family is that my uncle on my mother's side always had a very large family party on Christmas Day. He even had a Christmas tree. It annoyed my father, but I just viewed it as our Hanukkah party because that's when we all exchanged Hanukkah gifts. I never viewed it as a Christian thing. Although when I met my wife and told her about it, she said, "You're opening presents around a tree on Christmas Day. Of course it is a Christmas party."

I'm the only one in my family who married somebody who wasn't Jewish. I can't tell you why, other than I didn't socialize that much. I didn't date a lot in high school or in college. Jenny was the first person I dated seriously, and I would say that contributed as much as anything else.

It was definitely a big issue to me that Jenny wasn't Jewish. I did say to her at one point that I wouldn't marry anybody who was not Jewish. My guess is that if I had pursued it, she would have converted. We did go as far as seeing a rabbi, and we talked about conversion. And my wife made lots of overtures. She participated in Jewish holidays. She joined Hadassah. It was probably my laziness and my not pursuing it that made her not do it. I wasn't real active in terms of Judaism. I kept up with the holidays, but I didn't do Sabbath things. I wasn't involved in a synagogue. I guess I always assumed that Jenny would just convert without me even doing anything. Anyhow, we continued dating for a year and a half or so. I never asked her to marry me, and she is the one who forced the issue. By that time, I wasn't willing to lose her. And so we decided to get married.

I always knew I would want to be married by a rabbi, and I knew that keeping a Jewish home was something I cared about. I think that for Jenny, religion has sort of gone in and out of importance in her life. But whether I practice it or not, my Judaism has always been extremely important and close to me. I have never rejected the notion of it, and I have always felt that it was a very, very big part of me. Why I didn't pursue a Jewish marriage, I don't know. That's probably a topic for years of discussion with a therapist.

Jenny and I never really talked much about kids. Like a lot of other people, we said, "Well, we'll work that out later. It won't be an issue." Of course, once we had our first child, Simon, we had numerous discussions, debates, and fights. A big part of the way in which we finally came to the conclusion we did is that we couldn't decide what to do. We both felt that we appreciated each other's holidays, and each other's background, and so we said, "Okay, we'll split the kids in half and we'll raise our daughter Catholic and the boys Jewish." We just kind of fell into it.

Even though the boys were given a Jewish education and Julie had a Catholic education, there have been a few of what I would call "crossover" events. Our temple has a retreat each year, and when the kids were younger we started going as a family. They would have all kinds of events at the retreat, and Julie would participate in them with her brother Gary. And then when Gary was in sixth grade, his class had their own retreat. Julie knew a lot of the kids going and was interested in the whole thing. So I asked the educators in charge if it would be possible for Julie to go along on the retreat with Gary. They were very creative and open people, and they said she could go. So Julie participated as an equal, if you will. There was even a big Havdalah service at the end of the weekend, and Julie was able to have a part in it.

The interesting thing is that I think my daughter actively participates in both holidays and both religions more than the boys do, although the boys have often said that they are going to celebrate all of the holidays forever. But I just see that my daughter tends to really understand and know the Jewish holidays probably better than my boys understand and know the Catholic holidays. She really knows something about them.

We tried to give all of our children an appreciation for honoring and observing and understanding each other's traditions. I think that's what made our family work. We never said that any part of one religion was better than any part of the other. Everything was done equally and with respect. The really difficult thing, though, is to say that along with participating equally in all the holidays, each of our kids was also able to maintain a religious identity of his or her own. That's the part we're not as sure about.

It is very important to me to see Judaism survive and continue on. If that is a concern for someone, then raising your kids in a family like I did opens you up for a loss. You know, my boys have less attraction to Judaism than I did even at their age and certainly less than I do now. Maybe later they'll come to it more. I don't know. They never really dated Jewish kids or tried to seek them out as friends. Chances are they probably won't marry Jewish girls either. And that would be a loss for me. That's the piece that for me would be the most difficult. It's just something to think about when you make this kind of choice.

Carol is a college professor. She is in her late forties or early fifties, and she grew up in New Jersey. Carol clearly feels that she and her husband have very different needs when it comes to spirituality and family.

✖ CAROL

* * *

I have to say that Dan has definitely been the dominating force regarding religion in our family. He is totally opposed to organized religion. His area is history, and he's got it all down pat. He brings up all the negative religious times in history, like the Crusades. And personally, I feel like he has never had a positive religious experience that he felt he wanted to pass on.

* * *

I met Dan the first day of college. We started going together right away. Dan's Jewish. My family is Catholic. I went to Catholic school through fifth grade and then to public school after that. The reason I stopped is that the nuns were pretty brutal, and even though my parents liked the idea of a Catholic education, eventually they decided enough was enough.

Dan and I were together a long time before we got married. I remember we would talk about having kids and what we might do with them in terms of religion. We basically put off deciding and just said, "Well, we'll work it out." When we did finally decide to get married, the period leading up to our wedding was an emotionally chaotic time. Dan really wanted to just have a justice of the peace, but my family was so against it, and I was afraid of crossing them. We ended up being married by a minister of the Assembly of God. The wedding was at a little historic chapel at a state park in Connecticut. It was a beautiful park, with this really old white clapboard church. I thought it would be perfect, but it ended up causing some problems. A few days before the ceremony, it suddenly became an issue that there was a big cross right in the front of the church. I think that maybe Dan realized it was there and told his mother about it. His mother became very upset that their family was going to come in and there would be a cross. So we spent two days of wondering if we could get something to cover it up. But of course that would be really insulting to my family. Then there were a few days when we thought, "Why did we ever agree to get married? We should have just kept putting it off." It was very difficult. I'm not sure how we decided, but we ended up with the cross not being covered. The wedding ceremony itself was very short. And that was it.

There are things about Catholicism that I really dislike. I have a problem with a lot of the teachings. Even going into a Catholic church makes me feel guilty and weird. But still there is something that is important to me about having a religion and a connection with God. I like what I know about Judaism and told Dan I could consider converting. He told me there were a lot of negative aspects to Judaism that I didn't know about. He said it really discriminates against women. So I started looking into different types of churches. I tried some Protestant ones that seemed okay. And at some point I went to a Unitarian church. Either of those could have been nice for me. I think I could have gotten something out of either of them. But I didn't join either of them.

There is one element that has colored my feelings about participating in religion since I've been with Dan, and it puts him in a bad light. Maybe if I told him how I felt, he would say, "Oh, I never meant it that way." There have been times when I felt I wanted to go to church, like on Christmas or Easter. I just wanted to go. Those are moving times to me, and the services are special events that I wanted to be a part of. Dan would always make fun of me because I wanted to go to church. And he would do it enough that I would stop wanting to go. I'm sure if I said that to him now, he'd say, "Oh, you know I was just kidding, and you took it too seriously." But he always made me feel foolish. "How stupid of me to want to go to church."

I have definitely felt a loss as a result of not being really involved in a religion. I think it is easier to deal with until you have children, and then it gets very difficult. Once I had children, I felt that I wanted to at least have some expression. I wanted to celebrate holidays and keep up some of the traditions. Dan just doesn't seem to be interested in traditions at all, which is very hard for me, and he pokes fun at me for wanting to have them. It is very difficult to get him to join in. At Easter I like to color eggs with the kids. Dan might grudgingly do one, but it is always clear that he doesn't want to be involved. Christmas of course is hard, although recently Dan started helping the kids and me decorate. Christmas is the most difficult holiday for him because of the whole idea of the birth of Christ. I look at that as just a nice tender little story. I never portray to the kids that Christ is the son of God or anything like that. I talk about him more in the way that other religions view him, as being sort of a really special enlightened person.

I always wanted to teach the kids not just about my traditions but about the traditions in Judaism as well. Some years we would do both Christmas and Hanukkah, but the thing is I had to do the Hanukkah part too. I know so little about Judaism. I would try and read about the holiday, and I'd ask my friends about it. Dan really didn't want to do anything. So the years we did it, we would just do a little bit. It was always me making it happen and trying to drag some information out of him. "Tell me about Hanukkah." Last year on Purim, some people I work with gave me a little gift with hamantaschen, and I brought it home. We had it on the table and the kids were asking about it. I said, "Dan, tell us about Purim. You know about this holiday. Tell us." But it isn't something he wanted to do.

It's hard because we don't have any family here. Occasionally we have been invited to someone's house for one holiday or another. There were a few years where we did Passover with friends, and I thought it was wonderful. I loved it. It was just great. I remember also a few years back when our kids were pretty young that we were invited to a Purim party. Everyone dressed up. It was just a lot of fun.

Each year at Christmas, I say I'm going to take the kids to church. When they were younger it really didn't happen. And now that they're older, they would have to be choosing between Dan and me. They'd be stuck in the middle. They see choosing to go to Mass with me as siding against Dan.

They are very sensitive to his feelings. They don't want to hurt either of us. I just don't want to put them in that position.

There has definitely been pressure from my family to at least raise the kids in one religion or the other. My sister, who is very religious, is always pushing us. "Raise them to be Jewish. They need to have something." My parents took more direct actions. I didn't baptize our kids when they were born. My parents eventually told me that they had baptized each of the children on their own. You can just do it yourself, and part of me knew that the minute I left them alone with a baby, that is what they would do. You just use water and you do the prayers. Then you save the soul. When my mother told me about baptizing them, she said that all she could see were these poor babies' souls in limbo. It was just so painful for her. Part of me was so angry that they did that, but basically I considered it to be pretty meaningless, so I didn't really care.

We go back to visit my family a couple of times a year in New Jersey, and each time we go, there is actually a lot of tension. We are usually there on the weekend. At the beginning when we went, the kids and I would go to church with everybody, and sometimes Dan would come too. Then eventually he stopped. This is the aspect that is really the most difficult issue for me now. My mother wasn't always able to go to church when I was a kid. At this point in her life, going to church with her family is an extremely big deal to her. So for me it is a very stressful, horrible situation because I always feel like I'm choosing. I choose to be with Dan, or I choose to be with my parents and my siblings. I feel like it is a very awkward, awful choice that I have to make. When the kids were little I would just take them with me. But now there are times when the children don't want to go either, and that to me is the absolute worst. Then I have to decide if I should stay home with them or go with my mother. It's really awful. It's always such a struggle for me because I see my parents only twice a year, and this is important to them.

There is another dimension to all this, which is that when we are visiting my family, and I have to make that choice, I don't want my family to say, "I told you so." I don't want them to say, "Your husband won't support your religion. We told you this would be a mistake and that this wouldn't be a good marriage for you. Welcome back. We knew you would come back eventually." Part of me thinks that if I go to church with them too much, that's what would happen. So that's something I'm fighting as well.

Dan and I have had fights over this in the past because I feel it would be so much easier for me if he would just come with me. "Just be there. It would make my life so much easier." But, no, he can't do that. Actually, the very last time we went to visit my family was the worst. I really regret the decision I made. What happened is that my sister is married to a man whose uncle is a priest. Father Mathew conducts all the weddings and baptisms in the family. He will sometimes do a special Mass at my sister's house on Sunday, which is considered to be a big honor. Last year when we went to visit, Father Mathew did the Mass at my sister's house and I went by myself. Dan and the kids stayed back in the hotel room. I felt horrible. I really wanted them with me. It was even more of a difficult thing because I felt it was an insult to my sister for them not to come. I knew she had probably arranged the Mass because of our visit. This year when we went back to visit, Father Mathew again came to do the Mass. But this time, I just didn't feel I could go without Dan and the kids. So none of us went. I made up this big excuse. It was awful. We all walked in when the Mass was over, and everyone was clearly mad at me and felt that I had snubbed them. They were right. Here was this family member doing a special Mass for us. So it's just a very difficult situation for me.

It's a shame. I feel sorry that being with my side of the family has become so awful. I think that what I have to do is work it out so our visits don't involve a Sunday. It's just too hard otherwise. And I know this has all been pretty confusing to our kids. I feel sad because I think there are some really positive things that can be gotten from religion, which just haven't been passed on to them.

Barbara is in her forties. She grew up in the Boston area. Barbara and her husband don't really care about providing their children with religious experiences. They just want them to have good values. But for some of their relatives, that isn't enough.

✄ BARBARA

* * *

I guess you'd say our family was pretty religious. Our house was kosher. My mother used to make really nice dinners for all the Jewish holidays. She worked so hard for them. And for Passover, she would make sure to do every last thing you're supposed to do. She definitely did more than anybody else I know.

* * *

I started out going to a Jewish day school, but eventually I changed to a different school because I didn't like it. I didn't like being in such a totally

Jewish world. As I got older, nobody ever said I should only go out with Jewish boys, but I think that's why my parents had us at the day school. Some parents think that if they make sure you're with Jews most of the time, you'll only date Jewish people. But it's not true. You'll meet people at all kinds of places.

Jay and I met when I was in the tenth grade. He's Irish Catholic, but he had no strong religious beliefs. It didn't bother me at all that he wasn't Jewish because religion to me is just not an issue. It's an issue to my family but it isn't to me. Jay and I started spending time together. I didn't tell my parents about him because I knew they'd be really upset. My mother met him once but didn't know he was anyone important to me. And then what happened is that my mother passed away. She had a heart attack and she died. By that time, she knew I was seeing him, but it was never talked about.

I didn't go to college. I started to work. I became friends with a number of other people who weren't Jewish. Most of the people I knew when I was younger were Jews, so they are the ones I was originally friends with. But I never really was very comfortable with the Jewish friends. I didn't like the way they acted or the ways their parents acted. And once I started to pick friends on my own, none of them were Jewish.

Jay and I were together a long time before we got married. Since my mother had passed away, religion meant even less to me. It was something I just didn't want to deal with. I finally told my father about my relationship with Jay, and fortunately he got smart about it pretty quickly. I had said to him that if he wanted to be a part of my life, he would have to accept us. And that's what he did.

We were married by a Jewish justice of the peace. He wore a yarmulke, and he had us do the breaking of the glass. But he wasn't a rabbi. He was just a justice of the peace who happened to be Jewish. We paid him a little extra for the yarmulke and the glass. We didn't do those things for me. None of it was for me. It was basically just to please my father.

Jay and I have three sons. They all had brises, and again, it was because it made my father happy. Jay's mother had already passed away, and his father wasn't a part of his life, so we didn't have to worry about any Christian rituals. We do always go to Jay's sister's house for dinner on Easter. And we put out lights and have a tree at our house for Christmas. It's not for anything religious. My husband just likes the look of a tree. He likes having it. To me, it's a big mess to have it and clean it all up. But I do it because he likes it. I do things for him, and he does things for me.

Jay goes with me to my brother's house for the Jewish holidays. I like to go because all of my family is there. I'll have Thanksgiving at our house, but I don't make the dinners for the Jewish holidays. I know I'm not really practicing Judaism, and it wouldn't feel right. It's been getting harder and harder to go to these dinners at my brother's house because some of my relatives are extremely critical of me. They think I should be leading a much more Jewish life than I am. My older brother and his wife think it's terrible that we have a tree. They're upset that my children don't go to Hebrew School. They're very judgmental. And I think their attitude pushes me farther away from wanting my kids to do anything Jewish.

Jay and I honestly don't care about raising our sons in a religion. We just want them to be nice boys. We want them to be good to others. We want them to do well in school so they can get somewhere in their lives. I have actually thought about having a bar mitzvah for my oldest son. He'll be thirteen next February. Some of his friends have been getting bar mitzvahed. Also, he and his cousin are exactly the same age, and she is having her bat mitzvah soon. I'm afraid he might feel that he's missing something by not having one.

I've been thinking about the bar mitzvah for a while. I even got my son started in Hebrew school. But I decided I was being a hypocrite. A bar mitzvah ceremony doesn't mean anything to me, and I know it wouldn't mean much to him. I'm not doing enough for him in the house to have a bar mitzvah make any sense. It would all be for the party. And to me, just having a bar mitzvah so you can have a big party is not the thing to do. There has to be something more behind it. What I am thinking about doing is taking my kids to Israel and doing a very small bar mitzvah ceremony there. Despite the choices I've made, I would like to pass some part of Judaism down to my kids, if I can do it in a way that feels right. I don't want to do something for the wrong reasons. I think that going to Israel and having a very simple service might be just fine.

I think that if my mother were around, I might have done more in terms of Judaism. She would have helped me and made it more enjoyable. It would have made a whole lot of difference.

Rachel is probably still in her thirties. She is a psychotherapist who grew up in New York in an area that was "not religious, but very Jewish." The only way Rachel and Stephen could come to an agreement about how to incorporate religion into their lives was to look outside both of their own religious experiences to something completely new.

✖ RACHEL (TO BE FOLLOWED BY HER HUSBAND, STEPHEN)

* * *

My family called ourselves Reform, but we almost never went to synagogue. As my older sister jokes, "The only time we would go to the synagogue was when they had the bazaar," and that was once a year. Still, we identified strongly as Jewish. Everything was, "Is this one Jewish? Is that one Jewish?" Not when we talked about our friends. But anytime there was a famous person who turned out to be Jewish, it was always noted.

* * *

We did celebrate all the Jewish holidays. We also celebrated Christmas, even though my father never let us get a tree. I always used to kid him that one of the reasons I married a Christian was so that I could celebrate Christmas without guilt.

My father was a survivor, and that was a very strong part of my upbringing. I knew all about the Holocaust. My father was one of the ones who did not talk much about his experiences. Some survivors talk a lot, but he was one of the survivors who told us very little. He did not dump his stories on us. But we still knew about what happened. We grew up knowing about it. It was very, very present in our lives.

All my life, the way being a child of a survivor affected me was to make me feel as though being Jewish wasn't safe. I personally don't look all that Jewish, even though my mannerisms might make you think I am. I remember there was a professor that I knew in graduate school who was also a survivor from Poland, like my dad. She said to me one day that every time she would comment on my not looking Jewish, I smiled. I wasn't really aware of it. But I think I was glad I didn't look Jewish, because it felt safer. And I believe that on some level, that's why I married a Christian. I think that it made me feel safe.

From the time I started dating, I went out with guys from different kinds of racial and religious backgrounds, and my parents were fine with that. My sister married a Catholic man, and I got to know his brother Stephen. Stephen and I were friends for a number of years before we started going out. He used to tell me that he was sure he was going to marry someone Christian, and preferably Catholic. He didn't expect to get stuck with this brash New York Jew.

Stephen has always been very much a practicing Catholic. He went to church every week. As we got more serious, this situation got harder. Our relationship became an issue with my father. It had been less of an issue for him with my sister, because she and her husband had agreed to bring up the children Jewish. Stephen and I didn't know what we were going to do about children. He wanted them brought up with some religious background, and it made the most sense for them to be Catholic, because that's what he is. I knew I didn't want that, but since I was not religious and he was, it felt hypocritical to say, "No, they have to be brought up Jewish even though I don't go to synagogue and I'm an atheist." We argued back and forth about this for years. We talked and talked and talked, and we really didn't resolve it. Finally, I agreed to bring them up Catholic.

Stephen is British. We lived in England together for four and a half years, and we were married there by a rabbi and a deacon. Before we could get married, we first had to get permission from the Catholic Church. We met with a wonderful priest whom I absolutely loved. He said, "I need to ask you if you're going to try to bring your children up Catholic," and then he sort of smiled and said to me, "But that doesn't mean you're going to succeed." When our son was born a few years later, this same priest did the christening. He also happens to be a Hebrew scholar, and he offered to do the whole thing in Hebrew, but I told him none of us would have understood it. My parents came to the christening, and he was incredibly sensitive to my father's Holocaust experience. He was just a wonderful guy who helped make everything easier.

Even though I knew my son was going to be baptized, I also wanted him to be circumcised. I would have preferred to just have the procedure done in the hospital. But at the time, we were mistakenly told that he would have to be under general anesthesia. So instead of having a circumcision in the hospital, we decided to have a bris. We found a mohel who was also a doctor, and he ended up doing it.

The whole issue of religion was much more difficult to work out than I thought it was going to be. Most of the interfaith couples I know raise their children in the mother's religion. It was hard for me that Stephen was so determined that our kids were going to be Christians. Even though I had agreed before we got married that they could be Catholic, I pretty much knew even at the time that I wouldn't be able to go through with it.

It's amazing to me how visceral my reaction was. On the one hand, I had never been very active in Judaism. I didn't go to Hebrew school. I never had a bat mitzvah. And yet I identified so strongly as a Jew that the idea of raising my son as a Christian was making me impossibly uncomfortable. I just couldn't do it. It wasn't even that I would have been expected to really participate in any of the religious activities for the kids. Stephen would have handled all of it on his own. But the idea of having my children go through the Catholic education programs and rituals at the church was something I just didn't want to happen. I had gone to church with Stephen, and the more

I found out about Catholicism, the less I liked it. It was way too rigid for me and seemed very much shame-based. It didn't feel like something I wanted my kids to be a part of. So when our son was about two years old, I told Stephen that I couldn't go through with raising him Catholic.

For a while, nothing was really settled. And then there eventually came a point where I said, "Let's try to find something that we can both share in." That was also what Stephen wanted. He felt very isolated going to church without his family. I'd heard about Unitarianism ten years previously when I was in graduate school. I never knew much about it except that it was kind of a liberal-faith religion. There was a Unitarian fellowship not far from where we lived. And I said, "Why don't we just check it out?" This was almost six years ago, when I was pregnant with my daughter. And from the day we walked in, we felt at home.

Unitarianism is nondenominational. They talk about Christmas. They talk about Hanukkah. We have a seder there each year. If they didn't acknowledge the Jewish holidays, I would feel uncomfortable, but they do. Every religion is talked about. And unless they're focusing on a Christian holiday, they're not talking about Jesus. When Jesus is mentioned, they refer to him as a prophet. Whether or not you believe he was the Messiah depends on whether you are Jewish or Christian and how religious you happen to be. You can be Unitarian and still be either an atheist or a believer. It's a place where you can be whatever you want.

This really hasn't been such a big leap for me. My kids are probably learning as much about Judaism as I would be teaching them on my own. And I still consider myself Jewish. I just practice Judaism in a Unitarian context. You can stay whatever you are. You don't have to give up your own religion.

I don't like when someone refers to the fellowship as a church. That makes me very uncomfortable, and I think every Jew who belongs there feels the same way. There are some Unitarian places around the country that do call themselves churches, and if ours did, I probably would not have gone to it in the first place. Because they called themselves a fellowship, it was to me a place where I could feel welcome.

As a family, this has been the best thing we've ever done. It's given us a community. That's the biggest thing. We feel like it's our place. We go every week. Stephen goes as devoutly as I do. We're both involved in doing volunteer projects there. I teach in the Sunday school, and the curriculum is wonderful. It focuses on the values and ethics that I want my children to have. This year the curriculum dealt with world religions. We had two weeks where the kids were learning about the Muslim religion. One of the teachers had some students come in who are from Pakistan and who are Muslim. They talked all about Ramadan and Muhammad and explained what their religion is all about. I'm so glad my kids are being exposed to things outside of their own insular world.

For Stephen, this has been a very big change. At the beginning he was willing to try it. He was surprised at how much he loved it, even though he finds it a little bit lacking in some of the theology. The community was just so welcoming to us. About a year ago, I asked him what he would do about his religion if I died. And he said he'd continue to be involved in Unitarianism. For a guy who was so traditionally Catholic, that's an enormous change.

My dad died just when my son turned two, before we discovered this fellowship. It was very hard. My dad liked Stephen so much. But he was not happy that I married a religious Catholic guy. He never knew what we found, and I feel badly about that because I think he would have liked the philosophy of Unitarianism and what it teaches. My mother thinks it's wonderful. For Stephen's parents it's been difficult, because they're such devout Catholics. And it's also been an issue between my sister and me. My sister divorced Stephen's brother a number of years ago and became Orthodox. She and I see life very differently. She's very disapproving of the choices I've made and not quiet about sharing her disapproval. But we still love each other, and our bond is very strong. And she's learned to shut up about her opinions, so we get along pretty well.

Even though their father is Christian, I consider my children to be Jewish because I'm Jewish and they are my kids. My daughter will say that she's Jewish, but my son tells me that he's Christian. I keep telling him he's Jewish. "No, Mom, I'm Christian." I chase him around and tease him and say that he's Jewish whether he likes it or not. I hug him and kiss him and tell him every kiss I give him makes him more Jewish. I know my son wants to identify with his dad. I completely understand that intellectually. But it bothers me that he wants to think of himself as Christian.

I know that a lot of my feelings are tied up with the Holocaust. I want my children to hold on to their heritage. Their grandfather was persecuted because of who he was. Even if I'm not religious, I want my children to identify, really culturally, as Jewish. I know their heritage is also Christian. I guess that when they're older, they'll have to figure out for themselves what they want to do.

Stephen is in business. He grew up in a religious family whose outlook towards others was one of acceptance. Because his religion was such an important part of his life, Stephen approached his relationship with Rachel from a perspective that was very different from hers.

✖ STEPHEN (PRECEDED BY HIS WIFE, RACHEL)

* * *

I was raised in a religious Catholic household in England. I went to Catholic schools and have always continued to practice Catholicism on my own even when I was away at college. Religion has always been a part of my life that I am comfortable with and that I like.

* * *

When I was growing up, I knew that my older brother would sometimes go out with non-Catholic girls. My parents were never very happy about that. I wouldn't say it was a major deal. They probably worried about it a bit, and it was occasionally discussed, but not all that explicitly.

My brother married Rachel's older sister. That's how Rachel and I first met and got to know each other. I was still living in England, so we started a long-distance relationship. For quite a while, I was somewhat ambivalent about letting the relationship progress very far. Having been through the experience of growing up in a Catholic family, I wasn't entirely convinced that things were going to work out particularly well if I married someone who wasn't Catholic or at least of another Christian denomination.

It's not that there was that much Judaism explicit in Rachel's family. Her parents were not religious. The way she grew up, being Jewish was valued much more from a cultural point of view than from a religious one. As Rachel and I gradually did get more serious and talked about how we might possibly handle religion in our household, it was clear that she probably could have been comfortable raising kids without much of a religious structure. But I definitely wanted my children to have some sort of a religious framework. I had gotten a great deal from my religion while growing up. I knew I wanted my children to be given something along those lines as well.

This is something that we really were kind of stuck on for a while. Rachel's take on all this was that she wanted her kids to grow up with a sense of Judaism, just from a cultural point of view because she herself is an atheist. So then, you know, you've got me, the religious person, saying, "Well, hang on a minute. What's the point in trying to follow any part of your religion if you're an atheist? What's the bloody point?" And because I was more religious, we did eventually sort of decide that we might raise the kids as Catholics. But we really didn't make a firm agreement.

Once we were married, this didn't become much of an issue again, even right when our first child was born. But as he got older, it started to get harder. Things really do get more complicated when kids are involved. Let me tell you that even if you were the kind of person who thought you'd never want to go into a church or temple again, when the kids come along you'll be bloody scratching your head thinking, "Now, how do I really want to do this?" All of a sudden, any feelings you have about your own heritage and your own traditions will all come back out again. And the importance of it can't be underestimated because this is your culture. This is where you come from.

Rachel had thought that maybe she could have the kids be Catholic, but when it came down to it she just couldn't do it. So for a long time we didn't know what to do. And really, this was a major sticking point in our marriage. I kept going to church on my own, and the rest of my family was kind of just ignoring that. Then Rachel started talking about Unitarianism. This was something she had heard about a number of years ago, and there happened to be a Unitarian fellowship in the town that we live in. So we decided to try going to that. I walked away almost after the first time we went to it thinking, "This is the answer to my prayers." Instantly, that's how it felt to me. It was a ready-made solution.

Theologically, Unitarianism is very different from Catholicism. They only talk about Jesus from time to time, when it is relevant to a particular holiday. There are no crosses in the building. Really, the only religious item you'll see there is the chalice. Unitarianism is officially a non-Christian denomination. From Rachel's perspective, she can very comfortably be a part of the fellowship. When she says, "Well, I don't believe in God," there are a hundred other people who will say, "Well, neither do we."

As a couple, participating in Unitarianism gives us a church, if you like. My wife doesn't like that term, so I would say instead that it gives us a place to go where you can worship. You can celebrate, and you can be inclusive of all types of religious beliefs and cultures. It teaches nothing but acceptance for who you are and the value of the innate worth of every human being. Now, if those aren't basic Christian tenets, I don't know what are. Those are things that I think our kids will be able to grip on to and make sense of. The community atmosphere and the values that are a part of Unitarianism, and in particular the focus they place on the religious education for the kids, are wonderful.

Definitely, for me, when you get into the theology of Unitarianism, it is somewhat lacking. But I was always a very liberal Catholic in any case, so I can go there and I can tolerate what I consider to be the theological short-comings. And having said that, what you learn about Unitarianism really depends on whom you talk to. You could line up ten Unitarians and you'll get ten different answers in any given theological discussion. I personally find that healthy. I'm really coming around to being even more comfortable with it than I was or ever suspected that I could be. I think these days I consider myself Unitarian, with a Catholic theology. Given where Unitarianism is, that's perfectly acceptable.

Some things from Catholicism have been hard for me to let go of. And to a certain extent, I haven't let go of everything. I do have comfort in the fact that my kids were both baptized. One of them was baptized in a Catholic church by a priest, and the other was baptized by a Unitarian minister. Having them baptized is something that I considered to be very important. Essentially, from a Catholic perspective, it is the only sacrament that really matters. So that gives me a comfort, yes it does.

This is all essentially a late-in-life shock for my parents, because if you had asked them thirty years ago, they would have assumed their kids would do just what they themselves did. It's turned into a very different world for them. My parents have four grandchildren. My brother's kids are being raised as Conservative Jews. And then there are my two kids. As my parents said to us recently, "Four grandchildren, and not a First Communion in sight." I know that it's been hard for them.

I do still have some mixed feelings myself about all of this. But, you know, I think I'm doing the best thing for my marriage. I think this particular denomination has enabled us to do that. And I think I'm lucky to have found it and for it to work for us. Because I think that for a lot of people, this kind of thing can really start to rip you apart.

5 Deciding to Convert

All of the people in these stories who convert choose to do so specifically because of issues related to marrying someone of a different religion. It is not a step any of them were planning to make on their own had the marriage not taken place. In some stories, a man or woman converts because it is so important to their spouse, whereas in other stories there is pressure to convert from the in-laws. There are people who seem truly happy after they make this choice, while others express feeling hurt that they were in some way "not good enough" in the eyes of their spouse's family until they did convert.

The level of commitment of the person who converts varies greatly, as does the way the person feels about the conversion after it has taken place. Some people feel very connected to their new religion whereas others feel they are converting in name only, and the act has no real meaning for them. There are stories in which people seem very comfortable about fitting into their new religious community, and other stories in which people feel they still have to prove themselves in some way. It is dramatically less common for Jews to convert to Christianity than it is for Christians to convert to Judaism.

Rebecca grew up in a city on the East Coast. She has several siblings, and her entire family has always been supportive and accepting. When Rebecca and I first met she seemed to be completely comfortable in her role as a Jewish wife and mother. But when we sat down to really talk about this subject I found there was far more below the surface than I had realized. I got the feeling that if Rebecca were to live her life over again, she might not make all of the same choices.

✠ REBECCA

* * *

My family was Catholic, observant and practicing. I really didn't think of us as very religious, but we did go to church every Sunday and there were a bunch of rules that we followed. It drove me crazy from the time I was about twelve. I just began to have a lot of questions and to see how many parts of it I didn't believe.

* * *

In elementary school I knew a lot of Jewish kids, but I really didn't know that much about Judaism. I knew what most people know about it. You can't eat ham, and things like that. I didn't know any Jewish-Christian intermarried people. Intermarried to us meant Catholics who married Protestants.

Josh was a much more observant Jew than anyone I had ever known. He had gone to a Jewish day school all through high school. When I met him, he was keeping kosher. He would go to synagogue for High Holidays. He was strongly identified as Jewish, and for him to be keeping kosher in his twenties, when he was still in college, showed me something about him that I really liked.

We went out to eat a lot. Josh would eat fish, and not much else. He never ate meat. He says that on our first date I asked him if it was true that all Jews are smart. That was something my mother had said, which I really didn't believe. In fact, I don't remember asking it. But I was very interested and impressed with him. Josh has this huge knowledge base and background from his education, which I really admired. And also, just rigorousness of practice is impressive to me. I would always respect the kids who would bring hard-boiled eggs and matzah for lunch during Passover, and who wouldn't eat anything else.

Religion was simply an immediate topic in our relationship. I would ask Josh questions. It was very hard for me to understand some of the things he felt. I wanted to know more about what he believed. As I got to know him, it became clear to me that the Holocaust was a big factor to him and his identity. Both of his parents were survivors. He had actually grown up in this whole community of friends who were survivors.

Fairly early on, when we realized that we were in a relationship and not just something that was going to last two months, Josh said in a completely straightforward way, "Just understand that we will never, never get married. It is not even a remote possibility. If you want to get married, let's break this off right now." He was totally emphatic. He was never going to marry anyone who was not Jewish.

I didn't believe it. He said it and I heard it, and I just said, "You know I don't want to get married. That's not why we are in this relationship. Let's just have fun. If we get to a point in our relationship where we want to get married, obviously we'll deal with it then." What I meant was, of course, it will work out then. We'll get married because our feelings about each other will be more important than religion.

This was the last thing in the world I would have expected to be a problem. Here I was in a relationship with an educated person whose views about the world were very similar to mine. Our outlook on almost everything was completely identical. I never would have expected this.

What intermarriage means in the Jewish community was something I did not understand at all. There's this whole tradition that intermarriage is just like the worst possible thing a kid could ever do from the Jewish point of view. I didn't know how some parents might actually sit Shiva and never speak to the kid again. I just didn't know about any of this.

Well, after a couple of years I realized that I did want to get married. Josh still said the same thing. It was not a possibility. Okay. Fine. What we actually decided is that we were going to live together. Josh supposedly lived with his parents, but most of the time I was dating him he just stayed at my apartment. He ended up moving in with me. At first his parents didn't seem that upset. They still weren't taking our relationship all that seriously. It turned out that we needed a new refrigerator, and so Josh and I went out and bought one together. He mentioned it to his parents, and that's when they absolutely went crazy. I guess the refrigerator made them realize that things were more involved than they had thought. I just remember that Josh's brother and his wife were coming to my house for dinner that night, and they were about two or three hours late because there had been this family explosion because Josh and I bought a refrigerator.

As far as I know, there were no objections about me other than the fact that I wasn't Jewish. At that time, we had been dating for almost three years. I saw his parents frequently. It wasn't like I had met them a couple of times. I saw them a lot more than I saw my own family. I had been to their house many, many times. I always went to their seders, which I loved. I totally felt like part of the family and I thought everything was great. Then it all just exploded. It was unbelievable.

The thing that hurt me the most was that I went from considering myself as part of the family to being a nonperson. Nobody would talk to me after Josh and I bought the refrigerator. They realized that what he had been telling them for years, that we would never get married, that he wouldn't dream of doing that to them . . . that it wasn't true. They thought I was a perfectly nice and wonderful person, and then when it became possible he was going to marry me, I was just unthinkably bad. I was like the evil enemy. The way I processed it, I felt they had always hated me and I was just too dumb to notice. I became paranoid.

What happened next is that Josh got his own apartment and moved out of mine. We tried to end our relationship, because at the time he was working in the family business. He didn't even have a checking account. He was completely dependent on his family financially, and he couldn't just leave the business. There was no way we could continue at that point. We went for a couple of years just trying to work things out in different ways. We weren't really together, but we were always talking.

It's funny, but even during this time I was sort of keeping kosher. I had started when Josh began spending time at my apartment. I didn't have two sets of dishes, but after a while I had started going to the kosher butcher so I could cook food for him. And I didn't mix meat and milk. It was very clear to me that I wasn't Jewish and I didn't feel Jewish even though I knew kind of a lot by that time. I was learning and getting interested, but I was very far away from even thinking about converting. I don't actually know how his family felt about the whole issue of conversion. No one ever mentioned it. I never felt from them that it would be okay with them, and that everything would be all right if I would just convert.

And then everything changed. After a year of living apart, Josh took a new job and moved to Washington, D.C. Gradually, we started talking again, and I visited him a couple of times. He finally seemed more willing to consider a future with me, even though I wasn't Jewish. We went on a trip together and decided to get married. And we finally did it. We got married. We had a civil ceremony. We were married near my parents' house, by a retired sea captain who lived in their town. My parents were fine about our marriage. They tried to help. They wrote a letter to Josh's parents. They said they would do whatever we wanted. Josh's parents didn't come, but everyone else did. I know that his father actively pressured everyone not to go, but Josh's brother was the best man, and everyone came. The wedding was very nice, but it was hard.

Josh always wanted me to convert, but he never asked me to do it. I don't think he felt able to demand that I convert. And I just wasn't willing. All the stuff that happened left me with a very bad feeling towards Jews. I felt like I had been the victim of some kind of discrimination. I remember going to a friend's wedding and just wondering if people would be looking at me and noticing that I wasn't Jewish and thinking bad things. I was very uncomfortable.

On one hand, I didn't really have a religion so it seemed reasonable for me to convert. I had pretty much given up Catholicism. But the fact that I didn't believe in Catholicism didn't mean that, "Fine, I'll just do this other religion instead." Most of the things I didn't like about Catholicism were pretty uniformly applicable to all religions. They're not good on women's issues, and all of that stuff. Also, who needs another way to divide people up? I had this Utopian vision of this beautiful world in which everyone could get along. My true vision ultimately would have been to do both, to be everything. Because I think it's all the same anyway.

I also think that when you convert, what you're really doing is making yourself acceptable to people who don't like you the way you are. What you are isn't good enough for them. That's exactly it. I think that is often true, and I think it's horrible. I think it's really horrible.

But on the other hand, I had gotten married and moved to Washington. Everything in my life had changed, and a lot of good things were happening. I felt so badly for Josh. I really did. I had this whole terrible experience for two years, but now his parents wouldn't talk to him. They wouldn't have anything to do with him at all.

I started lighting Sabbath candles. I learned to make chicken soup out of a cookbook. I started leading a fairly observant Jewish life the minute I got married, even though Josh wasn't doing that himself. He didn't ask me to do it. I just felt like I wanted to do this for him because if he had married a Jewish person he would have gotten these different things. That's not necessarily true, I know, but it's still something I was thinking about. So I just started doing all of the Jewish practices. We started having a special dinner on Friday nights for Shabbat. We would say the prayers and light the candles. Believe me, I initiated it. And that is something we still do.

The thing that was funny is that I could do anything in terms of practice, but when it came to making a statement as to who I was, that was really hard. It was just very interesting, but I didn't want to convert at all.

We had gotten married in May. By the time of the High Holidays at the end of September, Josh's parents still weren't speaking to him. He called them at the holidays, and they wouldn't talk to him. Unspeakable. You would hope that you would never do anything like this. Anyway, they didn't talk to him. But around Thanksgiving they finally came out and we basically made up. And shortly after that his mother died.

I started to actively think about converting that fall after she had died. By the time I went to see the rabbi I had already made up my mind. It was very hard for me. I still know this rabbi. I've heard him tell this story at parties about how I came in and threw myself in a chair and said, "Well, I guess I'm just going to convert." I was very negative and hostile about it. I felt that I was having to do violence to myself, because I was doing something I just didn't believe in.

The reason I decided to convert at this point was really never spoken. It is very clear to me in retrospect that Josh wanted me to convert because he wanted our kids to be Jewish. He wanted to have children, and he wanted them to be Jewish, so it was important to him that I convert before we had children. If I had not converted, I don't know that we would have had children. We didn't start trying to have kids until after I decided to do it. Honestly, I think if I hadn't converted, it's very possible we just would not have stayed married.

Ultimately, I tried very hard to do a sincere conversion, but I really don't feel that I did. I took all the classes. I studied hard for eight or nine months. I would read everything I could find about Judaism, and I tried to learn all about the laws. I went to services. I did find many things in Judaism that I liked. But I found things that I didn't like also.

After I had actually converted, really, truly it's like I was defeated. I felt defeated. I felt like my vision of the way things could be was actually invalidated. Part of me still feels like I'm a wimp because I did it. I didn't just say, "Well, I don't really believe in Judaism. I'm not going to do it."

I knew even then, though, that I had won so much. I had this marriage with the person I loved, and we were going to have a family together. I can't really say what I gave up. That's the hard thing. It's not easy to point to. It's more like becoming something that you might not otherwise have become except for this. It wasn't inward driven.

One of my biggest issues was to what extent I was going to be mad at Josh forever about this. It's just like any relationship. You give and give, but if you give too much then you end up resenting the person even if they didn't ask you to give too much. But it was okay. At this time we didn't have many Jewish friends. There was no kind of Jewish community that we were involved in, which was for me probably better because it gave me time to just sort of work it out myself.

I converted and got pregnant maybe a week later, after six months of trying. One bad thing that happened, that I am just realizing now, is that I had my oldest daughter, Elissa, so soon after I converted. When she was born, I felt like I was just walking on eggs. I would have been a nervous mother anyway, but it was like, "Well, now I have to be a Jewish mother, and what does that mean?" I felt like this child belonged to Josh's family some-how, and I was going to mess this up. She was named for Josh's mother, which wasn't great. I was afraid that the things that would instinctively come to me as a mother would not be Jewish enough. My whole relationship with her as an infant was a little off.

What saved me is the synagogue we finally joined. It was the first time I had found a place that was really comfortable. It was a community that felt good to me. We had been a part of other synagogues before, but none that fit us as well. This community made me feel more confident and accepted. I became very active with it, and made a lot of good friends.

I think a lot of converts feel like they're not real Jews, and it's certainly understandable because we're not. The only way you can ever get to feel that you are really Jewish is by doing a lot of Jewish things. At least that's how it was for me. I always wanted to observe every holiday and do something spe-cial for it. For example, there's a custom of making little baskets for Purim. I would make homemade hamantashen to put in them, and I would have three other different kinds of food in there. I would bring the baskets around to all these people that I knew, because this is a Jewish custom. I just tried to do as much as I could.

One thing that I found is that a lot of Jewish people get very offended when they see someone doing more than they're doing, because they think (and literally, people have said things like this to me), they think you're try-ing to show them up. You're trying to be a better Jew than them. They think you're being self-righteous by doing all these things. The fact is that you're a convert, and you do have to do more. People who are born Jewish are just Jewish. If they breathe, they are Jewish. If they have a ham sandwich, they're Jewish. I felt like I had to do all of the right things all the time. I have been married for a long time by now, and we have three kids. A lot of the things are still nice to do, but I don't feel compelled to do absolutely everything.

Things still come up that surprise me, feelings I don't expect. My oldest daughter had her bat mitzvah two years ago. So this was fourteen years after my conversion, and I really was feeling like I was leading pretty much your exemplary Jewish life. My kids are going to a day school. We do all the holi-days. We celebrate Shabbat.

What I hadn't realized is that when you do your first bar or bat mitz-vah, it is the first time you're standing up in public saying, "I'm Jewish, and my family is Jewish." I started thinking about that months ahead of time, and it really started to affect me. I had a lot of emotional problems about it. My parents were coming, and they had arranged for all my siblings to be there as well. So I was going to have to stand up there and be a Jew in public in front of my whole family for the first time, and it was just too much for me. That's really what it was.

I think what happened is that I realized I had a lot of issues I hadn't resolved when I married Josh, and when I converted. But they were my issues, and my family was just fine. They weren't having any problems with this at all. I thought about it for a while, and I talked to my parents, and then everything was okay. And the bat mitzvah was wonderful. I felt very comfortable.

I miss my family. I feel sorry that we don't see them more often, and that we live too far away to share in many celebrations or events. They usually don't invite us to things like Christenings and First Communions, because I think they feel those are just not the kinds of events you fly half-way across the country for.

In my family, Christmas is the biggest event of the year. When Josh and I got married, we made this deal. He said we could never have a Christmas tree or any decorations at our house. What I wanted, and what he agreed to, is that we could spend Christmas with my family every year no matter what. But we almost never do. And that's something I think I'm going to try to change.

Initially, I thought going to visit my parents at Christmas time would be too hard for me, and I would feel too separated from them because of the religious issues. It seemed like it would be very painful. Then there was a time when maybe I had been afraid my kids would like it all too much. Christmas is a very attractive holiday. It's fun. I wouldn't worry about that now, because the kids are older and are very much Jewish. I know they could never be drawn into Christmas. In fact, the opposite is probably true.

I would have to say that my kids are pretty uncomfortable with Christmas and Christianity, and that definitely bothers me. I've always liked the idea of going to other people's homes for Christmas. It's a good thing to learn about other people's customs and traditions. I used to do that when I was a child. I remember going to temple a couple of times with friends for some holiday or event. I always enjoyed it. Anyhow, a few years ago some of our friends invited us to trim their tree. Josh and the kids sat in the kitchen the whole time and wouldn't go into the living room where the tree was. That was extremely upsetting. So I don't even know how happy they would all be visiting my family at this time.

What has tended to happen for a number of years is that we are rarely at home on Christmas Eve when my family is all together. I'm always trying to call them at the wrong time and it never works out. And I just get terribly emotional and frustrated.

It's not Christmas itself that I am missing. The only thing I would really want to do for Christmas is sing. We used to walk around our neighborhood and sing in front of the people's houses. I loved to do that. The issue for me is really more that my parents are getting older, and I think I just want to be with them. Of course, it's a religious time and they would all go to church, but we wouldn't do that. We just wouldn't go with them.

I'm not missing the religious part. I'm missing the family.

Lindsey grew up on the West Coast. She is in her late forties and is currently going back to school to get a graduate degree. Lindsey did a great deal during her marriage to accommodate her husband's religious beliefs and practices. But when her marriage ended, she was left to decide what part she wanted her own religion to play in her life and the lives of her children.

✳ LINDSEY (TO BE FOLLOWED BY HER EX-HUSBAND, MARTY)

* * *

What little religious training I had was at a Unity church. That was only until I was in the second or third grade. I liked it, but for some reason we stopped going. After that I probably was in church only maybe a dozen more times until I met Marty.

* * *

Marty and I both worked at a hospital in California, and that's where we got to know each other. He is a child of two survivors of the Holocaust. The home he grew up in was ultra-Orthodox. For most of his school years, he went to a very religious Jewish day school. But when he went away to college, he stopped doing as much. The year I met him, it was right around the High Holidays, and I don't think he even mentioned them. I didn't know what the High Holidays were until I converted to Judaism.

Before Marty proposed to me, he told me he wanted me to become Jewish. He handed me a book about Judaism and told me to read it. I read it cover to cover. He said, "All you really have to do is believe in one God." Well, I already did that. That wasn't an issue. Besides, I had a very difficult time with some parts of Christianity, especially the part that says you'll go to hell if you don't believe in Jesus. I can remember arguing with devout believers in the fifth or sixth grade that I didn't get that part. Marty said, "I need you to be Jewish. I want my children to be raised as Jews." The part about the children didn't seem to me to be a big deal. I figured I wanted the kids raised in one religion anyway. As long as they believed in God, I didn't really care which religion it was.

I agreed to raise the kids as Jews, and then Marty pressured me to go through the conversion classes as soon as possible. I said, "That's fine, but you're going with me." And he did. What actually happened is that I converted not once, but twice. I converted the first time to be Reform. We were married by a Reform rabbi while I was in the process of taking the classes. But then we had our kids, and it bothered me that I didn't know how to say the Jewish prayers. When you convert through Reform, you don't learn to read Hebrew. Marty would say the prayers, and it would sound like gibberish to me. Also, my kids started going to a Jewish pre-school at a Conservative temple. I went in for an introductory parent meeting with the rabbi. He asked who had converted, and I raised my hand. The rabbi basically told me he didn't consider me Jewish because I hadn't done a Conservative conversion.

I was definitely not happy with that rabbi's attitude, but I did decide to go back and convert again. I knew my kids would be going to a Jewish day school, and I wanted them to be accepted as Jews. I also wanted to understand what they would be coming home talking about. So this time I went through two years of classes without Marty. Then the kids and I had to drive to another city so that we could go to a mikva. When this conversion was finished, I figured that since I had done that much, I could go a little farther and have a bat mitzvah. And so that's what I did. I went through a bat mitzvah, along with four other adult women.

In some ways I felt very Jewish because my heart was in what I was doing. But I never felt completely accepted into the Jewish community. At times I actually felt shunned. I have blond hair and blue eyes, and I look very Aryan. I felt that some of the older members of the community in particular disliked me because they could tell right away I didn't fit in.

By this point two of my daughters were already at the Jewish day school. One daughter came home from school and said that her teacher told her she wasn't really Jewish. I said, "What do you mean by that?" This was a woman who knew all I had gone through to be Jewish enough. She told my daughter, "Well, this is a Jewish day school, but really, you're just half Jewish." And then my other daughter had a similar problem. The father of her best friend, who is Orthodox, told his daughter that my daughter really wasn't Jewish because I'm not Jewish. So things like that were very hard.

There were other things that were not easy. It took me about four or five years of going to the High Holiday services to really begin to understand them. There is so much Hebrew. I felt like an outsider. I think that even when you become familiar and comfortable with hearing the words, you feel a little left out if you can't really understand what is being said. And really understanding takes a very long time.

At home, we did everything. We had Shabbat every Friday night, and we really did the whole nine yards. I'd say the blessings and Marty would say some blessings. I lit the candles, and then the kids lit more candles. And then there were some prayers we'd all do together. Marty would participate, but I did all the preparations and all the work. And of course we did all the holidays. I made complete seders. To be honest, I think Passover is a nightmare from hell. There is a huge amount to do.

For me what was lacking in Judaism was spirituality. I felt we were so busy doing all the mitzvahs, and following all the rules, and doing the holiday preparations, and getting the Friday night dinner ready that I couldn't focus on anything else. I think that a lot of the traditions are beautiful, but they would fit better in a slower society because we really don't have the time to do what needs to be done.

I also had a problem with the attention Marty and his family gave to the Holocaust. We would get together with Marty's parents, and we'd all sit down and watch Shoah or something like that. To me it was dreadfully depressing and upsetting. They just wanted to relive it and relive it and relive it. I think that Judaism is a sort of "victim religion." People always seem to talk about the poor Jews, instead of trying to put the bad things behind them and move forward.

What happened is that several years ago we were planning my oldest daughter's bat mitzvah. And one day Marty basically walked out. He said he was leaving me for good. When he came to talk to me three days later he said, "You're going to pay for half this bat mitzvah." And I said, "From what I can see, your commitment to me is null and void. So as far as I'm concerned, my commitment to you is null and void. It is now your responsibility to raise the kids Jewish." So he did the whole bat mitzvah himself. I did nothing except take the girls shopping for their dresses. I went to the bat mitzvah and I gave a speech. Then I started going each week to a Religious Science church. And I said, "I'm not Jewish anymore."

This was very hard on my kids. They would say, "My mom really is Jewish." But I just kept telling them that I wasn't. I said that I no longer wanted to be Jewish, and so I had stopped. I told them, "I'll help you do what you want to do. I'll get what you need. And when you have Passover, I'll buy you special food and cook it for you. I'm not going to eat it, because I'm no longer Jewish. But I'm happy to make it for you."

The first year after Marty left, I wanted to put up a Christmas tree. But my oldest daughter said she would move out if I had a tree, and so I didn't do it. She was just too upset. We had some Hanukkah and Christmas decorations around the house, and that was it.

Initially my children were really angry with me. They'd say, "Well, you and your Religious Scientists. Religious Scientists are . . . ." And they'd make all kinds of nasty comments. I said, "What if I said that all Jews are those things? You say that you don't have any prejudice. You better listen to yourself talk." And they did. They got the message loud and clear that they were being very unfair. They even went to church with me a couple of times to see what it was like. I don't force anything. I just say to them, "If you want to go with me, you can go."

The next year I was able to put up a Christmas tree for the first time, and all the kids helped me decorate it. Marty was very angry. He said we shouldn't be having Christmas because I had agreed the kids would be Jewish. I didn't say anything. In my mind, I converted for him and raised our kids as Jews because it was all part of the whole package. If our marriage was over, that commitment was over as well. So I just did what I wanted to do, and let him jump up and down and yell as much as he wanted. The kids enjoyed the tree, and they opened up their gifts on Christmas day. They even put up stockings.

My kids will still be Jewish. There's no question about that. They identify strongly as Jews. But I think that what they will get from all this is more of an openness to other people. And that's something I'm glad about.

Marty is a doctor who grew up in the Boston area. His perspective of the religious aspects of his marriage to Lindsey is somewhat different from hers.

Marty (preceded by his ex-wife, Lindsey)

* * *

I grew up feeling that the single major event in my life occurred before I was born. My parents are Holocaust survivors. I was brought up in this strange community of survivors and their kids. I knew that people had suffered because they were Jewish. There was no other reason except for that. So I had a lot of mixed feelings about being Jewish myself. I didn't necessarily believe in God. My feeling was, "How could this have happened if there was a God?" I just didn't particularly have any faith.

* * *

My parents weren't very observant, except that they didn't eat shellfish or pork. We went to synagogue about three Friday nights a month. I had my bar mitzvah, and then I continued to go to Hebrew classes all the way through high school, and even into my first year of college. It was something my parents wanted for me more than I wanted it for myself, but I didn't put up a fight. It was okay with me.

I was married once before to someone who was Jewish. That didn't last very long. When Lindsey and I met, I didn't worry too much about religion because she really didn't grow up with any particular religious upbringing. She went to different churches every so often, and celebrated Christmas by gift giving, but that was the extent of her religious involvement. I had already been married to someone Jewish, and that had fallen apart. I thought that if Lindsey and I cared about each other, it would work out.

As the relationship progressed, and even when it began to get more serious, this really wasn't an issue. But when we started thinking about marriage and having kids, it was another story. I was very aware of my Jewish identity. I had a lot of Jewish education. I grew up in a house of Holocaust survivors. I always knew who I was. And if I forgot, somebody in my own family or in the community would always remind me.

I thought Lindsey needed to understand who I was. My perspective on what happened is different than hers. She says that I insisted that she convert. My recollection is that I insisted that she learn something about my background before we got married, or else she would not understand me at all. She wouldn't understand who I was, and she wouldn't understand my interaction with my parents and my family. I could never tell her what to do. I never could before the marriage or during the marriage. So that's my perspective.

There was this Reform rabbi who had a class for interfaith couples who were getting married. It either ended in a conversion ceremony or it didn't, depending on what you wanted to do. Lindsey converted at the end of that process, and then she went to another series of classes at a Conservative temple and converted again. I saw her conversion to Judaism as an act of love. She was trying to make me feel comfortable in my own skin with her, and I took it as an act of love. I was glad she did it. I have always said to her that she had to do what she wanted. When we had our first child, she asked me if she should go back to work or not. I said she should decide what she wanted to do. It was up to her. I was very careful about the religious thing. I was very careful never to say, "You have to do this." Her perception of what I told her was different, but I felt that she converted because she loved me.

In a way, Lindsey brought me back to Judaism. She took it seriously. I had mixed feelings about being Jewish. I was ambivalent about it. She wasn't.

She had made a choice for it and was not ambivalent. She lit the candles every Friday night. She wanted to go to services. When our kids were of the age to go to preschool, she wanted them to go to a Jewish day school. I wasn't sure about that, either. Sometimes I felt like she wanted to be too Jewish. There's a joke about this kind of situation.

A boy is going to marry a girl who isn't Jewish. He tells his father, and the father says, "You can't do that." "Dad," says the son, "she's going to convert, and we're going to raise the kids Jewish. We settled all the issues. Everything will be fine." Dad says, "She'll never be one of us. She'll never understand our ways. It will never work." The son says, "You'll see. It will be fine." So they get married and years go by, and they have kids. His wife lights the candles every Friday night. The son goes to work with his father in the garment business. And one Friday the father says, "You know, we have to do the inventory. We have to come in tomorrow." The son said, "Well, tomorrow is the Sabbath. She won't let me come in." "What do you mean, she won't let you come in? We've got to do the inventory." "Dad, she doesn't understand that. She won't let me work on the Sabbath." The father says to him, "See, what did I tell you? She'll never be one of us. She'll never understand our ways. It will never work."

Our kids did go to the day school. The guy who ran the day school was terrific. I've never seen a little kid sit through a prayer service and not fidget, but he'd have all the kids participating and interested and being very, very positive. I'd watch my kids read from the Torah, and that meant a lot to me. And in 1994 we went to Israel as a family. That was a very moving, spiritual experience. It was just extremely powerful. Gradually, I started to get more receptive to practicing my religion. But really, my parents had to die before I started to acquire any real faith.

What changed me was sitting Shiva, and going every day to the minion at the synagogue and finding that I was actually getting something out of it. Being Jewish, and practicing my religion, became a very positive part of my life. My parents had to die before I could get to that point. I feel like it was their gift to me. That really is the way I think of it. It was their last gift to me.

Religion was not a problem during our marriage. It became an issue after we separated. After we separated, Lindsey started going to church to hurt me. I think she would say she did it because she didn't feel she belonged in a synagogue anymore.

When the kids come to stay on my weekends, we light candles, we drink the wine and wash our hands and break bread. Once a month they go with me to synagogue. I tried to get my fourteen-year-old involved in a Jewish youth group, but she didn't care for it. That's okay. I know my kids consider themselves to be Jewish. They are not going to think of themselves any other way. They go to church with Lindsey once in a while, but mostly they hang around outside. They don't like to go in. The church is a different world to them. My older daughter did ask me once if she could go to a summer camp that was for Christians. I think that some of her friends were going to it. I said, "You can go, but I'm not paying for it. And it would have to be during your mom's weeks." So I'm pretty clear. I don't support anything that's not Jewish.

I feel that Lindsey has used Judaism as a weapon against me since we split up. It was a way she had of controlling something. It was tough for her to have me leave. It wasn't what she wanted. She made it clear during the divorce proceedings that she would not object to the wishes of her children, but she would offer them other things in terms of religion, alternatives. Just to get at me. A lot of my feelings are colored by the divorce. If someone asked me when we were married about whether this would ever be an issue, it's like another world. I mean, she used to want to go to services every Friday night. Even when the kids were busy, she wanted us to go. So it's all really turned completely around.

Regina is in her seventies. She worked as a teacher for many years before she retired. It is clear from Regina's story that even when religion is not a particularly important issue to the couple getting married, it can still cause problems if the couple's parents are upset about the religious differences. Regina couldn't do much to appease her own mother and father. She did go about as far as she could for the sake of getting along with her husband's side of the family.

✖ REGINA

* * *

My family lived in a very rural area in Oklahoma. The people I knew were against anyone who wasn't of their religion. They were all Protestant. And really, it wasn't enough to be the same religion. You had to belong to a particular church. Heaven forbid if someone belonged to the other church. Of course there weren't any blacks or Hispanics around, and there certainly weren't any Jewish people.

* * *

I met Jerry after I had finished college. I was working at a gym in Chicago, and he would come in a lot. Jerry is Jewish, but he wasn't religious in the least. We went together for almost two years. Sometime during that first year my mother came to Chicago and met him. She thought he was a great guy and enjoyed being with him very much.

After two years my parents both came to visit, and I told them Jerry and I were going to get married. My father was upset, but not as much as my mother. I thought my mother was going to have a heart attack. She was so furious. It wasn't anything personal, because they both liked him. But he wasn't what they had in mind for me. My mother told me that she was going to disown me because I was marrying someone Jewish. And then they left.

I had never really thought they would mind that much. It was a tremendous shock to me. It felt almost like there had been a death and I had lost my parents, and I was never going to get them back. But I was still planning to go through with the marriage. Jerry never pushed me. I just knew that I loved him enough to want to be with him. I knew I wanted to be with him more than I needed to be with my mother.

In my mind, I never really thought we would get married while his mother was still alive. Jerry's father had died several years earlier. His mother came from Europe, and had a very Old World background and outlook. We knew that our marriage was not going to be acceptable to her. But Jerry took me over to her house. He made me go into the kitchen with him to meet her. I said, "Hello," and she just nodded her head and didn't say anything. She wouldn't even look at me.

We kept moving forward. We settled on a date to get married, and started making plans. We talked about children. I said, "Well, I'm not that religious. It doesn't matter to me really. But if we are going to have children, I think we should raise them with one religion or the other." We agreed that the kids would be Jewish. Jerry called a rabbi he knew, who was Conservative. I met him and we talked. We sort of hit it off right away. He may have been part of a synagogue that was Conservative, but personally, he was a very liberal man. It was very easy and very simple because he made it that way. He talked to me about what I had to learn and gave me things to read. He said it wasn't important for me to keep a kosher home. But he did want me to go to the mikva, as part of the official conversion. I said, "Okay."

The day before I was going to the mikva, I called Jerry's mother and told her what I was going to do. I said, "Would you like to come with me?" It was very difficult to make that call. But she knew we were getting married and I wanted to try to make things smoother between us. She said, "I'll meet you at the bus stop."

So we met. It was a Friday morning. She didn't say anything to me all the way to the mikva. When I came out she spoke to me in a way that was less of a welcome and more of a demand. She said, "If you're going to be in this family, you're going to start right now. Come home." So we went to her house and she started saying, "You fix this, you cook that." And she showed me how to make the Friday night dinner.

On Friday nights, all of Jerry's family congregated at his mother's house. There was always a big crowd. And that night, I got an unbelievable reception from everybody. They were all delighted. There were only two family members who never accepted me, and that was his older brother and his sister. They haven't accepted me to this day.

That week Jerry called the rabbi and said, "We are ready to get married now." The rabbi told us to come over. Jerry picked up his mother and his brothers and sister, and we went to the rabbi's house and had the ceremony. And that was it.

It was very difficult for the first year. It was touch and go many a time because of my parents. I missed my parents. If my mother had accepted our marriage it would have been so much easier. It just was very stressful to me. And it was also hard, not because of Jerry's mother, but because of his brother and sister. It felt like they were taunting me. They were a lot of snide remarks. They made me feel I was just never right, no matter what I tried to do.

The first Christmas we were married I was pretty upset. We didn't do anything at all for the holidays that year. But once we had children, I decided I would like to have a Christmas tree. Jerry said, "Okay, we'll call it a Hanukkah bush." I think his family was a little upset about it, but Jerry was so open about it and supportive of me that they didn't say much. I just couldn't give Christmas up. It didn't mean anything religious to me. It was a tradition. It was happy memories from when I was a child. I didn't want to give up those memories.

Gradually, my parents began to come back into my life. It started when our children were born. Then Jerry was sick for a while, and my mother came to stay with us and help out. My mother was always saying things like, "Jesus loves me." Or she'd sing little songs about Jesus. The kids took it in their stride. They never said anything. They just went along with her.

My mother might have had a pretty good feeling that our children were being raised as Jews, but she didn't bring it up. And I never told her that I converted because she wouldn't have understood. Even when my son was bar mitzvahed, I didn't mention it to my parents. It wasn't hard to keep it from them because they live so far away. To them, a bar mitzvah ceremony would mean nothing. It would just be like pouring salt into a wound that had already started to heal.

Eileen grew up in Indianapolis. She is in her forties. Eileen's conversion to Judaism really had nothing to do with her religious beliefs. She converted simply in order to satisfy her husband's family. To her, it may have been a conversion in name only but for her in-laws it was enough. And it was something she could live with because she could see the positive results of her decision.

✷ EILEEN

* * *

I was raised as a Presbyterian. I was baptized in that church, and I went to Sunday school like a good little girl until high school. During my rebellious stage in high school I wouldn't go to church because I didn't want to spend time with my parents. In college I found myself pushing away from the Church a little more because I got to know some people who were really Bible-pushing, proselytizing types, and they offended me. I decided that I had my own beliefs and my own convictions, and that was enough for me at that time.

* * *

I met Larry when I was a junior in college. We started out just being friends, and religion was not an issue. It turned out that at the same time I was rebelling against my religion, Larry was also rebelling against his. He had spent hours and hours in Hebrew school and Sunday school, and pretty much decided that for at least the time being, he had had enough of Judaism.

Early on in our relationship Larry did something for me that always sticks in my mind. I had moved out to California. We were just dating at that point. It was my first Christmas away from home, and it was pouring rain. Larry went out and bought a Christmas tree for me. He brought it in and he set up. And while he was shaking off all the rain he was saying, "I can't believe I'm doing this. I'm Jewish." But he did it for me, because he knew it would make me happy.

When it was clear that we were getting really serious, our families started getting more involved. On my side, it was fine. My parents had a conversation with us about our relationship. They wanted to let us know that if we did decide to get married, they very much hoped that we would decide on only one religion and practice it together. They said they had known of several interfaith marriages in which each person tried to follow his or her own religion. Those marriages hadn't worked out particularly well, especially when kids came into the picture.

I felt fortunate to have parents who were supportive enough to say, "Do what you need to do, and choose either religion to participate in." But on Larry's side, it was much worse. Larry's parents sat us down at the kitchen table and basically told us that if we got married and I didn't convert, that they would disown him. And they pretty much said to me, "We love you, we want you to be part of our family, but we really want you to convert or we won't talk to you ever again."

After Larry and I got over the shock of what his parents had said to us, neither of us could say a thing. There was a somewhat long period where we didn't talk to them. We just had to kind of work through everything. For a while Larry felt, "To heck with them. If they don't want me in their family, then I don't want them in mine." But I know how important family is. I started thinking, "No, we can't have a one-sided family here. Your parents matter just as much as my parents. We have to work this out." I eventually told Larry that I had my own convictions and my own beliefs, and that I honestly felt I could make the change and convert without causing myself all that much stress. I felt I could do it. It was worth doing to keep the family together.

I don't know if this has anything to do with religion, or if it just has to do with personalities, but I was raised in a very forgiving family. I was taught to try to understand, and to learn to forgive. Larry was not raised like that at all. The members of his family all hold grudges against each other. I expect to be written out of somebody's will on his side of the family. Everything is very black and white, without any "in between," and there is definitely no forgiveness if you do something they don't want you to do.

From the time we told Larry's parents that I had made the decision to convert, their approach to me never really changed. They have always been very loving towards me. They didn't say, "Thank you for doing this." There was never any expression of appreciation. I think it was just something that was expected.

I did a Reform conversion. Larry went to all of the classes with me. It was sort of interesting because he relearned things he had learned before, but he was more receptive this time around. When I was in the middle of the conversion classes, we got married. The minister from the church that I grew up in actually performed the ceremony. He was sensitive to the mix of the religions, and even asked if it would be upsetting to Larry's family if he wore his collar. And then once the conversion was completed, we had a small Jewish marriage ceremony at Larry's parents' house, with his parents and some of their friends. There was a rabbi at that ceremony.

Like I said, I really did the conversion for the sake of the family. I still am a very independent person with my own beliefs. I feel like I'm a little Jewish and a little Christian. I believe in parts of both. For me, that's comfortable. Larry and I did agree that our kids would be Jewish, and that hasn't changed. We usually celebrate the Jewish holidays with some of our friends here in town. Our boys have been to temple a few times with us, but they've also been to church a few times with my mom when they've spent the night at her house. So they've really been exposed to both. The temple near our house isn't very welcoming, so we haven't joined and we don't go all that regularly. Now we are facing the fact that our twins are getting close to thirteen, and they have not studied for a bar mitzvah. So I expect another family blow-up soon.

One thing that we've come to a crossroads on is Christmas. Of course I grew up with Christmas. That was always a real special time. And since we've been married, we've just always done Christmas at my mom's house. It's been very easy. We would tell our kids that Santa went to grandma's house, the Christian house, and that we have Hanukkah. But my mom passed away last spring, so we just kind of skipped Christmas this year. We went on a cruise during the holidays to escape it all. I don't know what we'll do about Christmas from now on. We'll have to find another place to go if we want to be involved in celebrating it. We won't do it at our house, I'm sure. We did make the commitment that we would raise the boys Jewish, and I think having Christmas and a Christmas tree is very contradictory to that. Probably we'll just really start developing some more Hanukkah traditions at that time, and leave it at that. But I'll miss Christmas.

I think that in an interfaith marriage, flexibility is really important. My focus has always been on my family, meaning my husband and myself and our kids. Sometimes you have to be willing to be the one to move off the mark, to bend more than you might really want to. In my case I did have to do that, and I was willing to do that for my family.

Nick is in his fifties. He worked in the stamping industry for many years, and then retired early. Nick is living in a completely different kind of family and religious community from what he experienced growing up. He seems surprised to realize that not only is he participating in a life he never would have imagined for himself, but he is actually thriving in it.

❈ NICK

* * *

The first date that Sue Ann and I had, we went out for dinner at a 24-hour restaurant. She had been working, and it was 1:00 or 2:00 in the morning. I think the first words out of her mouth were, "I just want to have an understanding with you now. If we should fall in love, and if we should get married and have kids, I want your word that our kids can be raised Jewish." So that was the beginning.

* * *

At the time, on our first date, it didn't seem like such a big deal. Even though I had what my parents considered to be a good Catholic upbringing, religion never felt like a huge part of my life. It was just something I took for granted. And even though we didn't talk about it openly, there was definitely an expectation that my brothers and sisters and I would be Catholics for the rest of our lives. There was never any real feeling of the possibility of change.

Sue Ann and I were together a long time before we got married. When I met her, I was still going to church every Sunday. As the years went by I'd continue to go, but I'd get there as late as I could, and leave as early as I could. I did this until I was 30 years old. Then one Sunday morning I was with Sue Ann and I got up to go to church. She said to me, "What are you going to church for?" I said, "I don't know," and that was when I stopped going. But it's interesting. Even though I was no longer going to church, I still absolutely considered myself to be a Catholic. I just wasn't doing as much as I had been before.

The really big deal for me came about a year later. We lived in an apartment, and there was a park behind it. It was a Saturday afternoon and we were sitting on one of those merry-go-round things, just talking. Sue Ann said that even if we got married and raised our kids as Jews, she was having an extremely difficult time considering having a family with two different religions. She didn't necessarily think I had to be Jewish, but she did feel it would be difficult if I was in any way a practicing Catholic. Basically, I would have to kind of be off in some nondescript gray area. In any case, she thought we ought to try to come to some sort of a decision. This was really the biggest turning point for me, and it was very difficult.

Up until then, it wasn't much of an issue to me that Sue Ann was Jewish. For me, it hadn't meant a whole lot more than not going to church and not really being an active Catholic. But at this point, things changed. Now I had to make a conscious decision to give up my religion. During the next few days, I went through a lot of very painful emotions. But eventually I realized I was starting to think seriously about the idea of converting. It was beginning to make sense to me, and I thought it was something I could possibly be comfortable doing.

For me, the hardest part was just to get over the stigma of being Jewish. I had gone to a high school that had a number of Jewish kids, but they weren't the kind of kids I particularly wanted to be with. A lot of them were extremely obnoxious. I did have one Jewish friend, but we weren't all that close.

One thing that helped is thinking about Sue Ann's family. I had met her sister and brother and her parents a number of times, and I liked them. We first went to Indianapolis to visit her parents when we were still just kind of friends. I had never even been in a Jewish house in my life. I still wasn't close with any Jews other than Sue Ann. Her parents met us at the door. And almost immediately her dad pulled out the synagogue directory and showed me all the Irish names in the book. He pointed out all the names of Catholics who had intermarried or converted, and now belonged to their synagogue. Talk about being direct . . . . And the next day Sue Ann's mother cornered me in the bedroom and said, "Why do you like my daughter?" I'm thinking, "Is this how all Jews are?" But both her mom and her dad really are good people, and they have always been very nice to me. They struck me as the kind of in-laws I would want to have. Spending time with them, and getting to know them over the years, really helped any of the negative associations I had about Jews fade away.

Also, it helped that from the beginning I participated in Jewish events with Sue Ann. We hadn't been going out very long when Passover came around. There were nineteen people at the first seder I had with her. At the time, she was living in a little one-bedroom apartment. It was really small. Sue Ann was cooking, and my job was to figure out where to seat the nineteen people. The seder started early and went to the next morning. It was fun, and I loved it. We just had a great time. I still love that holiday.

Deciding to convert is not something most people do lightly. It was definitely tough for me. It took me a long time to get to the point where I was willing to do it, and this was for somebody that I was madly in love with. By the time I did decide to do it, I knew it was something I really wanted. Still, there were questions that would come into my mind, like "What are my brothers and sisters going to think?" or "What will all my old friends say?" The part that was really the most difficult for me was telling my parents. I considered not telling them. "Can I hide it from them? Is there any way they wouldn't find out?" But I decided I had to tell them.

Sue Ann and I went over to my parents' house one day to visit with them, which is something we have never done before or after. We don't just go and hang out with them. I told them I was converting. My mother was very unhappy and very outspoken. She went on about how I was leaving our religion and how terrible that was. My dad made it easy. He said, "My father was born in Nebraska, and he's a pretty basic guy. He always told me that there's one God, and it doesn't matter how you worship him. Just keep God in your life. You can be Jewish or Catholic or whatever you want. Just keep religion in your family."

What my dad said helped me. I didn't really care what my mother thought. I usually discounted a lot of what she said. But my dad was important to me. That statement he made . . . that was the turning point. I was ready to move ahead with everything.

I didn't actually convert until after we got married, but it was in the works. The wedding was held in the sanctuary at a synagogue in Indianapolis. We were married by the same rabbi that Sue Ann had been close to when she was growing up. It was a totally Jewish ceremony. The only thing that bothered us a little is that because I wasn't Jewish, we couldn't be married in the main sanctuary. We had to be in a smaller, secondary one.

What the synagogues will and won't let you do is very much a pet peeve issue for me. I think that the majority of people entering interfaith marriages are sincere. They obviously want some Jewish element in their lives if they are getting married in a synagogue by a rabbi. In my case, I was even planning to convert. So for the synagogue to make it hard for us by saying we couldn't have our service in the main sanctuary, or even use their chuppah, is just ridiculous to me.

My parents came to the wedding, and so did my grandmother. Everyone seemed to feel very comfortable. I think it was because the rabbi explained everything as we went along. He made it very easy for my family to accept me as a Jew. His whole attitude was just totally normal and relaxed. It felt great.

After the wedding I started to really move towards converting. Initially, it was pretty difficult. Sue Ann and I went synagogue-hopping for probably six months. It took a long time to find a synagogue where we felt comfortable. The congregants were always either too old or too Jewish or not Jewish enough. Finally we found a place we liked. And we started going to it. We didn't go really frequently, but I'd say we'd go about once a month just to get comfortable with the service and the people who belonged there. I liked the rabbi, so we approached him about sponsoring me for conversion. I started taking the classes, and I converted with him. The day I actually went through the conversion ceremony was a big day for my in-laws. My family never knew when it really took place. We had told them that I was going to do it, and that was enough.

I would have never in a million years guessed that I would end up here. I'm Jewish. Most of our friends are Jewish. They are very verbal, open people. I've come full circle. I'm more comfortable now with Jewish people than I am with Christians. And I am involved in the Jewish community, which I love. It's just a way of life that I think I fit into. The synagogue we belong to is very involved in social action projects, so our family volunteers at a soup kitchen on a regular basis. To me, being Jewish, and being married to the woman I am married to . . . my world has totally opened up.

It helps that Sue Ann and I are unbelievably compatible. We like to go to services on Friday nights, but we don't like to go every Friday night. We like to celebrate the holidays. I think we have a good level of participation that works for both of us. If I had been marrying someone different, for instance someone who always wanted to keep the Sabbath or who wanted to keep kosher, it would have been harder. I don't know if I would have converted as easily if it had been that regimented. I could do those types of things for Sue Ann, but they wouldn't be things I personally would believe in. So I think the key to my conversion, and feeling so good about it, is that I am married to a person whose level of religion fits with my own.

My mother is still not very open to my being Jewish, but I would say she has learned to live with it. My sisters and brothers send us cards for the holidays. My parents went to the temple for the naming of our children. And everyone in my family came to the bar mitzvahs of my kids. Those bar mitzvahs have probably been the peak experiences of my Jewish life. I found them to be better than I ever thought they were going to be. I went into the first one thinking that it was going to be a very commercialized type of event, but I was completely wrong. It was close and emotional and really the warmest occasion I had ever been to. Definitely, they can be pretty elaborate events. But when you think about it, many of the grandparents won't be around by the time their grandchildren get married. In many cases, a bar mitzvah is a celebration that all the generations are still there to participate in. And it was great because not only did Sue Ann's family participate, but my family was involved as well. My sisters and brothers and parents all came. And at each bar mitzvah, we gave them the honor of opening the Ark doors. They loved that. So like I said, bar mitzvahs are definitely highlights.

I think brises are great too. Don't ask me why, but I do. I like rituals. We light the candles on Friday nights. We do the blessings. We never miss, and I do it even if Sue Ann is out of town. It just feels like something we should be doing on Friday night. I think that with anyone who converts, things can sometimes go through your head like, "Are you really Jewish? Is it really a part of you?" Well, doing the candles on Friday night makes me feel, "Yes, I really am Jewish." I'm not doing it for Sue Ann. It's not like it's a chore. It's not something I have to do. I feel very natural with it. I never thought I'd feel natural doing things like that, but here we are. I also would never have imagined that I would put a menorah in my front window at Hanukkah time. I would have thought I'd be too embarrassed to do it, but now it's a part of my life.

There are some definite differences between Sue Ann and I that come from being raised in different religions. One obvious example is the way we each approach funerals and death. As a Catholic, I was raised for it to be totally normal to go to a wake in order to say good-bye to the person who died. I can just sit next to the casket and tell the person what I liked about him, and what I remember. And I like to see the body, which is something that is totally alien to my wife. She can't imagine why we would want to go and look at a dead person. But if we go to a funeral of someone I've known well, and it's a closed casket, I feel like something is missing. I mean, it's your last chance to talk to this person. He may not look quite the same, but at least he's there.

I've been Jewish for almost twenty years, so at this point going to a Shiva seems perfectly normal to me. But it's completely different than the experience of going to a wake. At a Shiva, what you're really doing is kind of working on your relationship with the ongoing family, and trying to help them. Instead of saying good-bye to the person you knew or loved or had a relationship with, you're really kind of communing with the family. I definitely feel more comfortable at a Catholic burial because I like to say good-bye to the person.

Everyone always asks me if I miss celebrating Christmas. Christmas was never such a big day to me. I hated decorating the Christmas tree. I don't really miss anything. It's hard for me to say that, but it's true. I'd like to say there was something about growing up Catholic that I miss. Probably the one thing I do miss the most are the people I grew up with. I miss my friends. Last week we saw some friends that I used to be really close to. I had spent my entire high school years with them, and several years afterwards. It's not like converting made me give them up. I just gave them up. It's kind of interesting to go back to them now because they look at things differently from the way I look at them.

My feeling is that when issues like religion are part of the relationship, you just have to take it slow and let your heart kind of lead you along. If something is going to be genuinely right for you, you'll know it. To me, converting was very comfortable and I just knew that it had to be this way. It happened naturally. The hardest parts were the points when I had to make conscious decisions to move things forward. Like the time when Sue Ann was on the merry go round and said, "I don't think I want two religions in our family." Times like that bring everything to a head. And then I think you're going to have two or three days of a lot of crying and soul searching, and then you just realize what it is that you really want and let it happen. For me, becoming Jewish was a great decision.

Francine is in her sixties. Before she retired she worked as a professor at a well-known university. Francine seems to have been attracted by the differences between her husband and herself and then gradually drawn into his religion without fully realizing what the implications might be.

✖ FRANCINE

* * *

My father's father was a rabbi. From what I can tell, his commitment to Judaism didn't really rub off much on my dad. I know that at the beginning of my parents' marriage, they were lighting candles on Friday night and doing some type of observance for each of the holidays. But as I was growing up, my mother kind of stopped doing most of that.

* * *

My parents certainly felt very Jewish, and had strong ties to their religion. I think part of the reason my mother didn't want to do much is because my father was away a lot. He was working. Sometimes she tried to persuade him to go to synagogue more to observe the holidays, but that didn't really happen. She didn't seem to care enough to do much on her own. She would occasionally light a Yortzeit candle as a memorial to a relative, but not the Sabbath candles.

My mother wouldn't have a seder at our house, but we always went to one. I remember that we always got new clothes for the holidays. Each year for Passover, I got a spring suit. I didn't go to services with my parents, but as I got older I would sometimes go with the families of my friends. One of my good friends in high school was Conservative, and I'd go to a synagogue with her. I wouldn't go to Hebrew school. I didn't want to go, and my mother didn't push it. Despite doing so little at home, I identified as Jewish. My family and friends were Jewish. Even if we didn't do anything in our house, the Jewish culture was all around.

We lived in New York. There were two colleges that weren't too far from where I lived. A lot of my friends and people from the neighborhood went to one of those schools. But I chose the other one. It turned out that the one I chose had only a handful of Jewish students. I didn't realize that when I applied. So without knowing it, I kind of was taking a few steps away from the Jewish world and the Jewish connections that were familiar to me.

Dale and I met when I started graduate school at Princeton. We were both in the same department. He is from Boston, and a practicing Roman Catholic. He looked so Irish. His whole demeanor and style were very different from the people I had grown up with. I think I found him to be very exotic. I was partly attracted to him because of the differences between us. Also, he is someone who can be extremely charismatic. He is very strongly opinionated and is usually arguing passionately about some issue or another. That's one of those things you find attractive before you get married.

At Princeton, everybody was an intellectual. There was a Catholic circle that Dale was a pretty big part of. This circle was made up of artists, philosophers, and historians. These were very interesting people. They weren't really talking specifically about religion all the time, but about all the things that go with it such as art and music and philosophy. So I was with Dale, and I was hanging out with these people.

For a long time, I didn't really know many specifics about the doctrines of Catholicism, or how the religion is practiced. My whole introduction to the Church was through literature and poetry. Dale would say to me, "This is really good stuff. This is something that you should read. You'll be interested in this." And I was receptive to all of it. He gave me novels and French poetry. A lot of the things he gave me to read had to do with being compliant, and giving yourself over to God or to Christ.

It was clear that I was being converted. I was converting emotionally at first, and then as soon as we discussed marriage, I formally began to prepare for conversion. There was a little class I went to. I studied catechism, which are the teachings of the Church. Of course I had to say I believed in Christ. But nothing was ever pressed on me. One thing that someone told me early on was that the key thing about the religion is your belief in God, and what that means to you. And that just about everything else is extraneous. Pretty much that was the way it was for me.

I didn't worry about belonging to any church organizations or doing any subsidiary things. But as a couple, we were pretty observant. We observed Lent, and we didn't eat meat. Dale and I went to Mass regularly, and celebrated all the holidays and various occasions throughout the year. When we went to church, people would smile at us and say to each other, "Oh, what a couple. This Jewish woman is converting to Catholicism. It is so great, so wonderful." It was exciting to me. We weren't talking at all practically about what our life was really going to be like. Everything was just sort of high up in the clouds. On the eve of Easter, I went through a baptism, and then a confirmation. So I was converted in April, and then we got married in June.

From the time I went away to graduate school, I didn't have that much contact with my family. I would talk to them once in a while, but not often. My way of dealing with things always has been and I think still is to avoid confrontation. I chose not to tell my family anything about my relationship with Dale or my conversion to Catholicism until a few months before the wedding.

I told them on the phone. They were appalled and outraged. They said I couldn't do it, that it was terrible. They sent me some letters, and then they just showed up. My parents are not very sophisticated people. They don't easily pick up and travel across the country, so this was something extremely important to them. They said, "We want you to come with us and talk to a rabbi."

The mistake I made was taking my parents to meet with the rabbi at the Conservative synagogue, which I chose simply because it was very close to where I lived. The rabbi at this synagogue was elderly and extremely traditional. I should have gone a little out of the way to talk with the more enlightened rabbi at the Hillel. At any rate, my parents and I had a meeting with the Conservative rabbi. My parents said, "She's a wonderful girl, she's Phi Beta Kappa, she has a Jewish heritage, and she's throwing her life away. What do you think, rabbi?" Of course the rabbi went on and on about what a terrible thing I was doing. He said, "The Church is going to take you and all of your kids."

I was pretty shocked when the rabbi said that to me. Dale and I hadn't even talked about kids. We were just thinking about each other and about my conversion. I guess that somewhere in my mind I knew that of course our children would be Catholic, but I hadn't yet dealt with the reality of what that would be like. Still, it didn't make me change my mind about anything.

My parents put up such a fuss, and really, that surprised me considering how little they did when I was growing up in terms of practicing Judaism. They didn't educate me about what it means to be a Jewish girl, but they wanted me to think of myself as one. Now they were saying to me, "This is a bad and evil thing for a Jewish girl to do." Maybe I was just a very naïve person, but I couldn't understand why this was so important to them. I thought their attitude was very unfair. My parents didn't come to the wedding. In fact, they virtually disowned me. They didn't sit Shiva or anything like that, but they just refused to have anything at all to do with me.

We had our wedding on the campus of a university, in a lovely little chapel. Dale's family planned the whole thing. I had one friend of mine who came, and nobody else. All the other guests were his relatives or people he knew through the church. I felt like an observer the whole day. The one thing that happened is that the chapel got very warm, and I started to feel faint and dizzy. Fortunately, a young priest sitting in the front row saw me and led me outside to get some air. Thinking back, I now realize I could have gotten away if I had had any foresight at the time.

A year after we were married, my oldest daughter was born. Even though my parents had vowed never to speak to me again, their attitude changed with the birth of their first grandchild. They wanted to see her. Ultimately, I had five kids. One thing I had never faced up to was the whole birth control question. The way Dale and I dealt with these things is that we didn't talk about them; we just let things happen. Birth control is something that was never discussed. I think that after about three kids it started to bother me that every time we had sex I might have a baby. As far as I could tell, Dale was not open to birth control at all. That did something to my whole attitude and probably had an effect on our marriage.

When our kids were growing up, Christmas and Easter were major family events. It always seemed to me an enormous irony that Dale is the one who married the Jewish woman, and yet I was the one out of all of the people in his family who ended up having to put together these big celebrations. For Christmas we'd have the tree and a huge amount of presents. For Easter there was always a lot of egg coloring and then an egg hunt and a big dinner. Really, the holidays were fun and I enjoyed them overall. It's just that I was the one who had to do all of the cooking and most of the work.

After we had been married twelve years, my husband and I got divorced. I had discovered that he had a girlfriend. Again, it was ironic. He was supposed to be the perfect Catholic. He was supposed to be so virtuous. It was a bitter, nasty end. So the marriage didn't take, and the religion didn't take either. I kept going to church for a little while. The kids were in public school at this point, instead of the Catholic schools they had originally started out in. And gradually, we just stopped going to church altogether. I still did Christmas and Easter with the kids, but day-to-day we didn't do much else. I felt that I was falling away from everything. I was a fallen-away Jew and a fallen-away Catholic. Really, that felt more natural to me than anything else. My belief in God was the same as it had been when I was a child. I felt that God is a presence in my life, but not anything that is deeply a part of me day-to-day.

My children are all grown now. I have three daughters and two sons. My sons don't do much in terms of religion, but my daughters are all practicing Catholics to varying degrees. I have mixed feelings about that. For a number of years after the divorce, my kids were pretty detached from the Church because they were living with me and I was uninvolved. I know it makes sense for them to want to reconnect with something that was such a big part of their lives when they were young. Catholicism was impressed upon them in a way that the Jewish religion was never impressed upon me when I was a child. My children were all baptized and brought up strictly as Catholics for a number of years. There are things about the Church and the rituals and the holidays that they really loved. So I know it makes sense that they would want to return to that. I think that what bothers me when I see my daughters turn to Catholicism is the realization that Dale's influence on them was so much more pervasive than mine. That bothers me, but there's nothing I can do about it.

At one time or another, each of the kids has expressed some interest in my Jewish heritage. And this year we actually had a seder. One of my daughters and her boyfriend were talking about Passover, and they suggested it. My first reaction was, "Oh, God. I have to do all that cooking." But my daughter said, "No, mom. We don't have to make every single thing. And I'll come over and make the matzo ball soup." So that's what she did. I got some hagadahs and some notes that a friend gave me, and we just sort of muddled our way through it. We really enjoyed it. We didn't do a great job, but we had fun. We did the Four Questions, which I remembered from all the seders I went to when I was a child. If any of my children ask me or show any interest, I would certainly do it again.

At this point, I would just like my children to know a little more about my own background. I would like to tell them about me, and about what my life was like when I was growing up. I feel they are a little reluctant to ask me too much, and I don't really know why. I don't want to push them. But I am perfectly willing to tell them anything they want to know when they do ask. And if my own children don't ask, maybe my grandchildren will. They haven't so far, but I'm hoping that one day maybe they will.

Michelle grew up in the Midwest. She has worked in different types of businesses over the last number of years. Michelle felt from the beginning that it would be better for their marriage if her husband would become the same religion as her. Although Andy couldn't promise that was something he would ever want to do, Michelle never stopped hoping he would come around to her way of thinking.

✖ MICHELLE (TO BE FOLLOWED BY HER HUSBAND, ANDY)

* * *

My family was very political. Our participation in temple life really fluctuated based on the leadership of that community at any given time. When the rabbinic leadership was extremely bright and very articulate and great sermon-givers, our life was quite active, and when the leadership was more administratively correct and not as dynamic, our relationship with the temple diminished. I personally felt quite enamored with the Jewish community, and was active in the youth group. I was actually more active than my parents in terms of the religious aspects.

* * *

My parents moved just after my bat mitzvah to a town where there was no Jewish community to participate in. My high school had 4,000 students and there were eight Jewish kids, and they were the only eight Jewish kids in town in my age group. So inter-dating was just what you did. My parents never had a problem with that. They just presumed their kids would eventually marry Jewish spouses, even though there really was no format to help that to happen.

I met Andy when I was still in high school. I was sixteen and he was twenty. At sixteen my parents were recently divorced after a twenty-five year marriage. I had an apartment and lived independently and went to school. I was a very mature sixteen-year-old. Andy was raised a Lutheran in an extremely Puritanical, anti-Semitic household. They were bigoted at all levels. They were against everything. They lived in a very poor community. His grandmother was of European descent and felt that Jews had horns and blacks were horrible scum. Andy had been active in his own youth group at a church, but he had fallen away from the Church on his own accord long before I met him.

Everybody knew we were dating. My parents had so many issues of their own at the time. They were in the middle of an ugly divorce. My relationship with Andy was pretty incidental. I know when Andy's family first found out there was a lot of difficulty. His brother made some very derogatory comments. His grandmother was insanely angry, and used the most hideous names not just about me but about Andy as well. She said she would never speak to him again because he was dating a kike. But Andy was already twenty years old. He was in his senior year of college. He certainly wasn't going to listen to this 4'9" grandmother who he knew was an anti-Semite and a bigot to begin with.

I understood inherently from the very start why it was important for Andy to become Jewish. I was really not capable at sixteen of articulating the issues very clearly. It certainly was never given to me why the reasons were that this had to happen. It wasn't because my parents wanted me to be with someone Jewish. I had never listened to them up until then, so why would I listen to them at this point? It was more of a, "This is just something that I know is right," kind of thing.

I wanted Andy to become Jewish because I just felt philosophically it was better. It's not that Jews were right or wrong. It was more a matter of operations. It was really clear to me that having so many disparities in our backgrounds was not conducive to a good long-term relationship. I felt that the differences between us were already so huge, that to lie on top of them the cavern between us about religions was just too much. And once we started talking about putting children into the fray it got even harder. I kept thinking, "Don't do this." So religion became an issue very quickly. I just felt that the more we could build in common between us, the better.

This issue of religion plagued us on and off. Or actually, it plagued me, not Andy. Andy knew right off the bat that I wasn't moving anywhere away from Judaism. He was very open to learning more about being Jewish. He did some reading, and he started to educate himself. The agreement was (and it was very one-sided), that he would pursue more information about Judaism because my moving towards a less Jewish household was not an option. Also, he really had no religious affiliation of his own, at least none that he could articulate. His feelings about religion were so personal he couldn't share them with me on any level. I'd say, "What do you believe?" and he'd say, "I can't really tell you. That's sort of private."

We moved to Chicago together. During the fall of my freshman year in college, Andy started doing more on his own accord. He took an introduction to Judaism class and started studying. I actually took the course with him, because I felt it was something I could do to be supportive.

This process is something that went on and on and on. Andy took a number of classes, but he was not ready to convert. We went back and forth a lot. There was no way I could be married to a non-Jew. Don't be ridiculous. I was active at college. I was way too Jewish. I was sent to Israel through JUF. There was just no way. So we separated. We had moved in together in 1978, and we separated in 1982 because there was no motion. This was one of several times that we separated over this specific issue. Andy was not moving towards conclusion.

And with Andy, the religious piece didn't really change. What happened finally was that over about a six-month period he kept saying to me, "You know, you are my very best friend. No matter what happens, you will always be my very best friend. That's not going to change." He said, 'Look. Really, honestly, there is no question we'll have a Jewish household. And I will get there, just give me time to get there." And I said "Okay."

Why did I agree to get married, when this was so important to me? Because if you love somebody, you just think, "We can work this out. This is not insurmountable." Andy, I know, went at it with that thought. I certainly went at it with the intention that he would move forward. Isn't that what women do all the time? You marry people because you think you are going to change them. You are sure they are going to change.

As far as Andy and I were concerned, we really always felt we were married the whole time anyhow. And the way we finally did get married one could question whether we are really married at all. We called several rabbis, and no one would officiate at an interfaith marriage, except one who wanted $2,500.00. Whatever we were going to do would have to be out of our own funding, so that wasn't going to work. Then I found out I had a cousin who is a minister of the Universal Life Church, and she is the one who ended up marrying us. There were about seventy people at the wedding. Andy and I wrote the whole ceremony. It was a Jewish ceremony with some accommodations, so we wouldn't make his parents too uncomfortable. There was a limited amount of Hebrew. We made a ring of flowers, and all stood around it. There were no chairs. We did the breaking of the glass. We did not have a chuppah. Again, we were working on zero money. We did have a canopy of trees, so we talked about the fact that we were really under God's chuppah. It was fun.

After we were married, there was never an ounce of non-Jewish life in our house. We never had a Christmas tree. We never celebrated Easter. We joined a Reform synagogue. I remember being appalled by the fact that mail from the synagogue was not addressed to Andy because he was a non-Jewish member. Mail was simply never addressed to the non-Jewish partner. I checked out a couple of other places in the area, and they were both the same. I understood why he couldn't be a voting member of the synagogue, or on the board. But I couldn't understand why they couldn't address mail to him.

Anyhow, Andy would go to services with me at the temple. I was a youth group advisor there for many years, and Andy would always hang out with me and help. I would run the seders, things like that. And after five or six years of doing it, with Andy helping me, it was kind of a joint seder-running by both of us. He fasted on Yom Kippur. If you didn't know he wasn't Jewish, you wouldn't figure it out. He acted like a typical Reform Jew. Most people we met just assumed he was Jewish. And as time went on it became hard to tell them anything different.

A lot of years went by before we had kids. One of the reasons we waited was because I kept saying, "Okay, so where are we here?" I wanted him to convert, but something was holding him back and it wasn't anything he could really articulate. He would get involved in a Jewish class for three or four months, and then kind of fall out of doing anything Jewish for a couple of years. I'd say, "Would you just do it? Just do it." And he'd look at me and he'd say, Well, I'm not ready to." I'm thinking, "What are you waiting for, a lightning bolt?" Sometimes I'd make a joke out of it. "You know, my birthday is in January. You'll be totally off the hook if you convert. You want to give me a gift? That would be the gift."

We had kind of a big meeting about it with the rabbi, who also met with Andy privately. He said to me, "Michelle, it's never going to happen." I said, "How do you know?" He said, "I'm telling you. This guy is never going to do this. So you have to find a way to accept it." It was very hard. Also, it was very incongruous in light of the way we lived to hear that Andy wasn't going to convert. It was hard to understand.

By this point, we were getting older and we did want to have kids. I'm about to make a major business decision and the decision is either to do the business or start a family. So Andy kind of says to me, "I'm not going to get there, so you have to get over it." I couldn't reconcile the way we lived and his degree of participation in Jewish experiences with what he was saying. I actually convinced myself that the problem was his parents. Maybe he couldn't become Jewish while they were still alive.

So we decided to just go ahead and have children. We talked about it. He was totally committed. He said, "Michelle, I'm not going to back off on the Jewish part. The kids will be Jewish, that's not an issue." I would say to him, "When the Nazis or some other group come one day and knock at the door and take me and the kids, where are you going to be?" I would use that analogy and he would look at me like I was nuts. And I'd say I know it sounds peculiar, but I remember the morning of my confirmation, we were sweeping up the glass from the four-story glass panes in the temple because they had been painted with swastikas. I said, "I can guarantee the time is going to come when you are going to have some anti-Semitic issues. I certainly grew up with tons of them. The world hasn't changed all that much. What are you going to tell your kids? Can you say to them, you have to deal with this but I don't?" I wanted us to be facing the same issues. "Are you going to be here with us? Make the leap."

But again, we moved ahead despite the same obstacles. And it really is the lifecycle events that seem to crystallize everything. Cheryl was born. We had a baby naming for her. I said to Andy, "You can't hold her for the naming. You can't be a part of that." He said, "What do you mean I can't hold her?" I told him, "You are not part of the covenant." A bris, or in this case, a baby naming, is a covenant between God and Abraham, and between God and the Jewish people. Its purpose is to cement the relationship of the newborn with God and with the Jewish community. So how can someone who is not a member of that community be a conduit for this child?

Andy was angry about what he felt was the injustice of not being able to participate as fully, but I really wasn't. I was angry at him, but not at the institution. He can be many things to the kids, but he can't be a part of a Jewish covenant if he isn't Jewish.

So in the ceremony when both of the parents are usually holding their child together, I held our daughter myself. The only people outside of the rabbi who knew why Andy wasn't holding her were he and I. Nobody else was aware of it. And it was painful. It was painful.

We went through the same thing with our next baby, Melissa. Then my son Brad was born and we had a bris. In each case there was the problem of what Andy's role was to be. It was very hard. Usually the baby is named in both parents' Hebrew names. But in our case, all three children were named only in my Hebrew name. The words were, "This child is the son of Esther." Again, nobody questioned that. I don't think most people realized that they were only talking about me, but I felt very badly.

So our family kept going along. Everyone, including our kids, always just assumed daddy was Jewish. From the beginning, I really didn't want the kids to know he wasn't because I kept thinking, "He'll get there, he'll change." By the time the kids were five or six they understood that Andy's family wasn't Jewish. We would go to see his parents on Christmas. And we'd always say, "We don't celebrate Christmas, but grandma and grandpa celebrate it. It's like when it's not our birthday, but we go celebrate someone else's birthday with them."

And the kids, even as they've gotten older, have never asked, "Did daddy convert?" Why would they even ask? He is just a part of what we all are. The outside world assumes he was Jewish. He never offers up anything different. If he were asked he wouldn't lie. But he has never volunteered the information. As time went on, it became more and more uncomfortable because our little secret, and the possible exposure of that little secret, was more and more peculiar. It was a stress to always have to keep up the façade.

About a year or so ago, several things started happening. In the first place, we started talking about bar and bat mitzvahs, because Cheryl was getting old enough that we had to begin to make some plans. And I said to Andy, "Do you understand that you can't have an aliyah?" An aliyah is when you are called up to the Torah, and you can't be called up to the Torah if you aren't Jewish. And he looked at me as if to say, "So what?" I said, "Up until now, the mask has been fairly easy to keep up. But Cheryl knows the parents of the bar or bat mitzvah child always go up for an aliyah, and when you can't have one, she's going to get it. She's going to understand why."

Another thing that happened is Andy's mother had a very severe stroke. And after the stroke, whatever restraint she once had, disappeared. She no longer controlled what came out of her mouth. For six months she used the word "kike" with some liberalism. And a lot of other issues about Jews kept coming up. The kids, especially Cheryl, were becoming very aware of all this. Cheryl said to me, "Grandma doesn't like us because we're Jewish, does she?" I kept saying, "That's not it."

My mother kept getting on my case saying, "How can you deal with her? How can you let your kids deal with her?" And I said, "She has been very good to us for twenty years. She has come a long way. I understand she's anti-Semitic, but I know that's how she was raised. She has moved mountains to deal with us. Do I think she's made it? No. But do I think she's moved a whole lot? Yeah, I do."

I did not want to restrict my mother-in-law from seeing her grandchildren because of this. I mean, she viscerally believes we will burn in hell. You can't disregard that. I said to her once that I know it is hard for her because she is worried about Andy going to hell. She said, "I'm worried about you too. But I really think that God knows you and Andy are good people. Maybe he'll look the other way." That may sound like an unkind comment, but it really isn't. From her, it was a stretch to try to find a way to accept the path that her son and daughter-in-law have taken. But since this stroke she's just been horrid. Like I said, Cheryl has become aware that grandma is an anti-Semite. And I've worked very hard with her trying to explain that sometimes it's hard to change how you were raised."

And then during this time Andy's brother was around and said some very unkind things about me along the same lines as his mother. Andy was there. And when his brother attacked me I expected him to immediately rally and say to his brother, "Are you out of your mind?" And what is interesting is that he didn't. He did not come to my defense. And I looked at him and I said, "Is that why you won't convert? Are you an anti-Semite underneath it all?" Andy said, "That's ridiculous." And I said, "Maybe it is and maybe it isn't, but I think you need to look at that." That moment seemed to somehow shock him into taking a look at why he wouldn't convert. What was holding him back? What was the deal? And within a couple of months, a fairly short period of time, he said, "I'm doing it."

He handled it in the same way he handled his own personal religion all those years ago. He shared nothing with me. He did it independently. He went up to the rabbi and said, "I'm ready to convert. Do I need to do anything?" The rabbi said, "Andy, you've had more classes than anybody I can imagine. There's nothing else you need to do. Let's make an appointment at the mikva."

Here's an interesting thing. Andy didn't want me to come. He said, "It's not your place. It's just something I'm going to do myself." I said, "I've waited twenty-two years. You're going to do this and I can't participate? Are you nuts?"

He said, "Well, you can come to the rabbi's office where we're going to meet." So I did, and there was another man there with his wife, and she was going with them to the mikva. So Andy said, "It's okay if you want to come, too." And I burst into tears. I cried through the entire mikva service.

I had a whole bunch of things I wanted to do afterwards, all of which were for me, not him. But it was his moment, and not mine. Besides, it wasn't easy to know what to do or say. Should we announce it to the congregation? That didn't make any sense. Andy has been operating as a Jew for years. And how do you deal with it with children with whom you've been fairly secretive on this subject? If the kids have asked anything about the events around that time, we will answer their specific questions. Otherwise, we tend to shade the area. So it has been a peculiar process.

Do I feel any different since he converted? Out of my mind with joy. Partly it's a feeling of unity. You know, when you get married, one of you may make more money. One may have more skills than the other. The key is, you both put a hundred percent in. Whatever each person has to bring, you bring a hundred percent. And for me, in terms of what I have to give, it's all there. "You've got everything. Good and bad. It's all there." But for Andy, I always felt there was this thing in the way. It wasn't all there. It wasn't a hundred percent. There was always something he held back, that made some wall. And I'm not sure that he felt that way. I really don't think he did. But I did.

It's hard to believe it really happened after all this time. But then, I'm an eternal optimist. And he did it. God bless him, it may have taken him twenty-two years, but he did it.

Andy is four years older than Michelle. He works with computers. Despite his wife's desire to have him convert, Andy felt strongly that he had to work his way towards this decision on his own, in a way that made sense to him.

✖ ANDY (PRECEDED BY HIS WIFE, MICHELLE)

* * *

I grew up in a Lutheran home. I am the youngest of three brothers. Religion for me meant that every Sunday I would first go to church with my family for an hour service, and then I'd go to Sunday school for another hour. When I was thirteen there was a special confirmation service where I stood up in a white robe and was congratulated that I had made it through all the years of Sunday school.

* * *

I didn't know anybody Jewish when I was growing up. I grew up in a city that had maybe a hundred Jewish families. We didn't have many Asians either. I came from a lower middle class neighborhood, and it was pretty much segregated into white poor people and black poor people. Those are the cultures I understood. Since religion was just one day a week, I didn't think too much about it.

When I got to high school and started dating, I was Mr. Rebellious. I did a lot of things just for the shock value. I dated an Asian girl, and my parents were kind of scared, but it didn't last long. My parents didn't openly prescribe to me or talk to me about their problem with the relationship because we didn't really go out for any length of time. I just knew their reason for being upset was that they didn't want me getting serious with someone different from us.

In college I met a lot of Jewish people, and began to finally have more of an awareness of different kinds of religious cultures. Michelle and I started going out. My parents knew she was Jewish. That was definitely an issue, particularly for my grandmother who, as my wife likes to say, believes that Jews have horns and tails. My grandmother was very vocal about how she felt. Everything she said was designed in some way to destroy or hurt or do damage.

My grandmother was expressing absolute unprocessed pure emotion, pure hatred. But with my parents it was more like, "We don't know anything about this so we are afraid of it." It was different from hate. It was fear. It was just fear of what was going to happen. Thinking about how I grew up, I know that what we are basically taught is that either you do what the Church says or you will burn in hell forever. So the whole concept of my deviating from our religion was really frightening for my parents.

From the beginning, the message I got from Michelle was "You have to be Jewish. Period." And I said, "I don't know if I can do that. I can look at it. I can investigate it to see what it is." I didn't say no but I didn't say yes.

So far, I didn't feel that organized religion had been a very good fit for me. I think religion is supposed to be something that helps us find ways to develop a relationship with God, and for me that really hadn't happened. Plus, the feeling I got is that you had to go to church or temple to be a good person. For me, it was more something you could do in order to interact with other people, to get ideas, to get support if you need it, or to get nurturing when you need it. But if I didn't feel a need for those things at a particular moment, being in a church or temple didn't mean anything to me.

Michelle would say to me, "I want my children to be Jewish." And of course, mechanically, they would be. But she meant much more than that.

So what I did say and what we did have to agree on before we could get married is that we would have a Jewish home. The symbols in the house that we had would be Jewish, the celebrations we had in the house would be Jewish, the education we would give to the children would be Jewish.

My objective in terms of religion was to seek God in any way I could. At the time, I thought that having a Jewish home would pretty much mean, "Go ahead and ask questions. Seek your own answers. Don't just accept an answer because somebody told you so." These were ideas that I associated with Judaism. I could live with those ideas. I didn't have a problem with them. I liked them.

After we were married I was willing to try to learn more about what it would mean to become a Jew. After all, you can't dismiss something that you don't understand. I didn't feel I could say, "I don't want this," if I really didn't know what I was talking about. You can do some reading, but the best way to start to get all the information is to take classes. I started going to an introduction to Judaism class, which was really the first in a series of conversion classes.

Before you can go through any part of the conversion process, you have to have a rabbi to sponsor you, and you have to be affiliated with a congregation. It used to be that whichever rabbi was sponsoring you would determine the curriculum that was necessary for you to convert. Then someone decided to standardize the curriculum. Now they offer a specific series of classes, so the onus isn't on one rabbi to try to decide each time what ought to be included. And the sponsoring rabbi is there to help explain everything, sort of like a private tutor.

I started out with a rabbi from a Reform congregation. He would ask me, "Why are you going through this?" I'd answer, "Because my partner is Jewish." He would say, "No, you can't do it for that reason." So then I'd have to say, "Okay, rabbi (wink, wink), I'm doing it because I really want to be Jewish." He wanted me to say the right words. He was always saying, "The ritual is the most important thing. This is what you have to do." I would say to him, "I don't just care about what you have to do. I want to understand why I'm supposed to be doing it."

So I took classes on and off for years. I kept waiting and trying to learn more, hoping something was going to finally kick in and make me really want to become a Jew. Eventually a different rabbi came into the same congregation, and I switched over to working with him. He was a much warmer person. He was more into the historical aspects of the religion. He would explain why something was done, and then I'd said, "I understand what you're saying, but that's not a good enough reason. It just doesn't make sense to me."

By the time our daughter was born, any of the formal learning pretty much went by the wayside because now we were just trying to get through the practical things. We had to go through the baby naming. We were trying to celebrate all the different holidays. And we were starting to build our own rituals within the family.

I still didn't feel like I had found any reason to convert to Judaism. I felt that anybody who converts was going to be at a disadvantage because they didn't have the whole series of foundations that you have if you are born Jewish. That bothered me a little. Also, I didn't particularly like Hebrew. I've never liked the way it sounds when it's spoken. It's difficult to learn. I am taking a Hebrew class right now partly because I have three children and I can't help them with homework or preparations for their bar and bat mitzvahs. I want to be able to at least understand what they are trying to do.

Michelle has been unrelenting on this issue of my becoming Jewish. And recently I said to myself, "Okay, what would actually change by me becoming a Jew? What would really be involved?" I decided that what it would basically mean is going on record and saying that I am going to be Jewish. That's all it is. There's no change in personality. There's no change in lifestyle. Nothing changes other than you're "on the record." Your name is "on the list." So then I thought, "Fine, just go ahead and do it. Stop waiting for something to happen. Just get it over with."

Once you decide you really want to convert, the rabbi at some point decides when you have enough information to be reasonably started on the educational path to learning about Judaism. It's not that you've learned everything. There's no final exam. The assumption is that you will be continuously learning. You're continuously finding out what's there. But now you have at least enough tools to understand where to look.

So the rabbi says, "Okay, you're ready." You go to the mikva, you strip down, and you shower. The level of this ceremony depends on how strictly Orthodox you are going to go with all this. The Reform movement has you showering for hygienic purposes, not for ritualistic purposes. For ritualistic purposes you would wash three times.

Anyhow, there is a mohel. He does what is basically a finger prick and draws blood from the skin of the penis. He has to see redness. He doesn't have to see blood, but typically he draws blood. He says this little prayer. He signs a certificate saying he has done a proper ritual on this particular individual, and then he's gone.

You descend into the pool at the mikva and you submerge yourself three times. Each time you submerge and come up you say a specific prayer. One time it's the Shema. Then you come out and everybody shakes your hand. You dry off, and you get dressed. You leave the area of the mikva, and you go out into the communal area where you are asked some questions. All of the questions basically are asking if you affirm the Jewish people. "Are you willing to support the Jewish people? Do you believe in the precepts of the Jewish people? Do you call yourself a Jew?"

You answer "yes" to each of those questions, and that's pretty much it. You sign a bunch of certificates that have your Jewish name on them, to certify that you are indeed doing this of your own free will. Those papers are sent off to some formal library where all of the information is copied down. That part is important because whether or not you are accepted as a Jew will always be in question when you are a convert. So the rabbis decided that the safest thing is to leave a paper trail that says each of the things you did.

For me, the act of converting was not a big emotional change or commitment. I know that Michelle still wants that for me . . . an emotional commitment to Judaism. "I'm sorry dear. It's just not there." I do hope the children have that. Maybe I don't have it because I don't have that earlier foundation, or maybe there are too many parts I don't believe in.

I do enjoy a lot of the Jewish experiences we have as a family. We have a lot of fun. Purim was a few weeks ago, and we all dressed up. Our daughter didn't quite want to go as Queen Esther, so she put on a formal gown and a jester's hat and she went as Queen Jester. I had a dark robe, fur collar, bald-headed wig piece, and an electric light bulb that I would stick in my mouth, so I was Queen Chester. Michelle dressed up with flowers, and she was Queen Astor. Our son was in a leisure suit and he was Queen Polyester.

For Simchas Torah, we go to the temple, and everybody is dancing around with the Torah. Some people get really emotional about it. I'm not so emotional. I am in awe to be looking at a document that is continually being copied and preserved century after century after century. But getting exuberant and dancing about it . . . I'm sorry, it's just not inside of me.

Joel grew up in the Midwest. He is a professional who is in his mid-fifties. Joel acknowledges how much his wife has done to support the religious goals he has for their family. And yet he still does not believe that a marriage to someone from a completely different background can ever really give his religious experiences the depth he'd like them to have.

✖ JOEL

* * *

I came from a household where there were a lot of mixed messages about being Jewish. My father had grown up in an Orthodox Jewish home on the west side of Chicago. He was very proud to be a cultural Jew, but he wanted no part of religious Judaism. In fact, he would work on Yom Kippur because he was sure there was no God. And just in case there was a God, he wanted God to know that his belief against the religious parts of Judaism was so profound that he was going to work on the holiest of days.

* * *

My mom was the one who would take all the kids to High Holiday services. In the 1950s and 1960s that was probably mortifying for her, because people would wonder where her husband was. But she always took us. The synagogue we belonged to was Reform, and I was bar mitzvahed there.

I met Holly in graduate school. She had gone to Catholic schools all the way through college. When she got to graduate school, she met Jews for the first time in her life. She found us to be people of conversation, of passion and argument, and a wonderful contrast to the very bland background in which she herself had been raised. We got together fairly quickly, and then lived together for a number of years. We talked about getting married. It was important to me that my kids be Jewish and it was important that my household be Jewish. It was part of the arrangement that if we got married, Holly would convert.

What prompted our marriage was the biological imperative. Holly wanted children. She sat down with me in probably June or July and said, "I want to have a baby. I want to get married." Holly's personality is pretty impulsive. When she gets an idea, she wants to do it. So we got married in fairly quick order, so we could start working on a family.

When we decided to get married, Holly had not yet converted. The conversion process takes a year or more. It was an issue between us that she would be converting, but it wasn't an issue that she be converted at the time of our marriage. We went to interview rabbis to try to find someone who would marry us. Eventually we were put in touch with a Reform rabbi who performed the ceremony. But initially we had gone to a Conservative rabbi, who advised Holly to go through the conversion, and then come back. Actually, I think that was excellent advice. If I were doing that piece over again, I would have the conversion before we got married. Just do that and have it done.

What happened is that we got married in December. Holly got pregnant in April or May. She was going through the conversion process at that point. I wanted her to convert before the baby came, but when our daughter Abbey was born in January, she was still going through the process. Part of the reason she hadn't yet converted was because of the way the classes were scheduled, but I think it also had to do with Holly herself and the way that she executes things. The fact that Abbey was born of a non-Jewish mother bothered me. It meant that Abbey wasn't Jewish. So when Holly actually converted, Abbey went with her to the mikva.

Holly comes from a very large family. That's something that attracted me to her, because my own family was pretty small. She has five kids in her family, and most of them also have large families. One of the things I looked forward to when I thought about getting married was being close with an extended family. By marrying a non-Jew, I didn't get what I was looking for in that regard. This was driven home to me one year at Passover, shortly after we were married. We were planning to have the first seder at our house, with my parents. And for the second night I thought briefly, "Well, we'll go over to the machetunim," which means my wife's relatives. Then I realized we couldn't do that. There wasn't a Jewish family out there on my wife's side for us to share the holidays with.

My in-laws did come to a seder once at our house. They had a nice time, but it wouldn't have been appropriate to invite them again. It wasn't their holiday. They have always been willing to participate in our events. I remember at Abbey's bat mitzvah, my father-in-law got up to do a reading, and he wore a tallis. I like my father-in-law a lot, but wearing the tallis was just a novelty for him. There wasn't any depth to it.

I married Holly at a time when I described myself as a latent Jew. I was never anti-Jewish. At the time we got married, I was becoming more aware of my identity as a Jew. I think if the timing had been different, and it had been a year or two later, I would not have considered marrying a non-Jew.

I know that not every Jewish woman is active. But I do think that if I had married a Jewish woman who was even slightly more active than me, our kids would have gone to a Jewish day school. I would have been really pleased with that. That was my fantasy. I think the fact that Holly grew up in parochial schools was a major hurdle for her, and she wouldn't allow her kids to be put in what she considered to be a similar situation. Also, I really think my own religious observance would have been greater with a somewhat-active Jewish partner. My willingness is there, but my discipline is not. By marrying a non-Jew, that's one of the things I didn't get.

I know that some of this has to do with Holly's personality. For example, I would have loved it, especially when the kids were little, for us to have more than just a brief dinner on Shabbat. I would like it if we actually hung around and sat together and read and talked and those kinds of things. No matter what religion Holly is, Holly would still have been Holly. If there was a soccer game, soccer took precedence. That's just Holly's personality. So what does that mean? Does that mean I should have been more thoughtful of what I was expecting in our Jewish home? Probably. I look at other mixed marriages. Some do have more extended Shabbats, and some do send their children to a Jewish day school. So it of course has to do at least partly with the personalities of the people involved, and what kind of a life they each want.

I know I'm lucky. Holly in fact did convert and she does not look back at Catholicism. She has embraced Judaism in the way that Holly embraces everything. She has been honest and receptive. We do have a Jewish home. As my kids point out, our family probably does more than most families. There is no question that my children and I are living in a Jewish household. But I feel there are differences between Holly and me that I think have to do with the fact that I was born Jewish and she wasn't.

There are deep ways that a person is Jewish. There's this whole set of cultural values and ethics that come, I think, more so with Judaism than any other religion that I'm aware of. These are things that our tradition is so richly steeped in. If you marry someone who is Jewish, all of that comes with them, so there is a bunch of stuff you have in common right from the beginning. I think there are a lot of cultural values and ways of doing things that come with being Jewish, at least middle-class Jewish in America, that don't come with non-Jewish. And that's the stuff that's missing between Holly and me.

A few years ago we went to Israel, and we were at the King David museum in the Old City. We're halfway through the tour with a guide named Shamone. He was an excellent guide. Anyhow, at one point Shamone announced that he's a convert, and the group was just shocked because he seemed so intimate with all of the Jewish history and stories he was telling us. It turns out that his family had converted hundreds of years ago, and that was his message.

I believe in the saturation of time. Things don't happen suddenly. Holly is Jewish, and she is just putting down Jewish roots. We'll see what happens to the next generation. If they marry Jews, then those roots will become a little bit deeper. My kids are not fully Jewish. I don't personally accept that they are. I just don't believe that a Jew by choice is the same thing as a generation of Jews. I close my eyes and there are generations back that were persecuted as Jews, and that died in the Holocaust. That's part of who I am, and that's not true for someone who is a Jew by choice.

The Holocaust haunts me. I am just fascinated by the enormity of it. God forbid, if there was a Holocaust in this country, I would stand with the Jews. If Holly could pass her children off as non-Jewish to save them, she would do it with nary a problem. And she would stand with her children for survival. I would be deeply conflicted at that point. I'm a Jew. I feel a deep connectedness with generations before me. Holly, by personality or by background, doesn't have that connectedness.

If I were going to marry again, I think that what I would do is just restrict myself from the very start to women who were born Jewish. What I've learned, and this is something I've talked to my kids about, is that there are a whole lot of struggles that just come with being married. If you bring similar cultural backgrounds and values to it, it becomes at least a little easier.

Theresa works in the medical field. From the time she was eleven her grandmother, who was a very active Catholic, lived with Theresa and her parents. Theresa's decision about whether to convert was complicated by her own acknowledged naïvety about what she would really be getting into, as well as an unpleasant feeling that she would never be fully accepted by her husband's family the way she was.

✖ THERESA

* * *

I met my husband when I was twenty-five. From the beginning, we talked about religion a lot. We would say, "What did you grow up thinking heaven and hell were? Did you have that? Did you have sins? How did your religion affect your morality and your values and things like that?"

* * *

Lowell grew up on Long Island in a community that was very Jewish. He went to a Conservative temple. Both his parents had grown up keeping kosher, but they didn't follow it for long with their own kids.

My own background is Catholic. I did all of it . . . First Communion, baptism, confirmation. I pretty much started questioning my religion by the time I was thirteen. I remember not liking the whole Jesus part because it seemed too patriarchal. And once I went away to college, I essentially stopped going to church.

Once we started to get serious, Lowell and I began to talk in terms of, "Well, if we got married and had kids, what would we do?" I knew I couldn't raise my kids as Catholics. I would especially never raise a daughter Catholic. But even though I didn't really like organized religion at this point, I knew that if I did have kids, I would want them to have something. Lowell ended up having feelings about being Jewish and wanting his kids to be Jewish. Basically, to me Judaism made a lot more sense than Catholicism, so it didn't really bother me to think of raising my kids to be Jewish. And that was kind of how we agreed that if we did get married and had kids, we would raise them Jewish and I would have to learn about it.

We decided to get married. We found a rabbi who didn't even ask us what we were planning to do about kids. His whole thing was interfaith understanding. My mother was having problems with all of this, but somehow she never could quite spit it out what she was really thinking. She did kind of say, "Well, aren't you going to have a priest at the ceremony?" I think she was feeling like I shouldn't deny my own background. But I told her, "I am not a practicing Catholic. I do not want a priest there."

The hardest part was Lowell's family. Now I look back and I think, "God, was I naïve." I assumed they would just welcome me into their family. They weren't really hostile, and I don't think his mother had too much of a problem about it. I know she really liked me. But his grandmother was upset. And his father was freaking out. His father almost didn't come to the wedding. The rabbi talked him into coming. I actually at one point remember saying to his family, "I'm really getting a feeling of what it must feel like to be black in America." I was different from them, and so I wasn't accepted. That's the way I felt about it.

I think that most people are pretty young when they get married, and they don't realize how important the other person's family is. Lowell was always telling me it didn't matter what his parents thought. "It doesn't matter. It doesn't matter." But I think what they felt about our marriage was always there between us. When you marry someone, you really are taking on a whole family. I honestly don't think Lowell realized that he was so affected by them. Things did improve somewhat over time, but you see, then I converted.

What happened is that after we got married, we moved out to California. And soon after that I decided to take some classes at a Reform temple. It wasn't in my mind to convert because I didn't know how I would feel. I just wanted to learn more. But I wasn't going to go alone. I made Lowell go with me because I realized that he didn't know that much himself. He actually enjoyed the classes. Even though he had been to Sunday school and Hebrew school, hearing it all from an adult perspective was good, and he learned a lot.

I was amazed at some of the people in the classes who considered themselves Jewish, but really weren't religious in any way. I found that fascinating. They didn't know much, but they were looking for something so they came to these classes. I understood more about the background and practices of Judaism than they did, and yet culturally they had a Jewish identity. Some of them had no idea if they even believed in God. It was fascinating to me that you would go and talk to a cantor or a rabbi about whether or not you believe in God. A Catholic would never do that. I took classes for a whole year, and then I took some time off. I took another class when I was pregnant with my daughter, and then I decided to convert.

Judaism is such an overwhelming religion. There is so much ritual and so many specific things you are supposed to do throughout the year. I think that part of the reason I decided to convert is because I was so comfortable with the rabbi and cantor at the temple where I took the classes. They were just very relaxed about everything. They would say to me, "Don't worry. One year you can do this, and one year you can do that." I had to come to grips with the fact that I would probably never feel really Jewish in any kind of a cultural way. It was more that I was making a decision about what religion our family was going to be. It did appeal to me that Judaism is a religion that seems so homemade. What I mean is that it feels like people are ultimately responsible for their own education, and it is up to the individual as to how he or she is going to practice. That's a very appealing part, and very different from the way things are done in Catholicism.

My parents already knew I was moving towards conversion. When I told them I was actually going to do it, my mother did say to me, "It's such a hard time to be a Jew." She sort of insinuated that people were going to come and kill me.

When my daughter was born, we had a naming ceremony for her at the temple. I used to work in a newborn nursery. I assisted on many of the circumcisions, and it was kind of difficult. I would always think, "If I ever have a son, I will never circumcise him." And then of course I married somebody Jewish and I converted and we found out that our second child was going to be a boy. I realized immediately that there was just no way this boy was not going to be circumcised.

I talked to the rabbi who had married us. And I said, "I don't want a bris and I don't want a mohel. I want him to have anesthesia. I want numbing." He said, "You know, I do naming ceremonies for boys that have already been circumcised all the time. Do it the way you want. You can always have the ceremony." So I did, and my son was actually circumcised on the eighth day by a friend of mine who is a doctor. Doing it that way felt all right to me.

In terms of what we did at home, sometimes we'd light the candles on Friday night. I have a few Jewish cookbooks, and I've made a number of things over the years. I even do Passover here. Lowell's grandmother has come to our seders, and she's very funny. I'd say to her, "Does it bother you that I don't have Passover dishes?" She'd say, "Don't worry. Go and get a rock and put it in the dishwasher with the dishes, and then they'll be O.K." She has turned out to be just a great woman. So that helped.

One thing I never could give up is Christmas. I'm one of eight kids. It's not that the whole family always gets together each year. But whoever could come always did. And there was always a special meal and presents and the tree and lots of decorations. When Lowell and I first met, it was around Christmas. My mother and a couple of sisters were visiting. Lowell had never really been around a tree or anything Christmasy before. It was all new to him, but I know he enjoyed it.

The first year we were married, we had been living in California for about eleven months, and I didn't know what to do on Christmas Eve. I couldn't decide. We had this little apartment. I was driving home from somewhere, and I passed a place where they were selling trees. I saw this one little, teeny tiny tree at the edge of the lot. I drove by and then I went back and I said, "I want that tree." And right near it was a tree stand that it would fit into just perfectly. So I bought that, and then I bought a string of lights and a few other things to put on it. I set it up, and when Lowell came home from work, he loved it. It was like a little Hanukkah bush. And that really started the whole tradition that we were just going to do Christmas. I realized that I couldn't *not* do it. We do try to make it much more low-key than it was in my family when I was growing up. The kids just think of Christmas as the time when Santa comes. They believe that Santa brings their presents and puts things in the stockings.

I also do Easter. It started because one year my brother and my sister were both here with their kids to celebrate Passover with us. The next morning was going to be Easter. So we decided that we would do a few things to celebrate Easter with all the kids. My kids were pretty young then, and I knew they'd love it. An Easter egg hunt is just kind of a fun thing. I basically love anything that makes life a little magical. The only thing is that, of course, Easter is such a big Catholic holiday. It represents hours and hours to me of being in church. As a child I didn't really like it. But now we don't do anything with the religious parts. We just do the fun parts.

My son has asked me, "Can we be Jewish and Christian?" And I looked at him and said, "Well, you kind of are. You have all these Christian relatives on one side of your family, and all of these Jewish relatives on the other side. You get all the good stuff from both sides."

What's happened now is that Lowell and I have separated. We've always been pretty typical in our household in that it's the woman who dictates everything in the home. At least, that's what I've always done. So now he's going to have to do a lot more when it comes to having a Jewish home and celebrating the holidays. This year, his uncle had a seder, so Lowell took the kids there. That made it easy for him. I'm not sure if he would ever have a seder at his own house.

I don't really know if I'm going to practice Judaism anymore myself. I'll definitely be involved in terms of the kids, and activities at the religious school, and bringing them to a Friday night service. Somehow it all doesn't mean as much to me now. There are certain parts of Judaism that I do really enjoy. I'm just not exactly sure what I want to do right now.

I think there were certain things about becoming a Jew that weren't positive for me. It felt like it was my decision at the time, but now I sometimes question it. I just think there was always a level of not being accepted for who I was. I think that was always an underlying issue that came out in little ways. It's an insidious feeling that I almost always had. Even when I converted, I'm not sure that feeling went away. I know Lowell's father was thrilled when I did it. And Lowell was very happy too, but I'm not exactly sure why he was so happy. I didn't know if he was happy for me, or if he was happy at somehow being relieved of the pressure he was under from his family. That's something I've wondered about, but I'll never really know.

Wendy is in her fifties. She recently took a part-time job in retail after years of not working much outside of the home. When Wendy decided to convert, she felt that she was making the final step in a long and difficult process. But she found that she still had a long way to go in order to feel anywhere near as relaxed with her new religion as the people who were actually born into it.

✷ WENDY

*　*　*

My family was Roman Catholic, and very religious. We went to Mass every Sunday. We all went to Catholic grammar schools. We said the Rosary after meals. Kids who came for dinner were always surprised that instead of getting up and going out to play when dinner was over, we would sit down and say these prayers.

*　*　*

When I graduated from high school I went and lived with a relative in Europe for a year. I think that because I was still living in a home atmosphere where everyone was going to church, I continued to go to Mass. I even taught catechism classes to little kids. But when I came back and moved in with my sister, it was like the best thing in the world was to not have to get up and go to Mass on Sunday mornings. And philosophically, I was moving away from the Church because I disagreed with a lot of what they said was and was not appropriate.

I started studying more and trying some alternative things. I read a lot about Buddhism and Eastern religions. I was no longer involved on a daily basis in Christianity. I mean, I would still go home for the holidays and spend Christmas with my family, but from the time I was eighteen I can't say that I was really a practicing Catholic.

When I was twenty-five, I was introduced to Jim through a mutual friend. I guess that from the beginning I knew Jim was Jewish. At that time, he didn't belong to a synagogue. I do know that he would fast on Yom Kippur. That was something that seemed unusual and odd to me, especially the year that we had season tickets to the White Sox games and the White Sox made it to the playoffs and he wouldn't go to the playoff game because it was Yom Kippur. I thought, "Come on, these are the White Sox." Of course, he probably didn't really care because he was an Orioles fan.

We went out for five years before we got married, and during that time we would occasionally break up. We would come back together and discuss issues and try to work things out, and then we'd break up again. Things went back and forth like this. The fact that I wasn't Jewish was definitely an issue for Jim. For me, not knowing Judaism the way that I know it now, it was kind of like "What's the big deal? If you love someone, you marry that person. That's what's important."

In the five years that we went out, I never once met Jim's family. Both our families lived out of town, but he met mine several different times. He even came to a family wedding with me and met all my cousins and aunts and uncles. I know that he didn't actually even tell his family anything at all about me until after his father died. He didn't want his parents, particularly his father, to know that he was involved with someone who wasn't Jewish. And in retrospect, that seems so odd to me. By this point, we were getting close to our thirties, and Jim was very independent in every other way, but this was still just something he didn't feel he could discuss with them. So from my perspective, it was significant when his father died. Jim does tell me that he was getting to the point where he was actually going to tell his parents about us, but I don't know when it really would have happened.

By this time we had decided to get married. And after his father died, Jim sat down with his mother. He told her that he was seriously involved with someone, and that we were planning to be married. I wasn't there when he talked to his mother, but from what I understand her attitude was "What's the choice?" She knew that the choice was either to lose a son or accept this person. Her choice was to accept me.

I agreed that we could raise our children Jewish. I did not agree to convert. That was something I really didn't even want to consider. As I had gotten older, my perspective on religion had become very political. I felt that religion had caused a lot of problems in the world. What seemed important to me was spirituality. I felt that you should have God in your life, but that God doesn't have to be identified with any particular group. So from that perspective I kept thinking, "Well, religion is really not that important."

Anyway, we decided Jim would be very involved in raising the kids to be Jewish, and I would help. I had gone to a public high school. I had known Jews. My best friend in high school was Jewish. I used to go to seders with her at her grandmother's. It didn't seem that it would be that hard to raise our kids to be Jewish, or that it would be any more challenging than anything else. I guess the big thing we agreed on was that we weren't going to do Christmas at our house, and that if I wanted Christmas we would go to my parents.

My parents really liked Jim, right from the beginning. I think they were glad that he cared about his religion, and they felt relieved that I was coming back into some fold. They probably thought, "Why can't it be our religion?" But the fact that I was going to be again participating in anything religious at all was I think very important to them. My parents are very ecumenical. They have the attitude, "It's like we're all a big, happy family." At times, of course, that's not true. Besides, it seems to me that Jews definitely don't want to be identified in this whole big group along with everyone else. They want to be seen as a separate entity.

When we decided to get married, I called the Chicago Board of Rabbis and asked them if they had someone on staff or knew of someone who would perform an interfaith marriage, and the woman on the phone laughed at me. I knew there were rabbis who would do that, but I never had much luck tracking them down. Finally, we talked to a Reconstructionist rabbi who agreed to get involved. He said that he could come to the service but he wouldn't actually officiate at it. He said he had contact with a judge, and he would ask the judge to marry us.

This rabbi did say one thing to us. He said, "I would be happy to find you a judge, but in good conscience I can't get involved unless you really think you might be considering conversion." At the very least he wanted me to take the introductory conversion class that meets about six or eight times, just to get some background about Judaism. So I agreed to take that class. I did it right around the time we got married, and Jim went with me. I thought a little about converting, but it still wasn't something I wanted to do.

I remember that very close to the wedding date my father wrote me a long letter and said that he really didn't care which religion we were married under, but he wanted us to be married under some religion. He didn't like the idea that we were going to be married by a judge. Knowing that we hadn't been able to find a rabbi, and also knowing that Jim was not going to agree to have a priest marry us, it was pretty much a moot point. I don't know if my father was hurt or not. I do have some extended relatives who think we were never actually married because the ceremony was performed by a judge. But to me, it was fine. Jim broke the glass, and we had some readings. It felt like what it was supposed to be.

From the time we were married, we were living this Jewish life. All of the life cycle events and religious events we participated in were Jewish. We didn't have Christmas in the house, and we didn't do Easter at all. I think that because our families were far away, there weren't a lot of obligations when it came to the holidays. There wasn't the feeling that on Passover we had to go to his family, and then on Easter we would have to go to mine. We would go see my parents at Christmas those first years. But it was strictly up to us what we wanted to do.

In the early part of our marriage, we went to services at a number of different synagogues. Jim was saying Kaddish for his father, and maybe a couple Saturdays a month we would try someplace new. Some of them were more interesting than others. The thing that really struck me at the beginning was how much activity and how much noise and running around there is at a Jewish service. And even now when I go to a bar or bat mitzvah, I always say, "If there were a nun in the room, it would be a whole lot quieter."

I think that at first I kind of resented the fact that Jim wasn't interested in taking the time to learn anything about Christianity, beyond what he already knew. I felt like, "Well, I'm learning all this stuff about Judaism. Don't you want to learn something about Christianity?" The truth of the matter is, no, he didn't. Why should he, because he was a Jew? He wasn't planning to change or adapt to anything else.

We had our children, two boys, and we of course knew they were going to be raised Jewish. They each had a bris, which was performed by a mohel who came to the house. Our intention was that they were also going to go to the mikva because it just makes their being Jewish all that more official. Like Jim said, "If they want to move to Israel, they will be able to move to Israel, and it won't be a problem." Even though I'm not Jewish, they would be considered Jewish. We didn't take them to the mikva right away, though. We just put it off.

When my oldest son was ready to start school, we decided to send him to a Conservative Jewish day school. Jim had gone to that type of school, and felt that was what he wanted for his kids. That was fine with me. So we had to go through an application process. On the forms they ask for the mother's religion, and they ask for the father's religion. During our interview with the Admissions Director I asked, "Are there any non-Jews at this school?" We used to live near a Reform day school, and people from the neighborhood sent their kids there even if they weren't Jewish, because it was a good school. She kind of looked at me and looked at my application and then said, "Well, there might be some fathers who are not Jewish, but the mothers are all Jewish, and the children are all Jewish."

I didn't say anything. The woman got up and left the room and I sort of scowled at Jim. "You were supposed to take care of this." Anyway, he wrote this woman a very nice letter. He told her that our intention was always to have our children go to the mikva to make them fully and completely Jews, but he had procrastinated about it because we belong to a Reconstructionist synagogue, which accepts patrilineal descent as long as the kids are being raised in a Jewish home. The woman very nicely wrote back a note. "It's fine, don't worry, you'll be fine." My son was accepted into the Jewish day school. And right about then we had both boys go to the mikva. Leon was four at that time, and David was two.

Not long after the kids went to the mikva, I started thinking that what would really make sense is if we were all the same religion in our family. So my initial decision to start pursuing conversion was that I felt it would be a good idea if our family all followed the same basic philosophy. There were two main issues that always got in my way when I thought about converting. The most important one was, "What am I going to tell my parents?" The other thing that bothered me was that I would have to go to the mikva. I didn't like the idea of being naked in this unusual place, with the rabbi and everyone else who has to be there. It made me uncomfortable to think about it. You would think that at a time like this a person would be worrying about the religious aspects and denying Christ and things like that, but with me it was going to the mikva and what I would tell my parents. Those are the things that I was thinking about.

I started taking all the classes. There were several different rabbis who were teaching the classes, so you could get a perspective on the different kinds of Judaism. We were still in touch with the rabbi who had helped with our wedding. He used to send me to one of the main Jewish neighborhoods in the city. He'd say, "Go walk around. Go into the stores and watch the people. Get a feel for things." And I did.

He also encouraged us to try out more types of synagogues. One Saturday we went to an Orthodox service, and it was horrible. As a woman, I felt ostracized having to be way up on the top away from the main things that were happening. I felt very out of place. I kept having this feeling that I was sitting there with a flashing sign above my head that said, "Not Jewish, Not Jewish." None of the women said anything to me. There was no transliteration, so I couldn't read anything. If you don't read Hebrew, you have no idea what's going on. I remember looking over the balcony and seeing Jim, just shmoozing away with all the men who were around him. I burst out crying. It was horrible.

I had to find a rabbi to convert with. This gets into something that I really resent, which is that there are all these different levels of being Jewish. You have to decide to be this kind of Jew or that kind of Jew. And I felt that since we were involved in a Jewish day school, and because Jim is a very strong supporter of Israel and wants us to spend time there, as well as to be able to go to Israel if something should happen, it would be better if I went through an Orthodox conversion.

I started out by talking to an Orthodox rabbi, who asked me different questions like why was I thinking about this, and what our family life would be like. I said, "We only do the Jewish holidays, and we do all the Jewish life cycle events." He asked me if we kept kosher. I said, "No, but I feel that with Judaism you always have the opportunity to move onto another level." Here I am talking to this Orthodox rabbi and trying to find my way through this. I didn't want to just say, "No, we don't keep kosher," or "I don't want to. I don't feel that it's reflective of my Jewish life."

What I did say to this rabbi is that I could not imagine going to my parent's house and not eating their food. I said I could not have my family in my home feeling uncomfortable because the food wasn't what they were used to. He said to me, "Well, you know if you're considering conversion, you really need to be reconsidering your position on keeping kosher." I said, "Okay, thank you." That was the end of my conversation with him. I decided I had to find a new rabbi.

I ended up doing a Conservative conversion, which is at least a step up from Reform, and was something I could live with more easily. I had been referred to this one rabbi, and he asked me less about, "Why do you want to do this?" and more about, "How have you been living a Jewish life?" I explained to him that we did all the holidays and that our children went to a Jewish day school. He said, "So you really have been living a Jewish life for the last six years or so?" And I kind of realized that, "Yes, that's what I've been doing, and I'm a Jew on all levels except for the fact that I don't have my papers." So that made me more comfortable. And he was willing to participate in the conversion ceremony.

The ceremony itself was much better than I had thought it would be. When I actually went to the mikva, I found it to be a very relaxing, soothing experience. At the mikva I went to, you wait in a room until a matron tells you a bathroom is available. You go in and shower completely. When you are ready, you put on a robe and call the matron, and she takes you into the room where the rabbis and anyone who came with you are. There is a small, very deep pool, with a fairly high wall next to it. Everyone turns around behind the wall while you get into the water, and when you are ready you tell them, and they turn back. The water was actually very warm and very deep, probably up to my neck. You have to say some prayers, you dunk your head, and then everyone leaves and you get out. After I did that part, we went back to the rabbi's office and said some more prayers, and he told me I was Jewish. I have to say that when I finally went through this process and even from the time I made the decision to convert, I really felt like I was coming home. I was at a place where I was supposed to be.

As for the part about telling my parents, it took me a while to figure out what to do. At the time I was seeing a therapist, and this was something that came up frequently. "How am I going to do this? How am I going to tell my parents I'm converting?" I kind of came to the conclusion in therapy that I didn't have to tell my parents anything. I'm an adult, and this is my choice, and I don't have to talk to them about it. I mean, there are lots of things I do in my life that I don't tell my parents. So I have never actually sat down with my parents and said to them, "I've converted to Judaism." I did tell my siblings, though. And my parents can see that we do all the Jewish holidays and our children are in a Jewish day school and we had a bar mitzvah for our older son. And when we're at family weddings or funerals or anything on my side of the family, I'll go to Mass, but I don't kneel down, and I don't go to Communion. So they must know. But deciding not to tell them saved me from the pain of having to sit down and say, "Mom, Dad, I'm not Catholic anymore. I'm Jewish." They know without me telling them that this is what I am, that I'm a Jew.

I think that when I originally made this decision to convert, I thought that everything else would just fall into place. But it doesn't. You are always making decisions based on your experience, and based on how it's going to affect both your immediate family and your extended family. That's what's been the big surprise to me. All these different little things come up that you have to have an opinion on or you have to make a choice about. For instance, there was a period when I felt like I couldn't tell my kids stories about my growing up or that I couldn't tell them more about who I am. Eventually I got to the point when I said, "No, this is my life, and this is who we are, and they need to know these things just as much as they need to know any other family history stories." So I tell them things now, and it's fine.

I don't feel so much that I gave something up by leaving Christianity. But what has always made me feel anxious and what I still don't feel very knowledgeable about or comfortable with is just that all these holidays seem so rote, so easy, for people. Every year at Passover I still have to look up what goes on the seder plate. I feel that for other people, all of that is so ingrained. I feel like I should know these things by now, but I'm still learning, and it's just not sinking in because I don't have the history. I don't have the context.

It's not just learning the religious part of things that's hard. It's all the little cultural things. I think. overall, that has always been the part that's the most interesting to me, even if it's the most challenging. It's not so much the religious aspects that I feel I want to incorporate for my family. The things I read about are not the technical things. I don't study Talmud. I don't know Hebrew. But what I read about all the time are memoirs about growing up Jewish. I read Isaac B. Singer, and books that tell you culturally what the Jewish people are all about. That to me is really interesting.

Learning to cook Jewish foods has been a challenge. I always said that I didn't have a grandma or a bubby to tell me how to make matzo balls and things like that. My mother-in-law would send me the Sisterhood cookbooks from her synagogue. I had a bunch of those and I would go through them all the time. My kids need to grow up with some of this stuff, especially since they're not around any relatives. For years I made potato latkes that were a

Julia Child recipe, and my friend said to me, "You know, these are really good. They're not potato latkes, but they're really good." I said, "What? They're potatoes and you fry them in oil. What's the big difference?" It was very funny.

I really do feel comfortable being Jewish. But I find it's much easier for me to identify myself as a convert in front of people who are Jewish, as opposed to non-Jews. I think there is a strong anti-Semitic feeling among Americans, and in the rest of the world. I remember one time driving in the car by myself and listening to a news report after the shooting at the Jewish Community Center in Los Angeles. I remember almost stopping the car and saying "What have I done? What have I brought my children to?" It's frightening.

Also, I just feel that some Christians would think, "Well, you know you're really going to hell because you're not right in what you believe." So why do I want to bring up that I'm Jewish? I was at a family baptism recently and the priest opened the service by saying, "You do this baptism because this is how you get to heaven, and this is your way to God. And if you're not baptized, you're not going to have eternal life, and you're not going to make it to heaven." And everyone in my family turned around and looked at me and laughed.

My family has always been great. They're very supportive of me. My parents were wonderfully involved with my son's bar mitzvah. My mother wanted to do something, and she came up with the idea that she would make Leon's tallis. My father at first wasn't sure it would be a good idea. He said to her, "Oh, they probably don't need that. They pass it down from father to son." I said, "You know, no, they don't really. Frequently men are buried in their tallis. You don't have another one." So my mother said, "I'll make him one."

My mother is an excellent seamstress. She made our Communion dresses, and she makes all those outfits for special occasions. Anyway, she decided to make this tallis, and she kept calling me back and asking what kind of material this or that part should be. My parents live outside of Philadelphia, and there's this area where there are a lot of fabric stores that are all run by old Jewish guys. She would tell me these stories, and I could picture her going into these stores and saying, "Well, I'm making a prayer shawl for my grandson, and what should I do?" So they would tell her all these things. "You can't have linen and cotton mixed together, and you can't do this or that. . . ." And she'd go home and call me on the phone and say, "What is this? I never heard this." So she made the tallis. And I went to a store I know that sells all kinds of Jewish items, and got her a little packet for the knots, or tzitzis, and she tied them. She practiced a lot before actually tying them until she really knew how to do it. The fact that she made the tallis was really, to me, very symbolic of being involved and accepting and saying, "This is what I would have done anyhow." This is the way that she participated. And my parents came to the bar mitzvah and had a good time. The combined families have always gotten along really well, so that when we do get together it's nice.

I never thought I was going to get married and have kids, and I think this has turned out so well. We have a great marriage. I love my family, and everybody seems happy.

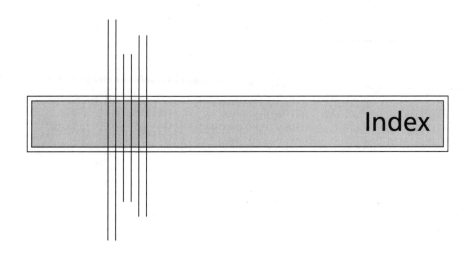

Index

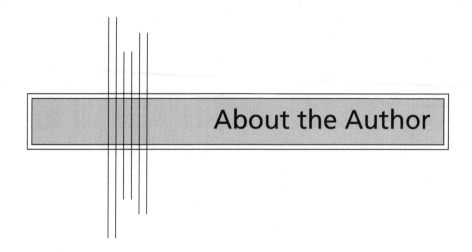

About the Author

JANE KAPLAN has produced a number of programs for public television and has independently created various films and videos. Her programs have concentrated on topics such as sexual harassment, parenting, the Holocaust, and mental health.